Corporate Finance

—Flotations, Equity Issues
and Acquisitions

Corporate Finance

—Flotations, Equity Issues and Acquisitions

Second edition

Martin Sabine, BA, MBA
Chairman of Somerley Limited, Hong Kong

Butterworths
London, Dublin and Edinburgh
1993

United Kingdom	Butterworth & Co (Publishers) Ltd, 88 Kingsway, LONDON WC2B 6AB and 4 Hill Street, EDINBURGH EH2 3JZ
Australia	Butterworths, SYDNEY, MELBOURNE, BRISBANE, ADELAIDE, PERTH, CANBERRA and HOBART
Belgium	Butterworth & Co (Publishers) Ltd, BRUSSELS
Canada	Butterworths Canada Ltd, TORONTO and VANCOUVER
Ireland	Butterworth (Ireland) Ltd, DUBLIN
Malaysia	Malayan Law Journal Sdn Bhd, KUALA LUMPUR
New Zealand	Butterworths of New Zealand Ltd, WELLINGTON and AUCKLAND
Puerto Rico	Equity de Puerto Rico, Inc, HATO REY
Singapore	Butterworths Asia, SINGAPORE
USA	Butterworth Legal Publishers, AUSTIN, Texas; BOSTON, Massachusetts; CLEARWATER, Florida (D & S Publishers); ORFORD, New Hampshire (Equity Publishing); ST PAUL, Minnesota; and SEATTLE, Washington

A CIP Catalogue record for this book is available from the British Library.

ISBN 0 406 00107 3

Typeset, printed and bound in Great Britain
by Latimer Trend & Co Ltd, Plymouth

To Maureen, for her continued love, support and guidance

Preface

Aim and scope of the book

The aim of the book continues to be to describe the theory, principles and practice of corporate finance, that is to say the major activities carried on by the corporate finance department of a large merchant bank or similar institution. The first part of the book contains an introduction to the characteristics of corporate securities which underlie all corporate finance transactions; the second part covers going public for the first time, commonly referred to as flotation or initial public offering, in the conventional manner. A new part three 'Alternatives and additions' describes other methods of going public and deals with the raising of further equity capital (subsequent to going public) in more depth than in the first edition; and the final part covers takeovers, mergers and disposals, perhaps the most glamorous area of corporate finance work.

Introduction for merchant bankers

Merchant banks have tended to encourage a mystique about their business. This is particularly true of corporate finance, ranging as it does from the complexities of prospectus documentation to the drama of public takeover battles. Reluctance to let 'daylight in on magic' creates difficulties for those who need to know (or are simply interested in knowing) about corporate finance in general or a particular aspect of it. As a practitioner, I believe this book describes the field in sufficient detail to serve as an introduction for executives starting work in merchant banking organisations. I have been told that the first edition proved a useful supplement to checking proofs, reviewing calculations, making the coffee and generally being thrown 'in at the deep end', which passes for basic training in many corporate finance departments and I hope the revised edition will continue to serve this function.

Handbook for professionals

The book is also designed to provide guidance to company executives who use the services of corporate finance specialists. This may be the company chairman pondering how his merchant bank will approach an underwriting decision or a finance director faced with an array of acquisition proposals. The book should also prove useful to professionals—accountants, lawyers, stockbrokers, fund managers, registrars, valuers and financial journalists—who are intensively involved in certain aspects of corporate finance transactions but do not always have the chance to see the overall picture. Technical terms have been kept to a minimum so that the book can also be readily understood by investors, students or anyone else who may wish to take an interest in the subject of corporate finance.

Practical emphasis

The book in its revised form is based on some 20 years' practical experience of corporate finance in the Asia-Pacific region, the UK and a number of other international financial markets. It has been written as a practical handbook and not from an academic or theoretical point of view. No formal survey of the available literature has been attempted, although a number of the topics covered in this book are dealt with in various works of reference which have proved useful sources. Colleagues and friends may recognise parts of cherished arguments and discussions held with them over the years.

'The more things change . . .'

The first edition of this book described the general principles of corporate finance work drawn from practical experience while avoiding a narrow focus on specific transactions. I believe this approach is the most helpful one and the second edition has retained it. The field is of course a dynamic one and the approach to each new transaction changes in response to varying market conditions, regulatory constraints, tax considerations and other factors. On the other hand, the principles underlying the different approaches remain much more constant. A technique may seem new but it is likely to prove a re-mix of traditional ingredients. Human motivation, which governs the 'sub-text' of many transactions, provides another constant, however much the means may vary.

This book is not intended to replace the need for specialist advice on individual transactions in country to country. What I hope it does is to provide the reader with a versatile framework for the analysis, implementation and understanding of corporate finance transactions which will remain valid as different markets and specific techniques evolve.

M. S.
November 1992

Contents

Part 1

Corporate securities: Characteristics, valuation and pricing

Introduction

(i) What is meant by corporate finance as covered in this book

The term 'corporate finance' in this book is used to refer to three major areas of activity. The first is going public, the initial public offering (IPO). The second covers alternatives to the straightforward IPO and raising additional capital once a listing has been obtained. The third is takeovers, mergers and disposals. These areas form the core of specialist corporate finance work in a merchant or investment bank. Other types of financing available to corporations such as bonds, syndicated lending, commercial paper and swaps are distinct subjects in themselves. Topics in financial analysis and capital budgeting also fall outside this definition of corporate finance.

The process of going public is reviewed in Part 2, beginning with the advantages and disadvantages and the reasons people embark on this some-times frustrating venture. A checklist is provided so that management can assess for itself without incurring substantial professional fees whether a company can go public. A guide to the structural changes which may be required is given. If a decision is made to proceed, it is necessary to form a team to co-ordinate all aspects of the flotation. The budget will be substantial but meeting the expenses is less painful if money is successfully raised by the operation. Meanwhile, the laborious process of putting together the nuts and bolts of a prospectus and a timetable for monitoring progress must also proceed. Correct timing and pricing are critical elements and difficult to get entirely right, even with a fair slice of luck. They are among the more glamorous and exciting problems of a flotation. After the preparations are complete, come the launch, allocation of shares and the start of trading.

There are other ways of gaining a listing apart from a full scale prospectus, such as acquiring a shell company or spinning off a subsidiary and these alternatives are reviewed in Part 3. Once a listing has been obtained, it is a much simpler process to raise further capital by way of rights issues to existing shareholders. Open offers and placings to new shareholders can also be carried out. Use may be made of equity-linked securities in addition to ordinary shares.

Part 4 of the book deals with takeovers, mergers and disposals. The wide range of motives for takeovers is discussed. They vary from carefully calculated financial gains to personal empire building. The first step is to identify acquisition candidates and subject them to a preliminary screening to avoid too much wasted effort. Despite this, a high proportion of unsuccessful projects is inevitable in the mergers and acquisitions field. When a likely candidate has been identified, a more intensive effort in collecting and evaluating information must be mounted.

The objective of gaining control can be tackled from various different angles.

There are also many options open regarding the structure of an offer and the terms of payment. After this review, there comes a moment when analysis and pre-planning must stop and action start. A skilful approach and sensitive negotiating style are important but sometimes the blunt instrument of a high cash bid is required. Winning a recommendation by any method possible is the single most critical factor determining the outcome.

For every aggressive move there are counter measures. Some need considerable planning to put into place, others can be used tactically in the midst of battle. Engaging in a contested takeover bid is possibly the most publicised event that a company and its management will experience. Willpower and personalities can become as important as fundamentals. Another area where the character of management, combined with innovative financing, becomes critical is leveraged buy-outs. In jurisdictions where a voluntary Takeover Code applies, much of the conduct of a bid will be governed by its terms. The formal procedures and techniques of how to carry an offer through require meticulous attention. Offer documentation is relatively complex. A number of specialist professionals have their own role to play in dealing with the technical aspects which arise.

It would be logical for management to spend as much time and energy on disposals as on acquisitions. This is rarely the case. The considerations relevant to disposals are the mirror image of the acquisition process but a deliberate policy is required on management's part if this important responsibility is not to be neglected.

(ii) How the subject is approached

The book contains sufficient detail to be of assistance to executives beginning their careers in investment or merchant banks. The material is drawn from practical experience of working on corporate finance transactions, alongside corporate finance specialists of various backgrounds, in different countries. Some of the detailed techniques are most closely derived from the UK or markets modelled on the UK. However, the majority of the principles discussed can be validly applied to corporate finance transactions worldwide.

The approach to the material should also prove suitable for professional advisers and company executives who are from time to time involved in corporate finance projects but whose main area of work and responsibility lies outside this area.

Institutional shareholders often hold the key to success of a corporate finance transaction either by being prepared to act as major sub-underwriters in an issue or by controlling critical blocks of shares during a takeover battle. They are increasingly being called upon to exercise responsibility commensurate with this power and it is hoped that the material presented will provide some relevant background. It may also prove of use to financial journalists and consultants in financial public relations along with shareholders and investors generally and those who simply have a passing interest in the stock market.

It has been the intention to approach the subject of corporate finance from as practical a viewpoint as possible. The book is not intended to be an academic survey of the outstanding literature on the subject but rather a summary of factors which have been found to be important from actual experience and a study of techniques which are in regular day-to-day use. Some of the theory of corporate finance is discussed but not beyond the extent to which it is relevant to these techniques. A complex exposition of a statistical method of evaluating risk which the average shareholder neither understands or trusts may boost an analyst's ego but has rarely advanced a corporate finance transaction.

(iii) Who is involved

At the level of the company itself, it is usual for senior management to be closely involved in corporate finance projects. The decisions being taken affect the future direction of the group, particularly as regards flotations and major takeovers. Further issues of securities may be handled by the finance director or the treasurer. In almost all corporate finance transactions, accounting staff will be involved in preparing and assessing up-to-date financial statements about the company. The documentation will require participation by legal and company secretarial staff. A team of analysts, researchers and co-ordinators may also be required, depending on the size of the transaction.

The staff of a corporate finance department in a merchant bank is usually young. Executives in their mid- to late-twenties will take considerable responsibility for transactions. They are stronger in educational qualifications than in business experience. On many occasions, merchant banks have found themselves out-manoeuvred by businessmen with shrewd instincts but little formal training. Some companies are adept at allowing merchant banks to feel they are running the show while keeping their own objectives firmly in view. The background of corporate finance staff is likely to be accountancy or business schools specialising in finance, the law, stockbroking or, on occasion, even 'real' banking.

Accountants prepare studies on working capital and profit forecasts and investigate and confirm key aspects of corporate finance transactions. Lawyers will be widely engaged not only in drafting, verification and documentation but often in negotiating with principals, devising bid tactics and dealing with regulatory and anti-monopoly bodies. Stockbrokers will mastermind market operations and provide critical input on pricing and underwriting decisions. The stock exchange and other authorities play a key role in holding the ring and setting the tone of what is or is not allowable in the context of each particular type of transaction. Property valuers, share registrars, receiving banks and specialist printers all have important roles to play.

(iv) What a corporate finance department does

A company only goes public once and therefore most managements will be novices in this particular field. They will look for overall guidance on rules, procedures, documentation and timing. Even inexperienced managements will have strong views on pricing, especially if some of their own shares are being sold. As the merchant bank is ultimately standing behind the underwriting it has considerable leverage in the pricing negotiations.

A company which has gone public will look to its sponsor for guidelines as to what is expected from the management of a public company. It may also wish an experienced party to monitor the market in its shares. The merchant bank which arranges the initial flotation should have a strong advantage when it comes to suggesting further transactions. If a close association develops, the bank may also act as advisers to some of the directors of the company in their personal capacity.

Takeovers tend by their nature to be one-off projects. The most valuable service is generating ideas and providing information about available companies. The merchant bank which is able to bring deals is likely to be given responsibility for that particular piece of business. Analysis of the market and the price to be paid will be required. The merchant bank may be involved in approaching the target company and opening negotiations. Most companies have little direct experience of negotiating with stock exchange authorities and bodies regulating takeovers. This will normally be left in the hands of the merchant bank or stockbroker.

As companies become more experienced in making takeovers, they may look to the merchant bank less for handling procedures and more for arranging a package. This will include offering or arranging suitable loan finance, handling purchases of shares and providing support through underwriting. Depending on the strengths of individual management, the merchant bank may also be involved in press and investor relations.

Fees are calculated on a percentage of the size of the transaction, perhaps $\frac{1}{2}$–1% on a largish transaction and up to 5% on a small one. In issues, market practice varies as to whether fees are paid outright or are included in a 'spread' between the price at which an underwriting syndicate takes shares and the price at which they are sold to investors. Fees for new issues of small companies can be as high as 10% for some very risky propositions but are normally perhaps in the 2–5% range, varying widely in different markets. Depending on what services are included, a documentation fee may also be charged.

In merger and acquisition work, it sometimes happens that a simple introductory fee is charged by the person putting up the idea. The detailed work is carried out by another house on a separate basis. Many merchant banks charge out-of-pocket expenses in addition. It can be irritating for a company to find it is charged with faxes and taxi fares on top of a very substantial fee.

Other categories of professional fees will normally be based on time spent at a certain rate per hour with a loading for urgency, complexity and general inconvenience. Corporate finance transactions can involve anti-social hours.

(v) Organisation of the book

The remaining two chapters of Part 1 deal with the characteristics of corporate securities and principles of valuation and pricing. These subjects are fundamental both to the issue side of corporate finance activity and to takeovers and mergers. Parts 2 and 3 deal with issues by public companies in the rough chronological order of the various steps involved and Part 4 follows the same basic format for the area of mergers, acquisitions and disposals. The processes should be more readily understandable if the chapters are read in order but a reader interested in only one aspect should find that the topics are more or less self-contained.

CHAPTER 1

Characteristics of corporate securities

This chapter deals with the characteristics of the different types of equity or equity-linked securities issued by companies. The characteristics described are those which are particularly relevant to corporate finance transactions. It is not intended to present an exhaustive account of all the rights attaching to each type of security.

Section I deals with shares, both ordinary shares (common stock) and shares with rights which differ in some way from those of the ordinary shares. Section II deals with loan stocks, particularly those which are convertible into ordinary shares. Section III examines the relevant features of warrants and options.

I SHARES

The shares which form the basic capitalisation of a company are called ordinary shares or common stock. Other shares are distinguished from them by having different rights in certain specified respects, notably as regards voting and preferred or deferred claims on income and return of capital.

(i) Ordinary shares

Ordinary shares are the most familiar type of security to the average investor. They are likely to be a greater number of shares and a greater spread of holders than for the other types of securities a company may have in issue. This makes them more marketable than other securities. A framework for analysing the worth of ordinary shares has become well established and widely understood, involving such measures as the price earnings ratio, dividend yield, asset backing and the variability of the expected return compared with the market as a whole.

(a) Cost of ordinary shares

Ordinary shares carry no fixed servicing obligations. Of course, shareholders are none too pleased if no dividends are paid but there is no legal sanction triggered against the company. Whether to pay or recommend dividends lies in the discretion of the directors.

This gives rise to different attitudes to the cost of ordinary shares. In theory, as ordinary shares (other than certain types of deferred shares covered below) carry the greatest risk of all the securities issued by the company, it would be expected that holders would demand the greatest return. Expressing this from the company's point of view, ordinary shares are in some sense the most expensive type of capital for a company to employ. However, in cash terns they are the cheapest, both in the sense that no dividends are actually required and because a normal dividend payment is likely to put a share on a lower yield than the interest rate on debt. From the point of view of cash servicing costs, it is cheaper and safer for a company to raise a given sum by issue of shares than it is by bank borrowings or issue of other securities.

Financial theory suggests that the difference between the cash returns on shares and the interest payable on loan stock or bank borrowing should be more than made up by the expected capital gain to holders of the shares. On the other hand, some managements may regard the share price of the company in the stock market as capricious, particularly in the short term, and largely beyond their control. Whether shareholders will actually reap a capital gain to compensate them for the lower cash income depends on many factors, including the timing of the investors' purchase and sale, the mood of the stock market and the economic cycle. What the directors of the company can control is the level of dividend payments. While theory tells them shares are the most expensive form of financing, they may be tempted to measure reality in terms of cash paid out.

(b) Timing and pricing of issues

Another paradox concerns the timing and pricing of issues of ordinary shares. Directors may feel that money raised by issues of ordinary shares is 'cheapest' when the share price is high. Issue activity tends to intensify at market peaks. To the shareholder, this may prove the most expensive time to increase his holdings. Shareholders may look back and rue an issue made near a market peak while the directors congratulate themselves on their foresight, having raised money for the company cheaply and at the right moment. This policy may expose shareholders to capital losses on their investment rather than the capital gains needed to supplement the dividend yield.

(c) Voting rights

A fundamental right of ordinary shares is that they normally carry the voting control of companies. In most takeover bids, the premium for acquiring control of a company attaches entirely to the ordinary shares. Preference shares or loan stock which may be more valuable on an income basis do not share in this bonanza unless they carry unusual rights to block or hinder a takeover.

A register of shareholders is usually maintained by the company, in which case the registered holder has the power to vote at meetings of the company or to appoint a proxy to vote on his behalf. Shares held in 'street names' and not yet registered by a purchaser cannot be voted by the new owner until transfer of ownership has been registered by the company. Some companies (mostly private) have issued securities in bearer form which allows the person in physical possession of the certificates to attend meetings and vote the shares he holds.

(d) Claims on income and assets

Holders of ordinary shares participate pro rata in the profits of the overall business attributable to them. The dividends they receive and capital gains they enjoy should be determined over a period of time by the performance of the company.

The articles of association of a company usually contain provisions preventing the dilution of shareholders' claims on the company's income and assets. In some jurisdictions, further issues of shares for cash are required (subject to any exemption previously granted by shareholders) to be made by 'rights', which ensure that the existing shareholders have the opportunity to maintain their percentage shareholding in the company.

(e) Bonus issues

Bonus issues, sometimes called 'scrip' or 'capitalisation' issues, are made to existing shareholders out of the company's share premium account or by capitalising reserves.

When a bonus issue is made, no cash is paid by shareholders or received by the company. In theory, the issue should leave the value of a shareholder's holding unchanged. For example, if a shareholder holds 100 shares with a market price of $1 and a one-for-ten bonus issue is declared, the total shares he owns will increase to 110 but the price should decline to approximately $0.91 ($1 multiplied by a factor of 100/110). However, in some markets bonus issues are well received, perhaps as a sign of favourable progress by the company, and the total market value of a shareholder's investment in the company may be observed to increase instead of adjusting fully.

(f) Repurchase/redemption

Ordinary shares, once issued, are regarded as part of the permanent capital of the company. However, it is normally possible for shares to be repurchased by the company with shareholders' consent. Such repurchases, made through the market or by a tender offer, can only be made (except by court sanction) out of reserves which are in any event available for distribution as dividends.

(ii) 'A' and 'B' shares

Standard voting rights call for each shareholder to have one vote if a resolution is to be considered on a show of hands, while if a poll is demanded the formula is usually one vote for each share. In some instances, usually for historical reasons relating to the founding shareholders' wish to retain control and raise new capital, shares will be created with differing voting rights. There may be 'A' shares with one vote per share and 'B' shares with say ten votes per share. The original shareholders can then raise capital by issuing more 'A' shares to the public while retaining voting control through their 'B' shares. The public may well value their shares in relation to the earnings, dividends and asset backing which would be identical to the 'B' shares, without much concern over the inferior voting rights. However, it may be naive to assume that value can be regarded as an entirely separate matter from control.

The attitude of stock exchanges to such voting rights is mixed. They may not grant listings to new issues on these terms. Where shares with different voting rights have been in existence for many years, it is difficult to insist on a change. Pressure may be applied by institutional holders for the directors voluntarily to propose that all voting rights should be made identical. Holders of shares with superior voting rights may be given a bonus issue (say on the basis one-for-ten) to compensate them for the loss of their voting advantage.

(iii) Preference or preferred shares

Shares which have generally superior rights to the ordinary shares are called 'preference' shares. Shares whose rights differ only in one area may be called 'preferred' shares.

(a) As regards income

Shares may be issued with rights to income and return of capital which are superior to those of ordinary shares. The dividend on a preference share is normally expressed as a fixed percentage of the par value or the issue price, for example 8%. This allows the company to issue a security which attracts fixed income investors but which is still classified as equity. Preference shareholders may, on occasion, participate in some percentage of the dividend paid to ordinary shareholders, giving holders some possibility of increasing income. Preference shares can be issued with a dividend linked to other variable factors such as the rates obtainable in the money market, but this is unusual.

The dividend rights of preference shares are normally 'cumulative'. If a dividend is not paid for one period, it must be subsequently paid together with the current dividend.

As with ordinary shares, there is no legal sanction on the company for failure to pay a preference dividend. However, no dividend can normally be paid to ordinary shareholders before dividends on the preference shares, and all arrears, are paid up to date. Missing a preference dividend may also trigger voting rights or other powers for the preference shareholders. Preference shareholders cannot usually vote at general meetings of the company except on matters which affect their rights.

(b) As regards capital

Preference shareholders have the right to have their capital returned to them in priority to the ordinary shareholders. However, the protection afforded preference shareholders as regards return of capital often proves illusory. If a company gets into serious financial difficulty, all the equity, both ordinary and preference, is likely to prove worthless. Preference shareholders therefore run the risking of limiting their potential gains while not significantly decreasing their chances of loss.

(c) Issues in place of ordinary shares

Issues of preferred or preference shares can be useful when it is difficult to issue ordinary shares. If the price of the ordinary shares is low, perhaps close to or even lower than the par value (in jurisdictions where a par value applies), an issue will not be possible. In such jurisdictions, it is not legal to issue shares at below par value. However, a new class of shares may be issued, designed to be valued at par because of its superior rights. This may also prove useful in a takeover bid, where there may be some doubt about the value of the ordinary shares or the bidder wishes to argue he is being generous to the target company's shareholders.

In situations where it is not practical to pay a dividend on the whole of the share capital owing to poor performance, it may still be possible to pay a dividend on a lesser number of preference shares. If new investors demand income, a rights issue of preference shares can be made in place of ordinary shares.

Preference shares are widely used in reconstructions. A company's equity needs to be increased but new investors are not willing to put in fresh money unless their investment ranks ahead of that of the original shareholders. As preference shares are counted as equity, an issue of preference shares serves to reduce gearing and to increase borrowing limits while giving new investors greater protection. An issue of unsecured loan stock, which might have similar rights, would not achieve this purpose.

(d) Ability to redeem

Preference shares are usually redeemable. This is a useful right in jurisdictions which prevent repayment of capital without court sanction and may restrict a company in purchasing its own shares. In such jurisdictions, it is possible for a company to redeem its preference shares out of a further issue of preference shares or if it has sufficient distributable reserves in its balance sheet and adequate financial resources. The possibility of redemption of a part of the share capital adds a flexibility in adjusting the overall level of gearing of the company. This feature has been found useful in some investment trusts to cater for the objectives of different types of investors.

(e) Treatment in takeovers

Shares which lack voting rights in normal conditions are largely ignored in takeovers and treated as part of a tidying-up exercise at the end of the day. However, as noted above, if a dividend is not current, preference shareholders are likely to have votes and, in some circumstances, may even have a majority of votes. In addition, provisions to protect their preferential right to capital may give them a veto over certain types of reorganisation planned as part of the takeover or merger.

Preference shares with special rights may be used specifically to put in place a 'poison pill' defence, giving the holders rights which make a takeover of the company prohibitively expensive to a hostile predator.

(f) Convertible rights

Preference shares may be issued with rights that they can be converted into ordinary shares. The method and terms of conversion are normally the same as those applying to convertible loan stock which are described below. Convertible preference shares are very close to outright equity. They would typically be issued in circumstances where the company would prefer to issue ordinary shares except for the technical or tactical reasons mentioned above.

(iv) Shares with deferred rights

Shares may be issued with deferred rights, usually as regards income. For example, a company may acquire by an issue of shares assets (such as development sites) which may not yield income for some years. The company may not be able to maintain its dividend if the new shares rank for dividend before the assets acquired can contribute income.

In this case, the shares may be issued on terms that they do not rank for dividend for a certain period of time, estimated to be the period before the assets generate profits. At the end of this period, the deferred shares will automatically become ordinary shares and rank for dividends equally with them.

This device may also assist in maintaining reported earnings per share. Shares which do not rank for dividends are not normally included in the earnings and dividends per share calculation. However, 'fully diluted' earnings per share, that is assuming all shares rank for dividend, should also be shown in the accounts, either on the face of the profit and loss statement or as a note.

Deferred shares have also been used as a fundamental part of tax schemes to lessen the amount of transfer duty. If the shares transferred have such inferior rights that their value may be argued to be negligible, their transfer may be effected with little or no transfer tax.

Deferred or preferred shares may become identical to ordinary shares on the triggering of some event to which their preferred or deferred status specifically relates. For example, preferred shares may be entitled to a higher dividend than ordinary shares initially. When the income on the ordinary shares increases so that it exceeds the preferred share dividend, the preferred shares automatically become ordinary shares. Deferred shares which, for example, do not rank for dividends for a certain period become ordinary shares when that period has elapsed.

II LOAN STOCKS

Holders of loan stock do not participate pro rata in the earnings of the company. The return is fixed at the level of the coupon on the loan stock and does not vary if the profits increase. If profits decrease or indeed are eliminated altogether, there is still a legal obligation on the company to pay the interest or be subject to various legal sanctions which may be taken by or on behalf of the holders of the loan stock. The rights of the holders are set down in a trust deed or other document showing the terms on which the issue is made.

(i) Unsecured loan stock

Issues of straight unsecured loan stock tend to appeal mainly to institutional investors, particularly pension funds and insurance companies. These institutions have long-term obligations which they seek to match with assets providing steady long-term income. Unsecured loan stocks have final maturities ranging from say 5 to 15 years or longer. At least for a proportion of their portfolio, institutions prefer a conservative investment, ranking ahead of ordinary shares and protected by various covenants. The degree of added security compensates such holders for the lack of any potential increase in their income. A serious breach of the covenants of the loan stock will constitute a default by the company on its obligations and will trigger repayment of the loan stock and other sanctions.

(a) Restrictions on issuing group

The trust deed which constitutes the loan stock contains restrictions on how the issuing company is financed and managed. These restrictions may include an overall limit on the borrowings of the company and its subsidiaries and a lower or 'inner' limit on borrowings which rank ahead of the loan stockholders. Loan stock may be issued by a holding company or a special-purpose off-shore subsidiary guaranteed by the holding company. If this is so, all borrowings by subsidiary companies conducting the group's main business rank ahead of the loan stockholders in practice, assuming the major assets of the group are held by such subsidiaries. The inner limit therefore includes both secured borrowings and borrowings of subsidiaries.

There is usually a covenant not to dispose of any major assets (unless the proceeds are reinvested in similar assets or used to repay debt) without the consent of loan stockholders or to make a major change in the nature of the business. It is assumed that stockholders will have made their decision to invest on the basis of the assets and business of the group at that time and might not take the same attitude if substantial changes are made. Trustees for the stockholders will represent their interests as a class and act as a representative available for discussions with the issuing company on points the company may wish to take up relating to the terms of the loan stock.

(b) Interest

The coupon on the loan stock is normally fixed and payable semi-annually. The stock will be valued by discounting the stream of interest payments and the final repayment of principal at maturity by the rate considered appropriate by the market from time to time for a stock of that particular risk and maturity. If interest rates drop, the value of the stock will rise and vice versa.

It is possible to set the coupon by reference to some floating rate, for example the rate of interest payable in the inter-bank market. Obligations of this kind are called floating rate notes. The interest rate may vary by reference to other benchmarks, provided there is some objective way of determining what the interest payment should be. Some floating rate bonds have a maximum and minimum payment built into their terms. Others may become fixed when the interest rate drops or rises to a certain specified amount.

More exotic issues are possible. In circumstances where cash flow is tight, payment-in-kind bonds may be used where interest is paid, at least initially, not in cash but by a further issue of bonds. Some bonds have been issued without any coupon payable at all, called, appropriately enough, zero coupon bonds. Such bonds are issued at a substantial discount to their face value. The discount is calculated to compensate holders for the lack of income until maturity by reference to the rates of return available on bonds of a comparable maturity and risk. This type of bond is attractive to some holders, as the 'income' is automatically reinvested at the same rate of return. If interest is actually paid, the recipient must seek a similarly attractive investment. Zero coupon bonds may be considered a speculative investment by bond standards. Their market value will fluctuate more than any other kind of bond for a given rise or fall in interest rates.

(c) *'Junk' bonds*

Unsecured loan stocks with low or poor investment ratings but high coupons have become extensively used to finance leveraged buy-outs (see ch 19). They are known in the market as 'junk bonds', although many are issued by highly reputable companies. Unsecured loan stocks have an important role in takeover offers, being used not only as a means of raising capital for the offeror but also to provide an increase in income to the target company's shareholders. The coupon on an unsecured loan stock will almost certainly be higher than the dividend yield of the target company's shares at the offer price.

(ii) Convertible loan stock

(a) *Rights and restrictions*

The rights and restrictions contained in the document which constitutes a convertible loan stock tend to be along the same lines as those for a straight loan stock. If anything, covenants may be less strict, as the holders of the convertible are likely to be regarded partly as shareholders as well as holders of debt.

Conversion: The right to convert will be carefully defined and protected. In particular, the conversion price will be adjusted in similar circumstances to adjustments to the subscription price of warrants, as set out in Section III below. Conversion rights usually start shortly after the stock is issued and last until it is redeemed. The conversion price may be at the present market price of the shares or at a small premium, normally not more than 10%. The holder converts by completing a form on the back of the stock certificate. The number of shares he receives is calculated by dividing the nominal value of the loan stock he tenders by the conversion price. If he tenders a stock certificate with a nominal value of $1,000 and the conversion price is $2, he will receive 500 shares. The market value of the stock and the shares is not relevant for this purpose. It should be noted that the stockholder pays no cash but simply exchanges his stock for shares. Likewise, the company receives no cash. However, its outstanding debt is reduced by the nominal amount of stock redeemed and its issued share capital (and share premium account, if appropriate) goes up by the same amount. A conversion therefore has a doubly beneficial effect on gearing, reducing debt at the same time as equity is increased. The conversion procedures normally contain provisions which prevent an investor collecting interest and dividends in respect of the same period.

Call provision: Many convertibles contain a clause which enables the company to force all holders to convert if over 75% of the holders have converted their loan stock. More controversially, conversion may also be forced if the share price exceeds the conversion price by a minimum amount (say 50%) for a minimum period. Such a provision puts a 'cap' on the value of the stock.

Variations in conversion rights: Most convertible loan stock is convertible into the ordinary shares of the company which issues the stock. However, there is nothing to prevent the stock being converted into the shares of another company if the issuing company has such shares under its control. In this case, a convertible issue could be a disguised method of placing out a significant holding in another company which might not be marketable as one block. The convertible loan stock could also be converted into, for example, straight loan stock or preference shares.

(b) Reasons for issue

As deferred equity: A convertible loan stock may be issued by a company which wishes to issue further equity but not at a discount to market price (as is usually necessary), or when it is unable to issue equity because of market conditions or other constraints.

As debt with a sweetener: A company may prefer to issue debt but is prevented because the straight debt market does not view its paper as of sufficient quality. In this case, the company may compensate for the additional risk by including an element of equity in the package.

To reduce interest costs: The coupon payable on convertible loan stock will be lower than that on a standard unsecured loan stock reflecting the value of the conversion right. Straight debt has no possibility of price appreciation in line with expected rises in the price of the shares.

In takeovers: A convertible loan stock can be used to increase the value of an offer while avoiding dilution in earnings per share. A detailed example of this is given in ch 15.

(c) Valuation

The valuation of convertible loan stock can be approached in two ways. If it is considered as 'deferred equity', it will be valued on the basis of the market price of the number of shares into which a holding can be converted, added to which is the income advantage in receiving for a period a higher level of interest than dividend. This differential in income should also determine the timing of conversion. Alternatively, a convertible can be considered to have a base value as straight debt, plus an option valued as a warrant (see Section III below).

If the convertible is regarded as deferred equity, the method of valuation will be as follows:

Coupon on convertible loan stock is 8%. Stock is issued in $100 amounts.

Dividend yield on ordinary shares at the conversion price is 4% and dividends are expected to grow at 15% per annum.

Tax on interest and dividends is ignored for this example.

Year	Interest	Dividend income	Differential	Present value of differential at 10%
1	8%	4.0%	4.0	3.64
2	8%	4.6%	3.4	2.81
3	8%	5.3%	2.7	2.03
4	8%	6.1%	1.9	1.30
5	8%	7.0%	1.0	0.62
6	8%	8.0%	—	—
				10.40

Conversion price is set at 21, a 5% premium to market price of 20.

Value on conversion is $\frac{100}{21} \times 20 =$ 95.2

Present value of income differential   10.4

Estimated value of convertible   100.56

(d) Timing of conversion

Experience shows that convertible loan stocks are generally converted. An investor will tend to convert when dividends rise on the ordinary shares to such an extent that the dividend income receivable after conversion (adjusting for the tax position of the investor) is greater than the interest receivable from the loan stock, provided that the investor believes the dividend level can be maintained. In the example above, other things being equal, the investor would convert after year 6 however long the maturity of the stock because he would increase his income by so doing.

The other reason for conversion before maturity is to increase marketability. The convertible loan stock of a company may be less marketable than the ordinary shares because of fewer holders, a lower amount in issue and a tendency for such issues to be 'salted away' in portfolios.

It should be noted that conversion will not necessarily occur simply because the market price of the ordinary shares is greater than the conversion price. Subject to marketability, the market price of the convertible will in this case rise above par and the investor can take his profit by selling the loan stock. He has no need to convert. The income differential should still be the main determining factor until the end of the conversion period approaches.

III   WARRANTS AND OPTIONS

Market dealing in warrants and options has become extremely active in recent years and much literature has been produced on aspects such as trading strategies and methods of valuation. However, apart from the special case of covered warrants discussed at the end of this Section, companies have very rarely issued warrants or options for cash. Instead, warrants are issued 'free' — by way of bonus issues or as sweeteners attached to loan stock, shares or other securities issued for cash, or as part of the consideration for a takeover bid. This suggests that despite the sophistication of the valuation techniques applied to dealing in warrants in the secondary market, in the context of an issue for new capital, companies regard warrants more as part of the supporting cast than playing a star role. The market in warrants is still seen as speculative and sometimes lacking in liquidity, so that while a particular warrant issue may be successful, this possibility is regarded at the planning stage as 'icing on the cake', not something to be relied upon.

A non-financial company is not normally in the position of issuing options on its shares, with the exception of share option schemes for executives. Such schemes form part of an overall compensation package for executives and are not usually evaluated as capital raising exercises. Traded put and call options issued by third parties do not directly involve the company concerned. No new shares are issued. If a company wishes to grant call options, it can do so in effect through issuing warrants to subscribe new shares. A repurchase programme of shares, whereby the company offers to purchase existing shares from shareholders, could be regarded as the company granting a put option.

Summarised below are the features of warrants which are relevant to corporate finance transactions, not to speculative activity in the market. The comments below relating to warrants apply in a general sense also to options, although the scope for their use in corporate finance transactions is more restricted, as noted above.

(i) Characteristics of warrants

A warrant represents a right to subscribe a certain sum of money for a company's securities at a fixed price for a stated period. Most usually, the securities in point are ordinary shares but they may also be, for example, preference shares or loan stock. Warrants can be listed on a stock exchange and traded. They impose no obligation on the holder and may be considered a type of long-dated traded call option. The rights of warrantholders are set out in the warrant certificate or other document. They are not as extensive as the rights of most other securities, concentrating on protecting the right to subscribe, the price at which subscription is made and the worth of the securities which can be subscribed for. Warrants are exercised by sending in a subscription form (often on the back of the warrant certificate) to the company with a cheque for the number of shares being subscribed for at the subscription price.

(ii) Terms

(a) Subscription right

There are two main ways of defining subscription rights. Some warrants carry the right to subscribe on the basis of one share for one warrant (occasionally, this is varied so that one warrant gives the right to subscribe for a multiple of shares). The second type of warrant gives the right to subscribe a certain amount of money for shares. The main difference between the two is the mechanism by which adjustments are made to the subscription price in the event of, for example, bonus issues by the company.

(b) Subscription price

This price is fixed initially at the time of issue and is often based on the market price at that time or a small premium to such price. It could be set at a discount to market but this is rarely done. A premium perhaps anticipates a future increase in share price. On occasion, a stepped-up formula is used, where the subscription price increases over time. This may encourage subscription just before the price increase is due.

(c) Exercise period

The exercise period determines the length of the warrant's life, for example three years. The length varies from market to market according to investor and issuer preference. Sometimes market regulations impose a minimum and maximum period. The longer the exercise period, the higher the subscription price is likely to be. A short-dated warrant with a relatively low exercise price has the characteristics of a deferred rights issue.

(d) Call provision

Most warrants can be 'called' if a large majority (say 75% or sometimes 90%) of the warrants have been exercised. If a company calls the warrants, the holders must either exercise their rights in a relatively short period (say one month) or allow them to lapse. This allows the company to 'tidy up' small minorities while presumably not prejudicing warrantholders since most have already seen it as in their interest to exercise their subscription rights.

(e) Adjustments to subscription price

The subscription price will be adjusted downwards in certain circumstances, the most frequent of which are bonus and rights issues. For a bonus issue of shares, the subscription price is simply adjusted by the ratio of the bonus issue. For example, in the case of a 1-for-10 bonus issue, the price would be adjusted by a factor equal to 10/11. The formula for adjustment for a rights issue is more complicated but based on a similar principle. The discount at which the rights shares are issued to the 'ex rights' price is in effect deducted from the subscription price on a per share basis (ie if the rights issue is 1-for-4, one quarter of the discount is deducted).

If the 'one warrant for one share' formula is used, warrantholders should also receive a bonus issue of warrants in the relevant proportion so that the percentage of the company's share capital for which they can subscribe remains constant. If a warrant is a 'money' warrant, giving the right to subscribe a certain amount of money for shares, warrantholders are automatically protected since the same amount of subscription rights now buys more shares at the lowered subscription price.

The particulars of the warrant will also define other circumstances in which an adjustment to the subscription price may be appropriate, for example, if shares are issued at below market price (other than by rights) or if capital distributions are made (other than normal dividends) for which warrantholders do not rank. There will also be a 'too difficult' clause, allowing the company to refer the question of an adjustment to the company's financial advisers or auditors for an opinion.

(f) Position in takeovers

The Takeover Code (as discussed below) provides that where an offer is made for a company's shares, an 'appropriate' offer should also be made for any convertibles or warrants outstanding. The Code stipulates that an appropriate offer would be one based on a 'trace through' value, that is the amount the warrantholder receives if he exercises his subscription rights immediately and accepts the offer. This ignores any time value, for which the warrantholder purchasing warrants in the market is likely to have paid a premium over trace through value.

To protect the warrantholder, a formula has been introduced into some recent issues which lowers the subscription price in the event of a bid. The formula for the reduction of the subscription price is

$$(A + B) - C$$

where A is the existing subscription price
   B is the market price (per share) of the warrants
   C is the offer price for the shares.

The new subscription price is in effect the offer price for the shares (C) less the market price of the warrants (B) so that the warrantholder receives the equivalent of the current market price of the warrants through application of the 'trace through' formula.

(g) Income

Except in very rare circumstances, holders of warrants (or options) do not receive any dividends or other income from the company.

(iii) Uses of warrants

(a) Potential for raising new capital

If warrants are issued with an exercise price of market or slightly above and have say a three-year life, a company with good growth prospects should receive further equity capital in due course. However, it is a feature of warrants that they are very rarely subscribed until just before their expiry date. Consequently, if stock market conditions are weak or if the company itself performs poorly so that the share price in the weeks before the expiry date stays below the exercise price of the warrants, no new capital will be raised. This means that warrants are not reliable as a source of new capital for the company.

(b) To sweeten a fund raising exercise

Warrants may be issued in conjunction with loan stock. The value of the warrants allow the loan stock to be issued with a lower coupon than would otherwise have been required. If the maturity of the loan stock and warrants coincide, the exercise of warrants may provide the capital to redeem the loan stock (but see *(a)* above). A convertible loan stock has the same elements but bundled into one package, which lacks the flexibility of the loan stock plus warrants formula.

Warrants are also used in conjunction with a flotation, a rights issue or a takeover. Here their function is to 'spice up' what might otherwise be seen as a dull diet. In flotations of investment trusts or property companies, warrants are a useful way of bridging the discount to net asset value at which such shares normally stand. The share plus warrant package will hold at or above the issue price (normally based on par or net asset value) in circumstances where the shares alone might not.

(c) As substitute for dividend

A bonus issue of warrants can be made to shareholders in circumstances where a company may not have the reserves or cash to pay a conventional dividend. Warrants have a value in cash but their issue does not affect the balance sheet. Nor is there always an adjustment to the share price when the shares go 'ex' a bonus issue of warrants as there is with a bonus issue of shares, as discussed further below.

(d) To increase shareholder value

Financial theory (and commonsense) suggests that value cannot be created by issuing a financial instrument for no consideration, leaving the assets and liabilities of the issuing company unchanged. Warrants with an initial subscription price equal to the underlying share's market price typically trade at 20% to 30% of the market price of the underlying share. In the case of a bonus issue of shares, a decrease in market price in proportion to the bonus issue is predicted by financial theory and, in round terms, observed in the market. However, in the case of a bonus issue of warrants, no particular 'ex bonus' adjustment is generally accepted or observable.

If the warrant subscription price is above the company's net asset value per share and above or at market price, as it usually is, shareholders suffer no immediate dilution. If the market price of the shares exceeds the subscription price when the warrants mature in say three or five years, the company and its existing shareholders will suffer an opportunity cost by issuing shares at a lower price than would have otherwise been possible. If the warrant issue is 'heavy' (say over 1-for-5), the overhang of shares may act as a dampener on increases in the market price. However, if the issue is kept to modest proportions, it appears that the value of the company's shares 'ex warrant issue' plus the warrants may exceed the previous value of the company's shares alone.

(iv) How warrants and options are valued

The factors relevant to valuing a warrant include the following:

(a) Intrinsic value

A warrant is said to be 'in the money' if the market price of the underlying share is higher than the exercise price. Thus, if the share price is $1.50 and a warrant carries the right to subscribe for one share at $1, the warrant is 'in the money' to the extent of $0.50 and has an 'intrinsic value' of that amount. In a situation where the exercise price of the warrant is higher than the market price, the warrant is said to be 'out of the money' and for the moment has no intrinsic value.

(b) Gearing

Warrants represent a convenient means for an investor to gear his investment. For example, if a warrant to acquire one share at $100 (current market price) is priced at $25, the gearing is 4 times, that is the investor has an exposure to 4 times as many shares by investing a given sum in warrants as he would if he used the same amount to buy shares.

(c) Maturity

Other things being equal, a warrant will be more valuable the longer its life. This value may be seen as a saving of carrying cost (since dividends on the shares will rarely equal the cost of funds to an investor). It may also be seen as a measure of the value of the period of time during which the growth of the underlying share and the volatility of its price and the market in general may combine to maximise the value of the warrant.

(d) Premium

Warrants rarely trade at their intrinsic value, except when near the end of their life or when the exercise price is so far below the market price of the shares that the warrants take on (for valuation purposes) the characteristics of a non-dividend paying share. In other circumstances, investors will be willing to pay a premium over the intrinsic value (if any) of the warrant. Any price for a warrant which is out of the money (and a warrant will always be worth something) represents a premium. The premium is in commonsense terms a measure of how much more it costs an investor to acquire one share by buying a warrant in the market and then exercising it rather than simply buying a share in the market. The formula for calculating the percentage premium is:

$$\frac{\text{Market price of warrant} + \text{Exercise price}}{\text{Share price}} - 1 \times 100$$

Thus, if the market price of a warrant is $0.80, the exercise price is $1.00 and the share price is $1.50, the warrant referred to in (a) above (which has an intrinsic value of $0.50) stands at a premium of 20% as follows:

$$\frac{\$0.80 + \$1.00}{\$1.50} - 1 \times 100 = 20\%$$

Premium is only a rough guide to whether a warrant is expensive or cheap. It does not specifically take into account maturity, which is an important element in the value of a warrant. It is also misleading where the warrant is substantially 'out of money' as any price for the warrant (and there will always be some price) will result in a large premium as calculated by the above formula.

(e) Growth rates and Capital Fulcrum Point (CFP)

The CFP is designed to measure the relationship between premium and maturity. Assuming the investor will in due course exercise his warrant, he is paying less now (ie the warrant price rather than the share price) but more in the future (ie the subscription price). At some compound growth rate, the future value of the amount saved now will exceed the subscription price. This percentage is the CFP. The formula is:

$$\left(\frac{\text{EP}}{\text{SP--WP}}\right)^{1/t} - 1$$

where EP is the exercise price, SP is the share price, WP is the warrant price and t is the maturity of the warrant in years (assuming annual compounding).

If the warrant described in the examples in (a) and (d) above had a three year life, the calculation of the CFP would be as follows:

$$\left(\frac{\$1.00}{\$1.50 - \$0.80}\right)^{\frac{1}{3}} - 1$$

$$= (1.43)^{\frac{1}{3}} - 1$$
$$= 1.125 - 1$$
$$= 12.5\%$$

If in this instance the investor believes the share price will grow at a rate higher than the CFP of 12.5%, he will prefer to hold the warrants rather than the underlying shares.

(f) More complex formulae

The most widely used formula for incorporating the various factors discussed above (including volatility and interest rates) is the Black-Scholes formula which first appeared in 1973. The formula depends, inter alia, on the estimated volatility of option and share prices and is based on the concept of setting up an option equivalent by borrowing money to buy stock. Professional option and warrant traders use this and other formulae (for which tables and calculator/computer applications have been developed) in making their trades so that they do influence market prices. Because of the degree of uncertainty involved, these formulae are more useful after the event (ie in the secondary market) than when a company is making a primary issue.

(v) Covered warrants

A covered or derivative warrant is a warrant issued by a third party which relates to shares of a company or to a market index, interest rate or currency. If it relates to a share, unlike the warrants discussed above, it is not issued by the company to whose securities it relates, and may not even be issued with their authority or approval. Consequently, the holder of the warrant has no rights against that company and the warrant does not involve that company in the issue of any new securities. The holder is dependent on the financial strength of the issuer and ranks as an unsecured creditor of that issuer. For that reason, issuers are typically major financial institutions. A holder of a covered warrant exercising his rights may have to pay his share of transfer costs, since existing, and not new, shares are being acquired.

A warrant of this type is in strict terms 'covered' only if it relates to shares of the company already owned or controlled by the issuer. An issuer will not always be in this position and a covered warrant normally contains a provision that the issuer may, at its option, pay a warrantholder cash equivalent to the market price of the share at the time of exercise of the warrant instead of transferring the share itself. Consequently, the issuer cannot easily be caught in a short squeeze. A warrant on an index can in practice only be settled in cash.

Covered warrants are similar to long-dated traded options. A covered warrant can be, in effect, a put option (the right to sell a share at a fixed price) as well as a call option, whereas a conventional warrant issued by a company is a call option. A warrant on an index can as easily be a put as a call. The holder of a put will benefit if the index falls.

A company which finds that a third party has issued warrants on its shares may feel that there is a potential opportunity cost. The company may have been intending to use warrants as a sweetener for a fund raising exercise of its own and may object that this could now be prejudiced if the edge is taken off investors' appetites. On the other hand, it may be argued that the covered warrant may actually increase investors' interest in the share. Issues of covered warrants frequently have larger capitalisations than warrant issues by a company and consequently tap into a larger institutional market.

The value of covered warrants can be assessed in the same way as the warrants discussed above. Covered warrants on shares tend to be issued at market price so that the price of the warrant is in effect the premium. Maturity is normally 2 to 3 years. The primary attraction of such warrants is hedging of portfolios, with some speculative activity. In some markets, the issuer will make a market in the warrants but if local practice permits, such warrants can be traded on the stock exchange, just as for conventional warrants.

(vi) Limitations to theory

Using warrant or option theory to analyse a transaction can be illuminating and works well in a trading context on a financial market. However, such theories remain too academic for most company managements. Few finance directors, in deciding whether their company should borrow money from a bank, consider that they are effectively disposing of the company's assets and acquiring an option to buy them back by paying off the loan, as option theory suggests. The assumption is that if the value of the assets pledged to bank declines below the loan value, the company can simply hand over the assets to the bank instead of repaying the loan. There are special situations – certain non-recourse loans or financial restructurings – where something like this may indeed happen but only as a last resort, not as a desirable feature of the transactions. Companies have to look further than the trading screen.

CHAPTER 2

Principles of valuation and pricing

An important part of most corporate finance transactions is valuing a company and putting a price on its shares or other securities. The two are obviously closely related as the valuation forms part of the basis of the price of an issue or, in the case of a bid, the price at which the transaction is carried out.

There is, however, an important distinction between valuation and pricing. Valuation tends to be at least in part a theoretical exercise. It is normal to consider a wide range of valuations. To claim that any one figure can be the precise valuation of a company is unrealistic. There are too many variables to be taken into account for absolute precision to be attainable. The weighting given to each factor in the valuation is largely a question of judgment, not mathematics. The valuation is therefore likely to be expressed as a range and to be partly subjective in nature.

Valuation will be affected by the attitudes of the people preparing it. A big project or a complex company would perhaps be approached cautiously by most purchasers but others might see additional opportunities rather than risks. Experience of a particular industry may have given some buyers encouragement, others burnt fingers. Value, like beauty, is at least partially in the eye of the beholder.

Pricing on the other hand is a much earthier process. It is disastrous to stray from the practical disciplines of the market-place. Whereas valuation can be a somewhat leisurely, almost academic pursuit, prices are fixed rapidly and tested immediately in the market. Timing is vital. Sentiment can change abruptly.

If an issue price is set too high in the opinion of the market on the day of subscription, the issue will flop; too low and there will be embarrassing over-subscriptions. In either case, substantial amounts of money will be lost and months of careful planning will be largely wasted.

In the case of a bid, the acid test is success or failure. Price is always a (if not the) determining factor. If the price is too low, the entire campaign may fail; if it is too high, funds which may later be badly needed are lost to the company. Whether the pricing of a corporate finance deal has been correct tends to be all too obvious.

I VALUATION

In a corporate finance transaction, valuation cannot usually be taken to very sophisticated lengths. There are two main reasons for this. First, there tends to be a severe constraint on time and manpower; second, the information available may be incomplete, out of date and not in the most relevant form. This is seen in its most extreme form in a contested takeover but holds true to a greater or lesser extent in most corporate finance transactions.

When investors refer to the 'worth of a company', they usually mean the worth of all the ordinary shares or common stock of that company. This is almost always the case with a public listed company, although care may be needed if other classes of securities are also listed. A private company often has a small share capital. The bulk of its funding will be provided by shareholder loans, which is a more flexible and perhaps more tax efficient method of providing the necessary base of stockholders' investment. In such a case, the definition of worth can be usefully extended to include any shareholder loans.

(i) Earnings multiple/price earnings ratio

'Earnings multiple' or 'price earnings ratio' has become a measure of valuation with which even infrequent stock market investors or observers are comfortable and familiar. However, some refinements in the way earnings are calculated and how the multiple is applied are necessary to ensure the earnings multiple concept is as appropriate as possible in a particular case. The main considerations include:

(a) How should 'earnings' be defined?

Earnings for this purpose can most usefully be regarded as the profits of the company and its subsidiaries and associates after deduction of the charges which rank ahead of the shareholders entitled to those earnings. Consequently, all interest charges owing to bankers or others should be deducted as these claims on the company's income and assets rank ahead of shareholders. Tax should also be deducted for this reason. If any proportion of income is attributable to outside shareholders of a subsidiary (for example if a subsidiary is not wholly owned by the company), this proportion, called 'minority interests' is also deducted. The above represents standard accounting treatment of 'earnings' as they would appear in an audited profit and loss statement in most countries, that is consolidated profit after interest, tax and minority interests.

(b) 'Attributable' earnings

The principle is to match what is being valued with the earnings attributable to it or generated by it. If there are preference shares outstanding which are entitled to receive a certain dividend, this should be deducted from the earnings before the ordinary shares can be valued. If there are convertible securities outstanding which are likely to be converted, the interest should be added back to earnings (with appropriate adjustments for tax) and the earnings related to the enlarged number of shares in issue after conversion.

(c) 'Recurrent' earnings

If a multiple is applied to a particular year's earnings to calculate a valuation, the implication is that the elements included in the earnings will be present in each year's earnings for the foreseeable future. Profits or losses which are made from activities which are not part of the company's ordinary business, such as the sale of a fixed asset used in the business, may be separately listed in the profit and loss account under the heading 'extraordinary items'. Such items should not be included in 'earnings' to which the multiple is applied for valuation purposes. However, there is also a category of 'exceptional items'—items which are held to derive from the ordinary business of the company but because of their size or other factors need to be disclosed separately if the accounts are to show a true and fair view. The distinction between extraordinary and exceptional items is sometimes difficult to draw clearly and different treatments of similar transactions are possible by different companies. As exceptional items are part of 'earnings', whether a particular profit is classified as extraordinary or exceptional can make a significant difference to valuation as well as clouding comparisons between companies.

'Recurrent' earnings imply that the business is a going concern. For this reason, depreciation should not be added back to earnings, as it is in a cash flow calculation. It is assumed that regular reinvestment at the level of the depreciation charge will be required to ensure that the earnings are indeed recurrent.

(d) Timing

Earnings are expressed over a single financial period, often a calendar year. Trading conditions may not fall conveniently into annual patterns. If a company has made a loss of 5 in the first half of the year and recovered to a profit of 10 in the second half, the accounts will show earnings of 5 for the whole year (10 for the second half minus 5 for the first). In this case, if the business itself is not seasonal, the year-end profitability is running at the annual rate of at least 20. To use the published figure of 5 for the basis of valuation is likely to be misleading.

(e) Forecast vs historic earnings

In assessing earnings, analysts will attempt to form as up-to-date a picture as possible. Past earnings are only of interest as a guide to the future. Reliable estimates and forecasts are much sought after. However, the degree of uncertainty in the estimates is likely to increase sharply beyond a few months in the future and the analysis will become more speculative.

(f) Other adjustments

The above are the first steps in identifying the most appropriate figure from a company's accounts to take as the starting point. No change is attempted to the numbers as presented by the company itself. At this point, the analyst must begin to think for himself what actual adjustments might be needed to ensure his valuation is soundly based. The valuation must also be comparable with valuations of other similar companies, a highly relevant consideration in most corporate finance transactions. The types of adjustments to look for include the following:

Accounting policies.   Have accounting policies been recently changed and with what effect? Most changes are linked to developments in accounting and auditing practice but the introduction of a change in accounting policy often seems to increase profits rather than the reverse. Popular areas are the valuation of closing inventory, the treatment of research and development expenditure, the life over which fixed assets are depreciated, and the circumstances when interest can be capitalised.

Components of income/profits.   In using a multiple of earnings to value a company, it is critical to ensure that all the elements included in the profits being multiplied are in fact appropriately treated in this fashion. This is particularly important where a very high or very low multiple is being used. Items which are not best treated in the manner include:

INTEREST ON SURPLUS CASH DEPOSITS OR INVESTMENT INCOME ON FUNDS UNDER MANAGEMENT.   Cash can hardly be worth more than its face value. If interest is earned at 10% on surplus cash of 100 and interest income included in earnings to which a 15 times multiple is applied, cash of 100 will in effect be valued at 150.

RENTS.   If a property is owned by a company but not for the moment used in its business, rent may be earned. In this case, it is preferable to value the surplus property separately and not include rentals in profits to which a multiple is applied. The multiple may bear no relationship to the capitalisation rate appropriate to the property.

FOREIGN EXCHANGE GAINS.   In times of unstable foreign exchange rates, a company with an international range of business may make substantial gains or losses from the timing of payment for its purchases and conversion of its foreign exchange sales income or simply by taking a speculative position. The company might argue that this is part and parcel of its regular activities. An analyst might well feel uncomfortable at putting a multiple on substantial foreign exchange gains (or losses) and risking distortion of the valuation. A better treatment is to exclude such items on the grounds that in the longer term gains and losses of this type will probably balance out. The same argument applies to say share dealing profits.

INCOME FROM SALES OF ASSETS.   Some asset-based companies regularly buy and sell major assets as well as utilise them in their business. Examples of industries where this is common practice are transportation (particularly shipping and airlines) and property development. The companies may argue that it is their regular involvement in a particular line of business that enables them to make sales of assets which outsiders could not achieve. Nevertheless, asset-based industries are often highly cyclical so that the reliability of such profits is hard to gauge. Differing accounting treatments by companies in the same industry complicate the picture.

ASSOCIATES.   If a company is accounted for as an associate, the attributable percentage of its earnings (rather than just dividends received) will be taken into the profits of the company holding the stake. Associated companies are defined as companies in which the holding company has a substantial interest (say a minimum of 20% of the equity) and some influence over management, evidenced for example by being able to appoint at least one board member. However, board membership may confer little control. The holding company has no access to the associate's cash flow which may be a weakness. There appears to be some merit in the verdict of a well-known City of London financier that 'associated company accounting is for the birds'. Certainly, caution is required if the contribution from associates (which may themselves be rated at a higher or lower price earnings multiple) is a significant proportion of the whole.

SALES AND EXPENSES NEAR YEAR END.   By accelerating or delaying shipment of goods or completion of projects, management can adjust profits to some extent from one year to the next. Many types of indirect or non-variable costs can be deferred by management on a short-term basis, for example an advertising campaign, a branch-opening programme or the hiring of additional administrative staff. It may well be legitimate to smooth profits to reflect underlying business trends but the analyst should beware of the effect on a single year's figures.

If a business is highly geared, increases or decreases in interest costs will have a marked effect on profits before taxation. Consideration should be given in such cases to applying the multiple to earnings plus interest paid and then deducting the amount of the debt to reach the valuation.

The underlying principle behind the above adjustments is that the multiple of earnings method is most satisfactory where the earnings are recurrent earnings generated from continuing business activities. If the earnings figure is substantially influenced by net financial income such as interest and foreign exchange gains, rents and sales of non-current assets, distortions are inevitable.

(g) Setting the multiple

When an adjusted figure for earnings has been established, it remains to set an appropriate multiple. Multiples vary by market, sector and individual company.

It is possible to try to calculate a suitable multiple on a theoretical basis. The major determining factors are the expected rate of growth, the perceived risk and the marketability of the shares. However, a more usual starting point is to identify comparable companies and use their multiples as a basis. Adjustments can then be made to reflect factors such as growth, risk and marketability. The higher the rate of growth which is anticipated, the higher the multiple. A company which is expected to exceed the average rate of growth for its sector should be accorded a premium. The estimate of risk should encompass if possible both commercial aspects, such as areas of business activity engaged in, and financial aspects, such as level of gearing. Most listed shares should be adequately marketable. A private company would be allocated a lower multiple than a public listed company.

The multiple appropriate for historic earnings figures will be higher than for forecast earnings. The historic multiple will reflect expectations of growth which are already being included in the forecast earnings. In addition, the forecast will contain some element of risk whereas the historic figures are definite.

A comparison of multiples may be distorted by different treatments of tax, when the apparent amount of tax due on the basis of pre-tax profits differs from the actual amount of tax paid. In financial statements, standard tax charges are normally applied but care must be taken if this is not so. Even if the deduction for tax is comparable, a company which is able to reduce or delay its tax payments by skilful tax planning may be able to achieve faster growth by use of the additional resources. This factor may also make it difficult to compare an average market multiple in one country with another. Tax rates may differ sharply, but not necessarily tax payments.

(ii) Net assets

An alternative way to value a company is to value its assets and then subtract its liabilities as shown in the balance sheet.

An example of a typical consolidated balance sheet laid out in vertical form is given below:

	$m	$m
Fixed assets		
land		25
buildings		10
machinery and equipment		15
		50
Associated company		8
Investments		7
Current assets:		
stocks and work-in-progress	28	
accounts receivable and pre-payments	13	
bank balance and deposits	20	
	61	
Current liabilities:		
accounts payable and accrued charges	15	
bank loans and overdrafts	20	
taxation	5	
proposed dividend	5	
	45	

Net current assets		16
Goodwill on consolidation		5
Intangible assets		5
		91
Less: deferred liabilities		
long-term loans	25	
deferred taxation	5	
		30
minority interests		13
Consolidated net assets		48
Consolidated net tangible assets		38
Net assets per share		
(75 million shares in issue)		$0.64
Net tangible assets per share		$0.51

In carrying out a valuation on a net asset basis, each item must be examined critically.

(a) Fixed assets

Most time will probably be spent on the fixed assets, typically the largest items in the balance sheet. If they have been owned by the group for a number of years, substantial differences may have arisen between book value and current market value.

A number of important considerations must be borne in mind when a company instructs a professional valuer or attempts to make its own estimate. In the case of a flotation or issue of securities, it must be assumed that the business in which property is used will continue as a going concern, otherwise the entire exercise would be in doubt. In this case, only an existing use basis can be used for valuation. Property which is of a specialised type may be difficult to value except as an integral part of the business.

Property which is surplus or which could be sold independently of the business can be regarded in a different light. The valuer should be asked to give his opinion of the best alternate use, that is the use which would produce the highest valuation of the property. The value of vacant land depends on what planning permissions have been obtained. A completed building may be valued on the basis of the income it generates from rental or on the assumption that it will be sold on the open market, either as a whole or perhaps floor by floor. Major income generating assets such as hotels, quarries and mines may be valued by discounting the net cash flow attributable to their operations.

(b) Associated companies

Associates are held at cost plus share of profits or losses since acquisition. It will be hard to check the validity of this figure without access to the associate's accounts. If advances have been made to the associate, they will also be included in the figure for associates. If the associate is a private company with a small share capital and large loans, the recoverability of the loans may be in doubt.

(c) Investments

Long-term holdings in companies which are not associates may be held under 'investments'. Such figures can sometimes represent the 'tip of the iceberg' if other transactions have been carried out to finance investee companies. Investments which are themselves listed or have an open market value should be valued at market.

(d) Stocks and accounts receivable

Stocks and accounts receivable are the most vulnerable part of a manufacturing concern's balance sheet. A fresh look at the real value of these items sometimes produces some startling differences of opinion. If the business is not continued, stock may become largely worthless and receivables difficult to collect. It is prudent to assume that some provision may be required in this area.

(e) Goodwill and intangible assets

Goodwill on consolidation represents a premium paid for control of a company over the fair value of its net assets. Most service companies can only be purchased at a premium to net asset value. Goodwill is regarded as an intangible asset although it might well be backed up by excellent earnings prospects. Other intangible assets might be expenditure on such items as trademarks, brand names, licences, patents and costs incurred in flotation or reorganisation. Some of these items will have more continuing worth than others.

(f) Loans

Loans may have clauses which trigger a right to call for repayment if control of the borrower changes. This may increase the cash demands on a bidder. Other terms of the loans, particularly currency, maturity and interest rate, may be relevant. If any listed loan stock is outstanding, its market price may be above or below par because of interest rate changes or other factors. In this case, the market value of the loan rather than the nominal value may be relevant.

(g) Deferred tax

A provision for deferred tax may be made when capital allowances for taxation purposes are significantly higher than the depreciation charges applied by the company in its accounts. A provision is made on the assumption that a lower tax charge now means more tax must be paid later. Some managements feel that they can manage their tax affairs so that the low tax charge will continue indefinitely and argue that deferred taxation reserves should be counted as equity.

(h) Minority interests

Minority interests will arise when a group owns less than 100% of the share capital of a subsidiary. This is also a warning sign that not all the assets shown in the balance sheet are wholly under the control of the parent company.

(i) Contingent liabilities

In addition to liabilities shown on the face of the balance sheet, there may be guarantees outstanding or other contingent liabilities. Liabilities can also arise through litigation, contractual arrangements, capital investment commitments, lease obligations, severance payments and unfunded pension plans. In some circumstances, liabilities may have been taken 'off-balance sheet' through use of joint ventures and associated companies and investments. Sometimes these liabilities are said to be 'non-recourse' whereas in practical terms it might be very difficult for a company to walk away from them and keep its banking relationships intact.

Net assets are of most relevance in acquisitions where the acquiror will obtain 100% control, conferring direct access to the target company's assets. The net asset value may be the single most significant figure for takeover exponents whose chief objective is to acquire assets at a discount to improve their own balance sheet or to sell off at a profit.

A holder of a minority interest has no direct access to the assets underlying his shares. The net asset backing in a flotation, where a shareholder is buying a small percentage interest, may therefore be less relevant. In some markets, investors prefer to see an issue price which is backed by net assets. It is felt that if the earnings collapse at least the net asset backing will provide some support for the share price.

The net asset statement will be scrutinised closely for the level of gearing which is shown. Net assets may be compared to total liabilities or just loans. Any cash resources will normally be subtracted from loans.

(iii) Composite basis

(a) Unconsolidated vs consolidated position

If sufficient information is available, a composite approach to valuation is often more satisfactory than taking an overall earnings multiple or net asset backing. Where a group consists of a number of essentially different assets or businesses, it is preferable to look at each on an individual basis. This requires constructing a valuation on an unconsolidated rather than consolidated basis. In a large company, this may have to be taken further involving a valuation of each major category of asset.

The main reason for building up a composite valuation on an unconsolidated basis is the different nature of businesses or assets which may be included in a group. Some businesses are able to make a considerable profit from a very low capital investment. They may require a high level of recurrent expenditure on, for example, advertising which is expended year by year without an asset base being built up. A well-known brand name with immense commercial value may not appear on a balance sheet. Other assets may have a high book value but a relatively small income. For example, the more prime the location of a property, the lower its yield.

(b) Adding earnings and asset valuations

If a group consists of these two types of assets, a consolidated valuation will result in an under-estimate of the worth of the group. On a consolidated basis, a group with a balance sheet and earnings as set out below may appear to be worth approximately $80–90 million, whether an earnings multiple or net asset backing valuation is used. However, if the components of the group are examined separately, it will be readily apparent that the group's value is greater.

An example of this principle would be as follows:

	$m	$m
Land and buildings		50
Plant and machinery		5
Investments		10
Current assets: stock	30	
accounts receivable	15	
cash	25	
	70	
Current liabilities: creditors	15	
overdraft	15	
	30	40
		105
Less: long-term debt		10
Net assets		95

For the latest financial year, the company reported earnings of $10 m and the current year's budget is for a small increase. A typical price earnings multiple for this industry is 8.

It would appear that a fair value for the above company is about $80–90 million representing an industry average multiple and a small discount on net assets. On further enquiry the following facts emerge:

(i) Land and buildings are factories only half occupied by the company itself. The remainder are vacant or rented to third parties.

(ii) Investment of $10 m consists half of an investment in a research and development company engaged in design work for the business and half of listed shares unrelated to the business.

(iii) Cash balances of $25 m are not utilised in the business but are managed separately by an investment adviser. There is no foreseeable requirement for additional working capital in the business.

A composite valuation of the business would be as follows:

	$ m
(i) Earnings	10
Less: Income from rentals and surplus cash	(2)
	8
Business valued on 8 times multiple	64
(ii) Surplus land and buildings at valuation	25
(iii) Surplus investment at market value	5
(iv) Surplus cash after a $5 m contingency	20
Total valuation	114
As compared with initial valuation	80–90

The composite method is likely to place the highest valuation on the group. It is most relevant where there is at least a possibility that the group might be broken up and sold to realise full value for each independent unit. When a hostile bid reaches this level, the directors of the target company have to consider whether it is in the shareholders' interests to continue to resist.

(iv) Other methods

As mentioned above, valuations can also be carried out by reference to various other methods. The main ones are discussed in (*a*) and (*b*) below:

(a) Dividends

The dividend paid on an ordinary share divided by the share price and expressed as a percentage is called the 'dividend yield'. It is normally expressed gross, without taking any account of the recipient's tax position. Income-conscious investors may place considerable weight on annual income received although they would acknowledge that capital gain is also part of the total return equation. Companies which pay out almost all earnings as dividend may be valued on this basis alone. As dividends and earnings are virtually identical in this case, valuation on the basis of dividends is also an earnings valuation.

In some markets, investors and other market participants will pay particular attention to the amount of dividend paid. They regard this as a more concrete return than the more speculative nature of capital gains. The fact that the company is able to pay out a substantial cash dividend is taken as a reliable test of strength.

(b) Cash flow

Using cash flow as a basis for valuation is essentially similar to using earnings or dividends. However, as the format of analysis based on cash flows involves setting out figures for a significant number of years ahead, the analyst is forced to spell out assumptions on such matters as capital investment and working capital requirements, inflation and timing of tax payments. In addition, risk can be incorporated more systematically by using expected values for the various components of cash flow rather than single point estimates. A computer model can be constructed by assigning probability distributions to each variable. A large number of possible outcomes are then calculated to produce a probability distribution of valuation estimates.

The snag of carrying out such a valuation in the context of corporate finance transactions is that there is rarely sufficient reliable data about a company and its many variable features to make the numerous assumptions required for the analysis. If general assumptions are made concerning estimated flows, little is gained by using the cash flow method. The net cash flow for an average year begins to look like an adjusted figure for estimated earnings. If it is assumed that cash flows continue indefinitely, the discount rate begins to look like a reflection of the multiple.

Relatively simple businesses owning a single major capital asset such as a hotel, quarry or mine may be usefully assessed by the cash flow method. The nature of the investment in such a company is quite close to a capital investment in its major asset. The discounted cash flow method has for a considerable period of time been widely used in industry to make decisions about capital investments.

II   PRICE

Pricing is essentially a practical skill whereas valuation is at least partially academic.

(i) Flotations

In flotations, pricing is chiefly based on comparison. An investor has a choice between buying a large number of existing shares or an unfamiliar one which is being floated. Although novelty can have some appeal, investor inertia and a sentiment of 'better the devil you know' may prevail unless there is a tangible incentive. The pricing of a flotation is therefore normally pitched at a discount to the ratings of the most comparable companies. The ratings of comparable companies are influenced by fundamental factors such as price earnings ratio, net asset backing and dividend yield. However, the price is set effectively at one stage removed from these fundamentals. It must also be remembered in a flotation or any other market exercise that the average investor is buying only a small number of shares and no premium for control or access to underlying assets is appropriate, as it would be for a takeover.

(ii) Rights issues

As rights issues are made to a company's existing shareholders, the question of pricing is not so sensitive. Most markets have a standard approach to pricing which again is based on the principle of a discount. In this case, the discount is not so much related to comparable companies as to the price of the company's own shares. Some incentive must be given to shareholders to take up the rights issue rather than simply buying more shares in the market which is a quicker and more convenient process. It is unlikely that fundamentals will be very relevant to the pricing of a conventionally sized issue. However, if the issue is so large it amounts to a virtual re-launch of the company, fundamentals will come into play in much the same way as for a flotation.

(iii) Placings

As in the case of a rights issue, markets normally have their own standard discounts which apply to a placing of shares to investors other than existing shareholders. In this instance, the position of the existing shareholders is highly relevant. They will wish to see the shares placed as close to market price as possible so that share price does not come under pressure. They will also be concerned if their attributable earnings or assets per share are likely to be significantly diluted.

(iv) Takeovers

In launching a takeover particularly if it is contested, some premium over market price is required if the bid is not to fall flat on its face. It is also helpful if it can be demonstrated that shareholders of the target company will receive an increase in their income. If it is possible to offer them an increase in asset and earnings backing, this will also be of some effect particularly as it deprives the defence of any argument about dilution.

If the price for success is too high and exceeds the valuation on a theoretical basis, the board of the bidding company must consider whether they should withdraw from the fray. In this connection it is useful to set limits in advance, even if they are somewhat flexible. On the other side of the table, the board of the defending company must consider whether they should accept an offer which exceeds their valuation of the company. Even if it could be successfully resisted, is it really in the shareholders' interests to continue the struggle?

The relationship between pricing and valuation is clearly a very close one with pricing in many cases beng the direct descendant of valuation. However, it may be that the price needed for a successful issue is, for example, too low to be in the company's interests. In these circumstances, it needs a strong will and determination to resist being carried along by the momentum and impetus a transaction can generate. In takeovers, one of the most difficult decisions is to recognise that the price necessary for success cannot be justified in terms of valuation. It is also a bitter pill for a board which believes it can resist an unwelcome bid successfully to acknowledge that they have lured an offeror too far and must lose in order to win.

Part 2

Going public

Introduction

SOME BASIC TERMS AND CONCEPTS

Part 2 of this book deals with going public. As with many specialised types of financing, a certain amount of jargon is used in describing the procedures, the participants and their role. This review is intended to introduce some basic terms and concepts and to present an overview of the more detailed aspects covered in the individual chapters.

(i) Terminology

The terms *'going public'* or *'flotation'* are applied to the situation where a company first seeks to obtain a listing for one or more classes of its securities on a recognised stock exchange. This process is referred to in the US as an *'initial public offering'*. Going public usually involves the raising of funds either by the company or its shareholders or both. Occasionally, all that is sought is a listing on an exchange without any further marketing of shares. This procedure is called an *'introduction'* and can only be used when a sufficient spread of shareholders to ensure adequate marketability is already considered to exist. This spread will be judged both by absolute numbers of shareholders – at least several hundred are desirable – and by the percentage of the total issued share capital held by the public.

The term *'prospectus'* refers to the formal documents which have to be filed with the relevant authorities when a company offers its securities to the public. The amount of information to be included in the prospectus is the greatest on the occasion when a company first goes public.

Prospectuses may well have to be filed when subsequent issues of shares or other securities are made. Much of the information required in the first instance does not need to be repeated. Subsequent issues therefore tend to involve less documentation and expense. In the US, it is now possible to have a prospectus on file with the authorities in approved form which can be used at short notice as the basis of further issues by a public company, normally of debt.

The procedures for an issue are likely to be simplified and considerable time saved if a prospectus does not have to be filed. The legal advisers to a company making a subsequent issue will devote considerable time and research to devising a structure for the issue which if possible does not involve filing a prospectus. However, this is not likely to be possible when a company goes public initially.

The term *'promoters'* has a legal definition in some countries. In this book, it is used in a more general sense to describe people closely connected with the company going public and who are the prime movers of the issue. Such people are likely to be existing shareholders or directors of the company,

'*Underwriting*' is a term derived from the insurance industry. It can be explained as a kind of insurance for the company and its shareholders if the issue does not prove popular with the market in general. The basic function of an underwriter is in return for a fee to take on the risk that an issue will not be fully subscribed by the investors at which it is directed. Flotations are open for subscription by the public at large, whose response may be difficult to guage. A flotation involves, by definition, the shares of a company new to the public so there is no existing market price to act as a yardstick for the issue price. Underwriting therefore requires a degree of judgment and willingness to accept risk, at least in principle. An underwriter will normally expect to be able to generate investment demand for issues that it underwrites, thus hedging its position.

The financial institution which takes the lead in managing and underwriting an issue is variously referred to as an investment bank, merchant bank or issuing house. Sometimes this institution may not be a bank at all but rather a stockbroker or other financial services company. For convenience the term '*merchant bank*' is used throughout.

Flotations represent attractive business for merchant banks, as they give prominence to the bank's name and enlarge the number of their public company clients. The relationship which develops between the lead manager of an issue and the top management of the company being floated can be close and long-lasting. This stems from the essential co-operation between them during the preparation of a prospectus and the detailed knowledge of the company which the merchant bank acquires during this period. If the issue goes well, the success is a shared one and the merchant bank in question has obtained a loyal customer. One of the problems with mergers and acquisitions from the merchant banking standpoint is that, at least on the vendor's side, the merchant bank tends to lose a customer at the end of the day however well it performs.

As well as the basic management and underwriting fees, there may well be benefits to merchant banks in terms of other financial services which can be offered to the new public company including insurance, management of pension funds, deposits and foreign exchange.

(ii) 'New issue' and 'offer for sale'

Going public normally involves the widening of the shareholder base by attracting a range of new shareholders. The mechanism by which this is achieved may be either:

(i)   an issue of new shares by a company to investors who subscribe for them in cash, referred to in this book as a 'new issue'; or

(ii) a sale of already issued shares by existing shareholders, referred to as an 'offer for sale'; or

(iii) a combination of the two.

In some jurisdictions, new shares are issued in renounceable form, enabling shareholders to renounce them in favour of a third party during a certain period of time without the payment of transfer duty. In such cases, a company going public via a 'new issue' will issue the shares first to the merchant bank which is leading the issue. The merchant bank will 'offer for sale' all the shares comprised in the issue, whether they are new shares just issued by the company or existing shares. The term 'new issue' is not used to distinguish between the two.

In jurisdictions where shareholders cannot renounce their holdings without the payment of transfer duty, there is no advantage in using the renounceable format. In such cases, interposing the merchant bank in a 'new issue' increases costs. The company going public will therefore offer new shares to the public directly, under the guidance of the merchant bank.

There are important differences between the position following a new issue and the position following an offer for sale. In a new issue, the company going public raises new capital whereas in an offer for sale, the existing shareholders selling their shares receive the proceeds. The company itself receives no cash. It is important therefore to establish from the outset whether the company requires or would benefit from new capital and how this is to be reconciled with the objectives of the shareholders.

The second difference concerns the size of the issue. In most countries, the stock exchange sets rules regarding the minimum percentage of the company's capital which must be in public hands before a listing is granted. This percentage is considered the most convenient measure of whether there will be sufficient shares available in the market to form a satisfactory basis for trading. Frequently the size of the issue will be determined by the need to satisfy this minimum which is typically around 25% of the amount of the security for which a listing is sought. If it is necessary to ensure that a minimum percentage be in public hands, the money amount involved in a new issue will be greater than for an offer for sale. This is illustrated below.

EXAMPLE

A company wishes to go public and is forecasting after-tax profits of $20 million. The terms agreed with the merchant bank are that the price earnings ratio will be 15 times the forecast earnings. The valuation of the company for the purpose of the flotation is:

$$15 \times \$20 \text{ million} = \$300 \text{ million}$$

The stock exchange requires a minimum of 25% of the share capital to be in public hands.

If an offer for sale is employed, existing shareholders will arrange to sell one-quarter of their shares and the size of the issue will be:

$$\$300 \text{ million} \times 0.25 = \$75 \text{ million}$$

If a new issue is employed, the position is different. It is assumed (for the purpose of the analysis) that with the addition of the amount to be raised by the new issue the worth of the company, previously assessed at $300 million, will be increased by exactly the size of the new issue. The size of the new issue (x) required so that 25% of the issued share capital will be in public hands is therefore found by:

$$x = 0.25 \ \$(300 \ \text{million} + x)$$
$$x = £75 \ \text{million} + 0.25x$$
$$0.75x = \$75 \ \text{million}$$
$$x = \$100 \ \text{million}$$

Consequently, the size of the new issue, at $100 million, is one-third larger than the size of the offer for sale, at $75 million. The company itself is worth $400 million in market terms, rather than $300 million, and has an additional $100 million in cash.

The above equation can be re-arranged to solve for the percentage of a company's share capital which would have to be issued to raise a given amount of money, which is sometimes the question which concerns the promoters more. For example, if $125 million were needed, the percentage of the company's enlarged share capital (x) which would have to be sold to the public would be:

$$125 = x(300 + 125)$$
$$125 = 425x$$
$$x = 29.4\%$$

To raise $125 million for the company rather than $100 million, existing shareholders have to accept a 29.4% decrease in their percentage shareholding rather than a 25% decrease. This type of decrease in a shareholder's percentage shareholding in a company is often referred to as 'dilution'. Dilution is also used to describe any decrease in shareholders' attributable earnings and assets caused by issues of new shares.

It is sometimes considered that investors are likely to be more receptive to a new issue than an offer for sale. The money raised by a new issue goes into the company to strengthen its balance sheet or provide funding for future growth. An offer for sale on the other hand puts money into the pocket of existing owners. If the owners (who may be presumed to know more about the company and its prospects than a new investor) are selling, investors may ask themselves whether they are well advised to buy. To counter this reaction, the company going public may issue some new shares even when the main purpose of the flotation is to allow existing shareholders to sell. In any event, the existing shareholders are decreasing their percentage holding in the company and so may be considered to be disposing of an interest.

(iii) Overview of topics covered

(a) Reasons for going public – advantages and disadvantages (see ch 3 below)

The factors involved in deciding whether to go public mostly have two aspects. Along with the attractions come responsibilities, constraints and costs. The pluses and minuses may appear to offset each other. The decision may well hang on the weighting that the promoters give to a particular factor. Some may consider their privacy is paramount and draw back. Others may emphasise the increased growth possibilities and press on. Where the balance of advantage lies will depend on the particular circumstances of the company and the personalities and ambitions of its directors and shareholders.

Chapter 3 is based on the assumption that the company's shareholders and management are considering going public from scratch, via a new issue or offer for sale. In Part 3 of this book, alternative methods of gaining a listing are considered which may be suitable if the promoters' objective is to obtain a listing and they are not primarily concerned with increasing the spread of shareholders or raising money at the initial stage. Other things being equal, the management of a company which is capable of going public in its own right will probably wish to do this rather than utilise the methods described in Part 3. However, most of the advantages and disadvantages discussed in ch 3 are also relevant to the decision as to whether to obtain a listing by other methods.

(b) Going public – is it a realistic prospect? – what structural changes are needed? (see ch 4 below)

After weighing up the factors involved, the promoters may conclude that the balance of advantage lies in the company going public. However, this does not necessarily mean a flotation is a practical possibility. Before committing their own time and starting to incur substantial professional expenses, the promoters need to take a hard-headed look at their chances. A list of the criteria which might be used to make this assessment is set out in ch 4 below.

It is assumed for the purpose of this chapter that the promoters wish the company to gain a listing on a major stock exchange. There are an increasing number of alternatives to full listings. A company which may not qualify for a 'big board' listing may nevertheless be suitable for trading on an 'unlisted' securities market or 'over-the-counter'. In these markets, the rules concerning degree of disclosure about the company, track record and the percentage to be held in public hands are likely to be less stringent.

Chapter 4 also deals with the structural reorganisation which may be needed in preparation for going public. Private interests are rarely formed up ready-made in an orderly group. The gearing, voting rights and number of shares in issue may also require some tailoring to suit market preferences. Some merchant banking and legal advice will begin to be needed at this stage.

(c) Forming a team and estimating expenses (see ch 5 below)

Once the review outlined in ch 4 below has been completed, the company and its promoters have come as far as they can on their own. If the decision is taken to proceed, a team of advisers must be formed, starting most probably with the appointment of a merchant bank.

The calls on the company's own resources of manpower are frequently underestimated. The involvement of senior executives cannot be avoided. It is important that their team of professional advisers be experienced in the specialist business of flotations and capable of working harmoniously together over a protracted period. Work on a flotation requires close co-operation and liaison in sometimes trying circumstances. The individual roles of the advisers are described in ch 5 below.

Expenses begin to mount rapidly and are considerable. With the appointment of advisers, the major categories of expenses (and who is responsible for meeting them) can be identified and the approximate amounts estimated. A list of estimated expenses will be produced by the merchant bank. Expenses can be reduced by careful planning. Interest on over-subscriptions may provide a contribution. The availability of funds from the flotation at least means a ready source of cash for paying the expenses is at hand.

(d) Components of a prospectus, timetable and list of documents (see ch 6 below)

The main components of a prospectus, the expected timetable and the documents required are set out in ch 6 below. A prospectus has a dual function. It provides information about the company and its management as required by law or the stock exchange regulations, so that investors will have sufficient information to make an informed judgment. Strict penalties apply if false or misleading information is given. At the same time, it serves as a selling document to persuade investors to take the plunge. These two functions sit rather uneasily with each other at times.

While much of the work can be left to the professional advisers, ultimately the contents of the prospectus, even the technical sections, are the responsibility of the directors of the company. The directors can delegate the preparation and supervision of the prospectus but they cannot delegate responsibility for it. The best strategy is to avoid giving any hostages to fortune in the statements made.

The timetable suggested by the advisers (a minimum of 4 months) may seem leisurely to the company's executives when the work is starting. Delays are the rule rather than the exception and the timetable should have some slack in it to allow for contingencies. No matter how methodical the preparations, the final stages seem always to be completed in something approaching a panic. In the last days before publication, it is difficult to make significant changes and the participants become locked into meeting a particular date, the alternative being a significant postponement.

To assist in meeting the timetable and monitoring progress, a checklist of documents is drawn up, with responsibilities assigned to the various parties involved in the flotation. This checklist should tie in with the timetable and vice versa. A sample timetable and list of documents are included in ch 6.

(e) How to judge timing and pricing (see ch 7 below)

The skill in timing lies in identifying when favourable periods in market and sector cycles coincide with a good performance from the company itself. Ideally, a 'window' of some months should be established as the cumbersome nature of new issue procedures makes fine-tuning difficult.

Pricing starts from the fundamental techniques of valuation, including forecast price earnings ratio and underlying net asset backing. However, underwriters cannot afford to let their analysis become too theoretical. Comparison with the ratings of similar companies already traded in the market is probably the single most important aspect of pricing. A shrewd feeling for what the market will stand, based on discreet soundings among potential investors, is a valuable cross-check. The most market-orientated method of pricing is by tender. This may inhibit large subscriptions by 'stags'. The realities of the market-place are ignored by issuers and underwriters at their peril.

(f) Marketing, applications and the start of trading (see ch 8 below)

Preparations for the launch must be set in hand well before the actual publication of the prospectus. Tell-tale signs of a company being groomed for flotation may appear some months in advance. Underwriting the issue guarantees receipt of the funds by the company and/or its shareholders and ensures a reasonable spread of investors even if the issue does not prove attractive to the market in general. As the company is an unknown quantity to the market, the underwriters do run a considerable risk.

Application procedures should be kept as simple as possible. Deciding on the basis of allotment is one of the more pleasant problems in a flotation, since the greater the difficulty, the bigger the success of the issue.

The first day of trading takes place in an atmosphere of high excitement with hectic activity in turnover as positions taken before the start of official trading are unwound. Turnover will subsequently subside to more normal levels. If the shares go to a discount on the issue price, a feeling of anticlimax will set in. It is interesting to compare the initial subscription list with the register of members of the company at some time later. The latter may be significantly smaller.

Opinions vary on what constitutes the success of a flotation, depending in part on the different perspectives of management, underwriters and existing and new shareholders. High levels of subscription and active trading at the opening do not always translate into satisfactory longer-term price performance.

(iv) Approach adopted

In approaching the subject of going public, emphasis has been placed on concepts and techniques which are valid in financial markets generally. To follow too closely the detailed practices of a single market at a particular time is not very helpful in an era of rapid change in regulations and investor preferences. Company law and taxation are in any event specialist subjects in their own right.

The basic questions facing a company and its promoters when it goes public and the appropriate responses have substantial common elements. In the following chapters, a practical approach has been adopted and the comments are based on actual experience. Sufficient detail is given to assist those actively involved in equity issues but the treatment is not tied to a unique set of market circumstances. Changes in local rules and practices and variations from market to market should not invalidate the principles discussed.

CHAPTER 3

Reasons for going public – advantages and disadvantages

Launching a public company is one of the major milestones in a successful career in business and finance. Going public represents a coming of age, and indeed the whole process may from time to time resemble an initiation ceremony of a rather primitive kind. Despite this and even as the regulations governing public companies as regards share trading, management and general disclosure become tighter in response to perceived abuses, the attractions of public companies to owners and managers of businesses appear to remain undimmed. What accounts for this allure?

The main advantages of going public are described below. Undoubtedly, the ability for the company to raise additional equity and for its shareholders to realise a profit are important considerations as is enhanced marketability for the company's shares. Less tangible factors, such as the increased prestige conferred by public status, also play a large part. At the same time, the process of going public may be an end in itself and may be the occasion to introduce fundamental changes in the management style of the company.

The attractions of going public carry with them concurrent obligations and restrictions. The most appropriate deity to watch over flotations would be the ancient god Janus, with his ability to look simultaneously in both directions. Managers aspiring to run a public company look back at the comforts of life in a private company and forward to the potential benefits of a public company and decide which direction to take. Management of a private company can run the business without significant outside interference or consideration of arms-length shareholders' interests. They are not constrained by listing agreements or insider trading rules or threatened by a possible loss of control. They do not have their breakfast spoilt by opening a newspaper each day to see their share price at levels they do not consider properly reflects the company's true worth.

Consequently, management and shareholders need to be thoroughly convinced of the merits of a flotation before embarking on the stony path to an initial public offer. It will be a time of great change for the company and all those associated with it. If a decision is taken to proceed, the reasons for doing so are likely to reflect not only the needs of the business itself but the character and ambitions of the people who run it.

Factors	*Advantages*	*Disadvantages*
I Outside investors participate substantially for the first time.	(a) From the company's point of view, increasing equity capital and raising new funds. (b) For the original shareholders, realising profits, securing tax advantages, diversifying, raising money and cancelling guarantees.	(a) Time and expense required. (b) Duties of directors become more onerous and the interests of public shareholders have to be considered. (c) Constraints on management's actions increase.
II Marketability.	(a) Shareholders may buy and sell more readily. (b) Value of the shares is enhanced. (c) Shares are more acceptable as security for loans. (d) Shares are more acceptable for use in acquisitions.	(a) Company and its directors must abide by listing rules of the exchange. (b) Care needed over dealings by 'insiders'. (c) Spread or gradual loss of control.
III Company becomes more visible.	(a) Extensive publicity accompanies the flotation. (b) Standing of the company increases and attitudes to it change.	(a) Level of disclosure increased. (b) Share price is taken as a barometer of the company's fortunes.
IV Changes of management style.	(a) Catalyst for development of professional management systems. (b) Recruitment of key managers. (c) Contribution by non-executive directors.	(a) Increase in formality. (b) Higher overheads. (c) Ruffled feathers.

I   OUTSIDE INVESTORS PARTICIPATE SUBSTANTIALLY FOR THE FIRST TIME

(i) Advantages

(a) From the company's point of view – increasing equity capital and raising new funds

If the flotation involves an issue of new shares, the funds raised are received by the company. It may be desirable for the company to increase its equity base to underpin business expansion plans, to introduce new products or to reduce borrowings. Forecast requirements for capital may exceed amounts that the original shareholders can contribute, placing limits on the company's development if further sources of capital are not tapped.

If the flotation raises new funds for the company and one of the stated purposes of going public is to reduce borrowings, this should make good sense to investors. In general, however, reduction of borrowings is considered by the market as one of the less exciting reasons for going public.

The initial flotation paves the way for fund raising exercises in future. This applies not only to the equity markets but to other capital markets. The company's public status in itself is likely to be an advantage. The increased level of information available makes credit analysis and assessment easier and more reliable.

(b) For the original shareholders – realising profits, securing tax advantages, diversifying, raising money and cancelling guarantees

Existing shareholders may have been financing the company for a prolonged period of time, often without a commercial rate of return on their funds. They may have been working without an arm's-length salary to compensate them for their time. Going public provides a convenient opportunity for the original shareholders to take their profits.

It may be more tax efficient for the original shareholders to realise a capital gain on their investment rather than to receive large dividends or salaries. Public company status may also offer tax advantages in countries where tax legislation includes a concept of a 'closely held' company.

Shareholders may wish to avoid having 'all their eggs in one basket' and sell shares in order to diversify their investments. There may be a need to raise funds to assist in provision for death duties or their personal matters. Bankers who have previously demanded personal guarantees from major shareholders to support the company's facilities can often be persuaded that such guarantees are no longer appropriate or necessary in the context of a public group.

Going public provides controlling shareholders with the opportunity to have their cake and eat it, i.e. to sell part of their interests while still retaining control of the company.

(ii) Disadvantages

(a) Time and expense required

The amount of time required to be devoted by top management to a flotation is very extensive and consistently under-estimated. Management finds itself distracted from the day-to-day running of the company at the very time when they would like it to be performing at its best.

The main expenses incurred in going public are discussed in ch 5 below. They can be divided into underwriting and professional fees and other charges such as capital and transfer duties. Some professional fees are likely to be incurred before it is certain that a flotation can proceed.

(b) Duties of directors become more onerous and the interests of public shareholders have to be considered

Once a company ceases to be private and becomes public, the responsibilities of controlling and managing it broaden and become more onerous. Instead of being answerable only to a small group, usually relatives or close associates, the directors must recognise a duty of trust to a body of public shareholders who will not necessarily be aware of or sympathise with the aspirations of the original shareholders. The precise duties of directors vary from country to country but two problems which can cause particular difficulty are:

(i)   The directors may well have been accustomed to deal with the company's liquid resources as if they were available for their personal requirements. The discipline of segregating the public company's funds may be irksome. The system to safeguard this money may be operated by relatively junior employees previously accustomed to carrying out the controlling shareholders' wishes without question.

(ii) In many private groups, there is a considerable amount of intermingling of funds and assets between companies. If money is required for a particular project, the assets of other companies may be pledged to raise it, as is most convenient and efficient. A considerable amount of inter-company and inter-group borrowing and lending may go on without security or formal arrangements about charging interest and repaying principal.

(c) Constraints on management's actions increase

Once a company has become public, certain corporate actions may require a meeting of shareholders rather than simply a meeting of directors. Transactions which are likely to be subject to a vote of shareholders include the issue of more than a certain number of new shares and the sales or purchases of assets which are significant in relation to the size of the business as a whole.

In a private company, even if a shareholders' meeting is required, the proceedings are likely to be similar to a directors' meeting. A general meeting of a public company on the other hand can be a very lively affair. If the matters under consideration are controversial, an intensive question and answer session and considerable press coverage can be expected. Even strong executives have been known to quail at the prospect of a stormy public meeting.

If a public body of shareholders needs to be consulted, relevant information will have to be provided to them well in advance, usually by means of a printed circular. The preparation of such a circular needs senior management time. If incomplete or biased information is presented, the results of the meeting may not be valid and the directors will be vulnerable to a charge of misleading their shareholders.

In some jurisdictions, any transaction or contract of material size with directors or substantial shareholders must be approved at a general meeting by a vote of the independent shareholders. This sometimes gives directors and major shareholders of a former private company their first taste of having to submit their actions to the veto of an outside body of opinion. The controlling shareholders and directors may be unable to force the proposals through, since, if they are interested parties in the transaction, they will be unable to vote their shares.

II   MARKETABILITY

(i) Advantages

(a) Shareholders may buy and sell more readily

Over the course of time a controlling group of shareholders (often a family) is likely to develop different interests and attitudes towards a company. Some will remain actively involved in the company and its management whereas others, perhaps through marriage or migration, may become remote from its affairs. Not only are the shares of a private company not traded in an organised way but the articles of association usually contain restrictions on the transfer and registration of shares. They will also include a 'pre-emption' provision, to the effect that shareholders wishing to sell must first offer their shares to the other shareholders. This procedure is cumbersome and may involve the price being set by a neutral party (perhaps the auditors) based on a formula which reflects the limited marketability of the shares. Once a company goes public, the articles of association will be amended to eliminate such provisions. The ability to sell shares freely provides a more satisfactory route for shareholders who wish to go their separate way.

(b) The value of the shares is enhanced

Marketability in itself will tend to increase the value of an investment. Some institutional investors are severely restricted as to their holdings of unlisted shares and may not be able to buy the shares at all before they are listed. All investors will look on the increased liquidity of their holdings favourably. In a valuation exercise, the multiple applied to the earnings of a public company would be higher than to those of a similar private company, resulting in a higher valuation.

(c) Listed shares are more acceptable to banks as security for loans

Once a share is listed, it becomes more acceptable to banks as security for loans, either on its own or as part of a portfolio. This provides an alternative for shareholders who do not necessarily wish to sell but need to raise money from time to time. Provided the shares are reasonably well traded, banks who engage in this line of business will normally be prepared to advance a percentage (say 50%) of the market price of shares pledged to them.

It can of course be very convenient for a major shareholder of a company to pledge his shares in support of bank loans. It can also be a source of serious difficulty. If the shareholder uses the funds to increase his stake in the company, his private interests can become highly geared. In addition, the loan would commonly contain a covenant that the value of the shares should exceed the loan by a certain amount. If the share price comes under pressure, the shareholder may be tempted to buy to support the price, potentially a vicious circle if the share price weakness continues. In addition, dividends from the shares rarely match interest payable, leading to further pressure on the cash flow of the private interests and a temptation to pay higher than desirable dividends from the public company or to extract funds from it by other methods.

(d) Listed shares are more acceptable for use in acquisitions

Sellers of assets or shares in companies are normally not willing to accept unlisted securities as a form of payment. Once a company is listed, it may use its shares as consideration in acquisitions, widening its financing options and allowing it to consider bigger targets. Acceptance of paper rather than cash may have attractions from the vendors' point of view, both from tax considerations and by allowing them to feel they still retain an interest in the asset or business they are selling.

In the early days of a public company's life, it may be necessary to make arrangements for vendors who receive securities in this way to place them on to third parties. As the securities become more widely held and actively traded, these 'back-up' arrangements become less critical.

Controlling shareholders and management must bear in mind that issuing shares in the context of acquisitions will tend to dilute their own control and bring cohesive groups of shareholders, sometimes of significant size, into the company. The new shareholders may have interests and attitudes which could lead to a clash of wills at some future occasion.

The information publicly available about the company will be sufficient to sustain a listing for, say, new loan stock or preference shares offered to the target company's shareholders, provided adequate details are given of the rights of the security to be issued. The security would need to have a minimum number of holders to ensure marketability, but this will be achieved if a reasonable proportion of the target company's shareholders accept it or satisfactory underwriting arrangements are made.

(ii) Disadvantages

(a) The company and its directors must abide by the listing rules of the relevant stock exchange(s)

By definition, the process of gaining a listing on a stock exchange involves compliance with stock exchange rules. A recognised stock exchange will require signature of an extensive formal undertaking to comply with the regulations of that stock exchange for companies whose shares are listed on it. The rules will include requirements that the company follows certain administrative procedures and provides relevant information promptly, particularly regarding results, dividends and other significant corporate developments.

(b) Care will be needed over dealings by insiders

Directors and other senior executives must accept that they will normally know more about the company than the general body of shareholders. This will restrict the occasions on which they can buy and sell shares. Restrictions are necessary to prevent them being exposed to criticism and possible legal action for dealing in the shares on the basis of privileged or 'inside' information. Such restrictions may include an outright ban on dealings during sensitive periods (for example, in the month before the company's results are announced) and the maintenance of a formal record of dealings at all other times, with appropriate public disclosure.

Directors of a company often feel that the market does not understand or appreciate properly the particular merits of their company. They may also feel strongly that purchases of the shares are an expression of confidence in the company itself. However, if purchases are made, for whatever reason, shortly before the release of price-sensitive information (for example unexpectedly good results), the actions of the directors may be questioned. Less frequently, directors may consider the market is unreasonably optimistic about the company's prospects, while they themselves have misgivings. They may feel an obligation to sell shares to protect the interests, for example, of wives and children for whom they are trustees. The same dangers apply to the sales of shares as to purchases.

(c) Spread or gradual loss of control

An anxiety commonly felt by shareholders and directors of a private company is the possible loss of control once the company becomes public. Although this is not usually an immediate threat, a potential danger may have been created.

Small shareholders in the context of a private company have little practical recourse if they are unhappy with the way the company is run. Once their shares become marketable, they may be tempted to sell so that for example an apparently solid family block may fall apart. Sometimes even the possibility of a group of outside shareholders appointing a director who is not familiar to the major shareholders seems threatening.

To counter the disintegration of a controlling block, at least 51% of the shares of the public company may be put into a separate private company and the control of that company vested in certain individuals. If family members want to sell they must then sell shares outside the controlling block in such a way that absolute control is not threatened. While for some purposes a 75% voting majority is required, even the most anxious of controlling shareholders normally accept that their control is secure if they can command over 51% of the votes at a general meeting of the company.

As the company grows and the spread of shareholders becomes wider, for practical purposes control of as little as 10 or 20% of the company may be sufficient to constitute control of the whole company. This is particularly true if there are a large number of relatively passive shareholders.

III COMPANY BECOMES MORE VISIBLE

(i) Advantages

(a) Extensive publicity accompanies the flotation

A flotation is a process which requires the publication of a high degree of information about the company. For a company identified with well-known branded consumer items or luxury products, the publicity may become an end in itself, an effective form of image advertising.

In the months leading up to the launch, the promoters will prepare the ground by a series of strategically placed press articles and announcements to arouse media interest. Coverage of the flotation when it actually occurs brings the company, its management and its products before investors' and the public's minds. Although some shareholders and managers dread this part of the transaction, other more flamboyant characters revel in it. Previously unknown businessmen may become national figures for a while at the time of flotation of 'their' company.

The attention drawn to the company and its business may increase awareness of its attractions as a business or joint venture partner. Sometimes a recently floated company immediately attracts a bidder. As the company will normally still be under the majority control of its original shareholders, any such bid could only be on a friendly basis.

(b) Standing of the company increases and attitudes towards it change

A public company is generally regarded as having a higher standing than a private company. Employees may take more pride in working for a public company than for an individual or family-owned business. A share incentive scheme may be offered to foster a sense of participation. Shareholders, whether employees or not, can become useful advocates if the company is threatened by actions of government such as unfavourable changes to legislation affecting the company. Customers may regard it as more prestigious to deal with a public company. For manufacturers or retailers of brand name products, the publicity surrounding a flotation is an extension of general corporate image building. Suppliers' level of confidence may be boosted and their credit checks are made simpler by the greater disclosure of financial information which listed status requires. Bankers too are likely to be influenced by this factor and the greater ease of increasing the group's equity base if needed.

Although it is difficult to pin down, there is perhaps a feeling that a company of a certain size and reputation ought to be a public company. Some general appreciation exists of the rigours and difficulties of going through a flotation.

The fact that a company and its management have passed this test is taken as a seal of approval.

There may be a strong streak of 'me too' as competitors see their rivals going public and fear that they may obtain some market or financial edge. A similar attitude can be observed among institutions. Once the ice has been broken by a successful flotation, a series of companies in that sector are often brought to market. Individual investors and institutions begin to feel comfortable with a particular type of company and sector of the market and the band-wagon effect is under way. After considerable research and investigation to learn about an unfamiliar industry, there is a natural tendency to try to capitalise on the base of knowledge gathered.

(ii) Disadvantages

(a) The level of disclosure is increased

Directors of public companies have to come to terms with a substantially increased level of disclosure of information. In a private company, only limited disclosure to 'outsiders' is necessary. In the context of a public company, the information to be published will cover important financial data including announcements of results and dividends, events which affect the management of the company, such as changes in the directors, and alterations in capital structure and shares in issue, which are relevant to investors trading in the shares. There may also be a sweeping provision in the listing agreement to disclose any information which is likely to have a material impact on the price or the level of trading of the shares in the market. Shareholders holding more than a certain percentage of the company will have to disclose the size of their holdings and any material changes in them.

Insistence on disclosure may sometimes be interpreted by management as a questioning of their good faith. They may consider holdings of shares and dealings by themselves and their families as nobody's business but their own. Disclosure of terms of employment such as salary and benefits may be a potential source of embarrassment compared with the anonymity of a private company.

(b) Share price is taken as a barometer of the company's fortunes

Once a company is listed, details of the share price movements and trading volume are released daily by the stock exchange. Arrangements may be made for the share price to appear in major newspapers. Share price movements reflect rumour and market whim as well as fundamentals. Management may experience pressure to promote good performance while feeling that the daily ups and downs of the market are largely irrational. Bitter comments may be muttered about the 'tyranny of the share price'.

If a company is seen as part of a market sector, its performance will be compared by analysts to others in that sector. This may lead to decisions being taken on a short-term basis. For example, if the sector as a whole has shown strong profit increases, actions a particular company might wish to take for long-term development of its business, but which might prove a short-term drag on profits, may be deferred.

If the company is performing well but the sector as a whole is out of fashion, it may be difficult for the market to accept a rating for the company much above the sector average. With the same results but located in a more glamorous sector, the company might be accorded a significantly higher rating.

IV CHANGES OF MANAGEMENT STYLE

(i) Advantages

(a) Catalyst for development of professional management systems

At some stage in a company's development, a change in management style tends to occur. The paternal attitudes often found in a small company give way to a more systematic and objective approach required to control and manage a larger group. Preparation for becoming a public company affords an opportunity and a catalyst for achieving this transition without the appearance of a direct attack on entrenched interests.

(b) Recruitment of key managers

A review of the depth and areas of expertise of management conducted by the underwriter and reporting accountants in conjunction with the controlling shareholders as part of the flotation preparations may identify a need for additional qualified executives such as a specialist finance director and a professionally-qualified company secretary. A professional middle management structure may be missing or inadequate in a private business. To assist in recruiting and retaining suitable executives, a share option scheme may be introduced. Extended service contracts may be negotiated for senior executives, giving them a greater degree of security and independence.

The more obviously distinct identity of a public company and the existence of outside directors and shareholders create the framework for strengthening professional management. This need may have been previously recognised. However, without the external stimulus of the flotation it can prove difficult to overcome internal inertia and vested interests.

(c) Contribution by non-executive directors

Prior to a flotation, a company is likely to appoint outside directors, typically one or two non-executives of standing in the political, business or financial community. These individuals bring a new perspective to the way problems are tackled and decisions taken. Perhaps for the first time, executive directors will have to explain their actions to independent individuals of comparable age, seniority and ability who should be unwilling to rubber-stamp decisions.

(ii) **Disadvantages**

(a) Increase of formality

Often a private group is run by one individual or a small number of executives who have grown accustomed to working closely with each other. Decisions can be taken quickly and efficiently. Introduction of more formal procedures may seem a short way removed from bureaucracy. It requires a delicate sense of balance to achieve the benefits of a more consistent and accountable decision-taking process appropriate for a public company without sacrificing the flair and flexibility partly responsible for the company's success to-date.

This problem arises in an acute form where the managing director has previously functioned also as finance director and consequently kept much delicate financial information to himself. This may be efficient in some sense – it certainly maximises the confidentiality of sensitive data – but it hampers the development of reliable information systems and the independent control function which is a cornerstone of professional management. When things are going well, the merits of shared responsibility may not be obvious. However, a management team will be much better placed to prove its worth when problems arise if they have access to all relevant information and have participated in past decisions.

(b) Higher overheads

Many of the changes in personnel and systems instituted during a flotation cause higher overheads without bringing any immediate improvement in performance or increase in profits. To attract an experienced professional finance director and a competent company secretary requires attractive terms to be offered. The cost may not be limited to one or two new recruits. There may be a knock-on effect as salary levels are reviewed to ensure that existing managers (some of whom may be family members) are being rewarded on a comparable basis. The result of such a review may be a one-time upward shift in personnel costs which will need time to show results.

(c) Ruffled feathers

There may be resistance from those who have experienced the company's growth from its early days and see no reason to change a winning formula. Their motto is: 'if it ain't broke, don't fix it'. There will always be some who are more comfortable with a 'family' atmosphere even if it becomes paternalistic or condescending to employees and limits the company's potential. Winning round those whom it is important to retain in the company will require careful explanation of the objectives of the flotation and no little diplomacy.

Throughout the process, it is important for the management to be alert to the swirling of company politics. Insecurity and jockeying for position may be engendered by the unsettling period of change. In the short term, the benefits of a change in management style are vulnerable as new executives find their feet and procedures become established. Awareness and support by senior management will be needed to ensure new procedures become firmly established.

WEIGHING THE BALANCE

The factors involved in the decision to go public and the pluses and minuses associated with each have been discussed under four general headings. Those taking the decision must weigh up where the balance of advantage lies and decide whether the compromises involved are worthwhile.

It seems a consistent experience that the time taken and the work involved in going public is greater than anticipated and that frustration, change and delay are the rule rather than the exception. At points of crisis, the determination of the principals that they are pursuing the right course will be severely tested. They must be convinced at the outset that the reasons for going public are sound and the underlying advantages strong enough.

Substantial amounts of management time and considerable expense are necessary if a flotation is to be carried through to a successful conclusion. Before large-scale commitments are made, it is useful as a first step to review briefly and from a strictly practical standpoint whether a flotation is a realistic prospect. Some criteria for doing this and for considering the need for reorganisation of the interests to be floated are discussed in the next chapter.

CHAPTER 4

Going public – is it a realistic prospect?
– what structural changes are needed?

Going public may be an attractive proposition but is it realistic, and how much will the structure and organisation of the companies being floated need to change?

A list of criteria to judge whether a flotation is a practical proposition or not is set out below. Changes which may be needed in the organisation of the group and in its gearing, voting arrangements and issued share capital are discussed in the second section of this chapter.

In some countries, a hierarchy of markets has emerged. There may for example be a major stock market, an unlisted securities market and an over-the-counter market. This chapter deals mainly with the requirements for going public on a major stock market where a company would be bound by a full listing agreement. The points discussed apply also to a company considering alternative markets, the main difference being the strictness with which the various criteria are applied.

I CRITERIA – NINE KEY QUESTIONS

A convenient starting point is to review recently issued flotation documents. This exercise serves to identify the main categories of information which need to be given to see how the group compares. Companies in a similar sector should be chosen if possible. While some elements in a prospectus are common to all flotations, critical factors and the emphasis which is placed on them vary from sector to sector. What is required for a flotation of a retailing chain will not necessarily ensure success for a computer company.

(i) Size and period of existence

Most stock exchanges impose a minimum size for the aggregate value of securities they are prepared to consider for listing. Size will be measured by the market value at the flotation price of the securities to be listed and is based on the whole class of such securities, not just the percentage in public hands. The purpose of the minimum size criterion is to ensure reasonable marketability in the security. Marketability is largely a subjective concept, so that the minimum size in force may be somewhat arbitrary. It depends in part on the type of security and varies widely from market to market. Within individual markets, the size criteria are updated periodically by the stock exchange authorities who will take steps to make sure they are known to market practitioners.

Many markets require a company to have been in business or to have recorded profits for a minimum period of time, say three to five years. A recently incorporated holding company used to reorganise a group prior to flotation is considered to inherit the track record of its subsidiaries. Recent significant changes in principal activities or top management are likely to raise doubts about whether the track record is adequate, as both stock market authorities and analysts want to be comfortable that they know the business and the people they are dealing with. Recent sizeable acquisitions may raise similar doubts.

(ii) Profit trend and prospects

If the company is likely to be primarily assessed on an earnings basis, the audited profits for, say, the last five years will be critical, together with a forecast for the current year. A smooth progression of profits is desirable. If there are departures from the trend, can they be readily explained? Are they due to cycles in the general economy or sector, or are they attributable to some special circumstances in the company? If a loss has been incurred, can the problem be clearly identified and factors responsible shown to have been isolated and remedied? If the loss or other problem arises in one particular company, could that company be left out of the group going public for the time being?

An accountant's report will form a key part of the prospectus. If the present audit firm is small and not widely known to the investing public, it is likely that a larger firm will be appointed, at least in a joint capacity, to carry out the report. The existing audited figures may be subject to adjustment in their report. Substantial adjustments or changes or inconsistency in accounting policies will detract from the quality of the figures and may jeopardise the flotation.

(iii) Sector/industry

What sector or industry would the company expect to be classified under? Is this sector in favour with investors? Are the prospects for the sector regarded as encouraging?

If a particular market sector is depressed, it may be virtually impossible for even a sound company in that sector to go public on acceptable terms. On the other hand, when the high technology sector is in vogue, flotation of a company with little more than a few promising projects on the drawing board is quite possible. Indeed, it seems that promise – allowing investors full range to their imaginations – is frequently preferred to performance. Pricing may even be based on a multiple of turnover if no profits have ever been made.

(iv) Undue reliance

Does the company's reliance on a single product, supplier or customer make it unduly vulnerable to events outside the company's control? Changes in technology or customer preferences could affect the company's line. Dual sourcing of key components or raw materials is highly desirable to offset the risks of shortages of supply or sudden price rises. A key customer could be exposed to changes in its own operating environment. In extreme cases, these factors may increase the risk to public shareholders to an unacceptable level.

(v) On- and off-balance sheet liabilities and litigation

Does an analysis of the balance sheet reveal any areas of weakness? The levels of gearing and the requirements for working capital should be examined to see if they are out of line with other companies in similar businesses. Are there any contingent liabilities, guarantees or litigation outstanding which could increase the company's financial obligations?

In certain industries, particularly banking and property, sophisticated techniques have been developed to finance projects without the full extent of such finance appearing on the face of the balance sheet. Litigation can be particularly damaging; in addition to the potential liability, law suits frequently involve a drain of top management time and damage to reputation even if the company is finally exonerated. Unfortunately, potential claimants may identify the period before a flotation as an opportunity to launch a suit in order to force a settlement.

(vi) Image and management

Does the company have some feature which will serve to identify it in the minds of investors? If not, is there some way that the company's attractions can be described so that it will be differentiated from existing investment opportunities? How can the promoters counteract the inertia which prompts investors to stick to more familiar shares?

Is the management known at all to the general public? Does it have a reputation for competence and integrity among its peers and in financial circles? Are there any non-executive directors of standing? Are there any obvious gaps in management competence, particularly as regards the finance and control functions?

(vii) Uncertainties

Major areas of uncertainty are likely to act as a significant barrier to investment. The market likes the extent of the risk of a new investment to be clearly established. If there is uncertainty for example in the outcome of litigation, the most likely reaction of financial institutions is to suggest a delay until the problem is resolved or at least until the maximum exposure can be quantified.

(viii) Timing

A prospectus requires the inclusion of audited accounts. In many markets, these should be not more than six months old. Even if the audit can be completed promptly, the available 'window' is quite narrow. A profit forecast is also likely to be needed. For prudence, management may wish to see some months' actual results and a reasonable level of business and orders on hand before committing itself for the whole year. Management may be torn between the need to be certain of their forecast and the flotation deadline. Other factors affecting timing include the state of the market and any queue of pending issues, with a danger of 'crowding out'.

(ix) Relationships with existing shareholders/directors

Are there any dealings between existing shareholders, directors and other related parties and the group which might be inappropriate in a public company but would be difficult to unwind? For example, any material amounts owing by such parties to the company should be cleared prior to the flotation. Amounts owing by the company to its shareholders may be repaid in cash or capitalised as part of a reorganisation of share capital for the purposes of the flotation. Do related parties retain control of any businesses which are in competition with the intended public group, creating potential conflicts of interest? The need for the public group and private interests to deal with each other on an arm's-length basis may involve unacceptable levels of complexity and expense.

If a clean bill of health can be given under headings (i)–(ix) above, it will be worth proceeding to the next stage, reviewing the structure of the group to see what changes may be required for flotation.

II STRUCTURE

Formal changes must be considered in the corporate organisation of the group. Market preferences on gearing, voting arrangements and share price must also be taken into account.

(i) Corporate organisation of the group

A business built up by an individual or family may grow in size and complexity in a rather haphazard manner. A series of companies may be established as is most convenient at the time. These companies may well be owned by the same or very similar sets of shareholders. The result is a number of private companies with common ownership and related lines of business which have not been formed legally into a group. There is no one holding company having beneath it a number of subsidiaries or associates in an orderly family tree. Matters for decision include the following:

(a) Choice of holding company

If the decision is taken to go public, a single company will have to be selected to have its shares listed on the exchange. A choice must therefore be made as to what company should be used. The largest or most well-known company may acquire all or some of the other companies or businesses and serve as the company which goes public. Alternatively, a new holding company may be established which acquires the companies chosen to form the public group. This company will derive its track record from its new subsidiaries.

(b) Choice of subsidiaries

Not all the companies which could be included may be integral to the business of the group to be listed. Small 'non-core' companies could be omitted if they add little to the overall picture; if they are loss-making, they are likely to detract from the market value of the group. Other things being equal, the fewer companies in the group to be floated, the simpler the documentation.

(c) Implications of transfer of control

Care must be taken over transfer of ownership of a company holding a valuable licence or agency agreement. The change of control may well require time-consuming consents to be obtained. In some circumstances, it could jeopardise continuance of the arrangements or lead to renegotiation of their terms.

(d) Method of forming the group

The method used for forming the group will normally be an exchange of shares. The companies acquired will become subsidiaries of the new holding company by their shareholders exchanging their shares for new shares in the holding company. Depending on the gearing of the new holding company and the preferences of the vendor shareholders, some subsidiaries may be acquired for cash. Cash may be provided from the company's own resources, by identifying cash subscribers for new holding company shares or by bank borrowings.

(e) Minorities

In general, it is preferable not to leave minorities outstanding so that the holding company may have complete control over its new subsidiaries and full access to their assets and cash flow. In some cases, the managing director of an operating company may have a shareholding in that company as a performance incentive which it may be better to leave in place. The incentive will be weakened if he exchanges shares in the company he runs for shares in a holding company with interests in companies he is unable to influence.

(f) Expenses

A reorganisation of this type is likely to involve significant potential expenses for capital duty on the share capital of the new holding company and transfer duty on acquisitions of subsidiaries or assets. The capital duty payable when new shares are created and issued depends on the tax regulations in the country where the holding company is incorporated. Some countries, such as Bermuda and the Cayman Islands, impose a minimal level of duties; in more 'advanced' countries, it may be a major expense. Incurrence of transfer duty again depends on the regulations of the country where the transfers are registered and can be minimised by adopting methods tailored to the particular tax jurisdiction. For example, a change of control may be effected by subscription of new shares. Existing shares will only be transferred after drastic changes in their rights bring about a corresponding reduction in their value. Schemes of this type may be vulnerable to periodic attack from tax authorities, so specialist tax advice is essential.

(ii) Gearing

The financial structure of the new holding company on an unconsolidated and consolidated basis should be reviewed. High gearing is a major reason for going public via a new issue to raise capital to retire corporate debt rather than offering existing shares for sale, with the proceeds going to the original shareholders. A group which is unusually highly geared may not be suitable for flotation at all until the level of borrowing can be reduced.

(a) Measuring gearing

The appropriate level of gearing depends principally on asset-backing and cash flow. An asset-based group, such as a shipping or property concern, or one which has highly predictable cash flows such as a utility, will be able to support a higher level of gearing than a business with unpredictable cash flows and little asset backing. It is important to measure gearing in terms of cash flow as well as the absolute amount of debt. A level of debt which looks reasonable as compared to equity and assets may nevertheless prove too high if interest rates rise. A rise in interest rates can also put asset valuations under pressure and create difficulties in supplementing operating cash flows with sales of assets.

(b) Covenants

Significant covenants in loan documentation require disclosure if they limit management's freedom of action or carry unusual risks of default. For example, apparent cash flow from pledged assets may be dedicated to servicing borrowings and not be freely available for the company's use. If covenants are too severe, some renegotiation may be necessary to permit a flotation to proceed. Since it will usually be in the bank's interest for the company to be public, particularly if its capital is increased, there is a reasonable prospect of being able to renegotiate.

(c) Market attitude

At times when sentiment is positive, fairly high borrowing can be interpreted as an encouraging sign that an aggressive management is using the capital structure to increase shareholders' returns. At other times, particularly during or soon after a financial crisis, even modest amounts of borrowing are seen to be risky and a company with an ungeared balance sheet is given a premium rating.

(iii) Voting structure

Private companies will sometimes include in their capital structure founders' shares or some other special class of ordinary shares designed to ensure that control remains with the original shareholders. The articles of association may restrict the interest of any individual shareholder to a certain percentage (sometimes as low as 2%).

It is not normally acceptable to investors and the stock exchange for a company going public to have ordinary shares with unequal voting rights. Prior to flotation, new articles of association will be adopted so that all ordinary shares carry the same voting rights and any restrictions on holdings or transfer are eliminated.

This approach is justified because control is a valuable commodity. This is most obviously seen in the premium offered for control of a company compared with the prevailing market price for a share transaction of ordinary size. All shareholders who run the ultimate risk of financing a business should participate in the benefits of control. They should also be able to exercise their voting rights as a check on management.

An exception with which stock exchanges would sympathise would be a nationalised concern which the government of the day wishes to privatise. It may not be 'in the national interest' for the company to be controlled by any particular group, at least for a minimum period of years. In such a case, the government may be issued with a 'golden' share conferring certain preferential rights regarding control, for example as regards votes cast at a general meeting or over the composition of the board of directors.

Older established companies may have gained listings at periods when voting rights were not such a sensitive matter to stock exchange authorities and major investors. Although it is unlikely that existing listings would be cancelled because of refusal to change the voting structure, there are a number of examples where institutional investors have brought pressure to bear on the directors to propose that voting rights should be made equal. As compensation, a small bonus issue of shares (say on the basis of one-for-ten) may be given to the class of shareholders foregoing the preferential rights.

Companies with existing listings may seek to introduce a new class of ordinary shares with superior voting rights as a defence against hostile takeover bids. This action is likely to be highly controversial and brings a risk of de-listing of the shares.

(iv) Share price

For reasons of historical accident, to save capital duty or because financing by shareholder loans is more flexible, private companies may have relatively few shares in issue. This would translate into a very high price per share if no changes were made prior to flotation. Many markets have a favoured price range at which popular shares tend to trade. Within markets, an appropriate price may vary depending on investor sentiment at the time and on industry sectors. A group intending to go public is often advised to aim at a share price in line with other similar public companies.

The expected market price of the share is found by dividing the valuation placed on the company by the number of shares in issue. The valuation will be negotiated between the promoters and the merchant bank and so for this purpose is a constant. The share price at flotation can only be reduced by increasing the shares in issue.

In order to achieve this, a number of measures may be taken. If the shareholders or other related parties have advanced money to a company under a loan account this loan account may be capitalised, i.e. cancelled in exchange for the issue of new shares. If the shares have a par value and this is relatively high, the shares may be subdivided so that, for example, one share of $10 may be converted into ten shares of $1 each. In addition, if there is a share premium account or reserves which can be paid up as a bonus issue, this may also be used to achieve the desired reduction in price. It may even be possible to use a share premium account created on the sale of new shares to pay up a bonus issue for which only the shareholders of record prior to the flotation are eligible.

EXAMPLE

For the purposes of flotation, a company going public via an issue of new shares has been valued by its shareholders and the underwriter of the issue at $480 million. Shares worth $120 million will be held by the public, that is 25% of the total issued share capital. The shares held by existing shareholders are valued at $360 million. At present, there are 1,000,000 shares of $10 each in issue, which would result in a market price of $36 per share. An amount of $40 million is owed by the company to its shareholders. Similar shares in that particular market trade on the stock exchange at between $1 and $2 per share. Set out below is an illustration of the steps which could be taken to produce a market price in the desired range:

		Shares in issue (000)
1.	Existing shares of $10 each in issue prior to flotation	1,000
2.	New shares of $10 each issued to capitalise the shareholders loans of $40 million	4,000
	Total shares in issue after capitalisation of loans	5,000
3.	Sub-divide each share of $10 into 20 new shares of $0.50 each (5 million shares × 20)	100,000
4.	Make 1-for-5 bonus issue out of existing reserves	20,000
		120,000

5. Make 1-for-1 bonus issue out of share premium
    arising on new issue (*Note*)   120,000
                                                         _____
                                                         240,000

6. New issue so that 25% of enlarged share capital is
    in public hands   80,000
                                                         _____
                                                         320,000

    Total valuation placed on company $480 million
    Estimated market price of shares $1.50 per share
    Target range for share price $1–2 per share

Note: On the above basis, 80 million new shares will be issued with a par value of $0.50 at a premium of $1 per share. Consequently, share premium of $80 million will arise, of which $60 million will be absorbed by making the 1-for-1 bonus issue of 120 million shares of $0.50 each.

CONCLUSIONS

A review of the basic requirements which must be satisfied before a flotation can be embarked upon with a reasonable prospect of success is essential if time, money and energy is not to be wasted. A decision, for example, to delay a flotation for a year may be frustrating but not so damaging to morale as a premature attempt which results in failure. Designing the correct corporate structure and selecting the companies to be included in the public group is a key element of success. Other factors considered in this chapter include the level of borrowings, voting rights and the means of adjusting issued share capital to obtain a desired price range. If the review is positive and a satisfactory structure can be put in place, the next stage is to begin selecting the team needed to get the project underway and estimating the costs involved.

CHAPTER 5

Forming a team and estimating expenses

A flotation is a team effort and the composition of that team will be a major factor in the outcome. Firms of advisers which individuals or the company have used in the past may not be best suited to the task because of the specialist expertise required. It is a question of 'horses for courses' and a flotation is more like a steeplechase than a sprint.

One of the potential benefits of going public is the wider circle of professional contacts which the company and its management forges during a flotation. These relationships, formed at a time of considerable pressure, often endure for a working life-time under the bond of shared experience and (hopefully) achievement.

The cost of the exercise is highly relevant to the decision as to whether to proceed or not. The second section of the chapter sets out the main headings under which costs are incurred. The costs are borne by whichever party receives the funds from the flotation which perhaps makes them less painful. Some commitments for expense may have to be made before it is certain that the flotation can proceed.

I FORMING A TEAM

(i) The company

The company team typically consists of about four people. The decision to go public is usually a highly personal one. Very often the founder, major shareholder, chairman or chief executive will be directly involved. In a private company, the same person may well fill all these roles. As it is easy to be discouraged by the length and difficulty of the process of going public, his determination and enthusiasm will be of the utmost importance.

As well as the vital involvement of a very senior company executive, there are many more routine tasks for the company to undertake. The accounting department will be heavily engaged in producing past and projected financial information in conjunction with the reporting accountants and it is usual for the finance director or chief accountant to take a leading role. The company secretary is likely to be responsible for reviewing the legal aspects of the flotation, including producing details of the corporate history and liaising with the outside lawyers.

In addition, it is useful for one or two junior executives to be assigned as progress-chasers and co-ordinators. As soon as confidentiality permits, they should be involved full-time as the more senior members of the company team will inevitably have urgent and unpredictable calls on their time during the period the prospectus is being prepared.

(ii) Merchant bank/issuing house

The first party to be involved outside the company is likely to be the merchant bank selected to manage the flotation and act as the underwriter. This choice is usually the first one as the merchant bank takes a central role in putting together the prospectus for the issue and may also assist in the selection of the other professional advisers involved. It can also give, in the preparatory stage, a view on whether the flotation is feasible and at least an indication or moral commitment on underwriting.

Merchant banks are actively involved in marketing the idea of flotation to potential candidates. Consequently it is quite possible that a company which is beginning to be known in its industry will be itself approached by merchant banks to discuss the possibility of going public. This is increasingly so as the competition between merchant banks becomes more intense. Some merchant banks invest in companies years before they are ready to go public and so have their own 'nursery' of companies being prepared for flotation.

There are three major criteria for choosing a merchant bank to manage and underwrite an issue:

(a) Experience

It is essential that the merchant bank or its senior staff members should have been actively and recently involved in the market. The number of flotations in a normal year is not very large and it may be surprising to find that even quite well-known names have handled rather few recent issues. Some claim an expertise which may barely exist in an active form and they will be, in effect, using the flotation of your company to brush up their technique.

As well as the number of issues, it will be relevant to look at the results. It must be recognised that the outcome of a flotation depends quite heavily on short-term market forces which may be outside the power of the participants to control. However, a series of under-subscriptions would be of concern as would large premiums on the first day of dealing, indicating that the promoters could have obtained a better price. It is also instructive to look at the price say six months after the start of trading, adjusting for movements in the level of the market in general over the same period.

(b) Size and reputation

A major role of the merchant bank, no doubt the single most important feature from the point of view of the company going public, is that it should be able to get the issue underwritten at a satisfactory price. This means it should either have the financial muscle and resolution to stand behind the issue if necessary and that it should be an effective marketer, with reliable institutional connections and other placing power sufficient to find a safe home for the issue. Most commonly, a combination of the two is involved. Once an issue is underwritten and receipt of funds guaranteed, the company going public can take the attitude of an interested spectator in the actual level of subscriptions.

(c) Chemistry

A flotation requires long hours to be spent by the senior management of the company with the merchant banking executives involved. There will normally be a team of say three or four bank executives. As the leader of the team may be more involved in winning new business than carrying it out, it is important to meet one or two people who would be involved in the detailed work as well as the merchant bank's 'point man'. Without a personal meeting, it is impossible to know whether a good working relationship can be established.

Many problems will have to be tackled during the course of the flotation. Some of these will be sensitive matters for people who have not previously had to disclose substantial amounts of information about their operations to the public. The merchant bank is expected to examine the relevant background of a company and its management, even (or especially) the incidents they might prefer to forget. A sympathetic approach is required to avoid turning meetings into confrontations.

The rest of the team of professionals to work on the prospectus may well be drawn from the traditional connections of the company and its management. The merchant bank involved will be able to offer suitable introductions if required. A number of companies, however, are uneasy at the idea of one professional adviser in effect appointing others and prefer to choose 'their own man'.

(iii) Reporting accountants

(a) Accountant's report

The accountant's report is the element of the prospectus which typically takes longest to produce and provides the raw material for much of the remainder of the prospectus. It therefore needs to be commissioned in good time. If the results show up some weaknesses, they should be highlighted as soon as possible so that the problems can be tackled or the flotation reconsidered.

The obvious candidates to produce the report are the group's traditional auditors who may be close business advisers to the private group. They start with the advantage of a good base of knowledge of the group and the way it has developed so that everything does not have to be explained from scratch. However, a flotation requires a great deal of accounting work to be completed under intense pressure and the company going public will need a wider range of services than before. The existing auditors may not be large enough to devote a team of experienced staff to complete rapidly the work which will be required. If the firm is not already well-known, its name may not be wholly acceptable to the merchant bank or give sufficient confidence to investors. It may therefore be necessary to appoint a larger accounting firm, either to replace the existing auditors, or to report on a joint basis. A joint appointment increases costs somewhat but allows the company to have the best of both worlds in terms of accumulated knowledge and reputation in the market. Usually little problem is experienced in establishing a smooth working relationship between the two firms of accountants.

A company which has an eye on eventual flotation may appoint an internationally known firm some years in advance or cultivate relationships with such a firm while not at that stage of appointing them auditors. In the absence of such contacts, the company will often rely on the advice of the merchant bank in the choice of reporting accountants.

The reporting accountants will be instructed to report to the directors of both the company being floated and to the merchant bank. In addition to their report for inclusion in the prospectus they may also (depending on market practice) prepare a more detailed 'long form' report. This covers not only the financial position of the company but describes its business, management and systems. Some recommendations for change may be made, particularly as regards internal controls and systems.

(b) Group reorganisation

The reporting accountants may be able to give valuable advice on any reorganisation of the group to be accomplished prior to flotation. There are two aspects in particular where accountants are likely to have relevant expertise. The first is how to put in place the transfer of assets, businesses and companies needed to create the group going public without incurring more tax liabilities than necessary. The second relates to the presentation of accounts of the group. If companies are purchased at above net asset values, goodwill may arise. Retained profits of companies acquired may be 'frozen', unavailable for distribution to the public company's shareholders. There are different possible accounting treatments of such matters as goodwill on consolidation, revaluation of assets and pre-acquisition profits. Steps may be taken with the advice of the accountants to minimise problems which can prove troublesome.

(c) Profit forecast

If there is a forecast of profits, the accountants will be heavily involved in checking and substantiating it. If a company is being valued primarily on an earnings basis, the profit forecast is arguably the most important part of the whole prospectus, as both the company and the underwriter will use forecast, not historic, earnings as the basis for the pricing. Even when the pricing does not depend on it, a profit forecast is highly desirable to give investors a better picture of the company's prospects. The accountants' particular responsibility is to confirm that the accounting policies have been consistently applied and that the calculations are correct. However, on most occasions they will be involved beyond this role and are in a position to judge whether the forecast is realistic or not. They will be unhappy to let any forecast go out without being entirely comfortable that it will be met.

(d) Other 'due diligence'

The accountants will also be asked to check the statement of borrowings, contingent liabilities and commitments and to provide comfort to the directors on their statement concerning the adequacy of working capital. Their advice may be taken on taxation planning for the company. If there is a trust deed or any loan agreement which contains limits on borrowings or other financial covenants, the accountants will check that these have not been breached. They will also have a major role in the verification of the prospectus in general and particularly as regards all figures and calculations.

(e) Statement of adjustments

The accountants will produce a statement of adjustments setting out the adjustments they consider necessary from the audited accounts as produced by the company prior to its flotation. If the reporting accountant has been the auditor to the group over the period it is unlikely that there will be any material adjustments, except if accounting policies have changed. The statement of adjustments is normally filed with the stock exchange or other regulatory authorities.

(iv) Lawyers

It is likely that the promoters will have their own contacts with lawyers. However, as with the accounting requirements, the legal work involved in a prospectus is specialised and not all firms of lawyers will have suitable specialists available to work on a full-time basis.

(a) Two roles

There are two separate aspects to the legal work in a prospectus, one for the company and its shareholders and directors and the other for the merchant bank. While it is possible for different partners at one firm to carry out the two roles, it is more usual to appoint separate firms to ensure that no conflict arises. For most purposes, the company and merchant bank have an equal interest in the success of the flotation. However, as regards pricing and the underwriting agreement, they are on the opposite sides of the table.

The work of the two firms overlaps. In general, the lawyers for the company will concentrate on the constitution of the company, material contracts it may have entered into and any current or pending litigation. They will also advise the directors and shareholders on their responsibilities as regards the flotation and how it may affect their personal position. The lawyers for the underwriters will draft the underwriting agreement and the verification notes, which underpin all facts and expressions of opinion included in the prospectus.

(b) Corporate structure

The legal work in the prospectus starts very early with preparing a group structure. Formal sale and purchase and other agreements will be needed to document any acquisitions of companies or assets. The lawyers may be able to contribute helpful suggestions for simplifying the methods used for the reorgansation and in minimising tax and other costs.

(c) Disclosure

As the work proceeds, the lawyers will be generally responsible for ensuring that all disclosures required by statute are included in the prospectus. Information which is not covered in other parts of the prospectus may be gathered for convenience in an appendix often headed 'Statutory and General Information'. This may include, for example, a summary of the new articles of association or bye-laws appropriate for a public company, details of material contracts the group has been a party to and disclosure of directors' interests. Lawyers will also draw up the company's board minutes for the various corporate decisions and approvals required and may also draft the share certificates and handle liaison with the legal authorities with whom the prospectus needs to be cleared or filed.

(d) Verification

An important discipline in preparing the prospectus is the verification of all material information included in it. A set of detailed verification notes will be drawn up, setting out each fact or statement of opinion and allocating to a particular party the responsibility for verifying it. The notes will be prepared on the basis of an advanced proof of the prospectus and form part of the final 'countdown' in checking its accuracy. It sometimes seems at this stage that all adjectives disappear from the prospectus. The notes will be circulated, discussed by the parties, amended as necessary in line with the final version of the prospectus and finally signed by the parties. The notes then become an integral part of the documentation of the prospectus.

(v) Stockbrokers

(a) Market soundings – pricing and sub-underwriting

The brokers should be closely involved in sounding out large potential investors to evaluate interest in the issue. On the basis of these soundings, they will also be in a position to advise on pricing and the formation of the sub-underwriting syndicate, which, depending on market practice, the brokers may take the lead in putting together. Often a general market view will emerge on a reasonable price for the issue which it is dangerous to ignore even if fundamental analysis suggests something different.

(b) Brokers' circular

The brokers may be able to set the scene for the issue by publishing a helpful background circular on the company going public, including sector and industry information. Care must be taken that nothing is stated on the basis of information supplied by the company which is not also included and verified in the prospectus. A broker's research analyst may however be free, for example, to make projections about future profitability beyond the profit forecast in the prospectus provided the projections are his own estimates and not the company speaking by proxy.

(c) Liaison with the stock exchange and the role of sponsor

In some markets, liaison with the stock exchange authorities is handled by a member of the exchange who will act as sponsor. In this case, the broker will make the formal application for listing and handle relationships with the executives in the stock exchange responsible for scrutinising new listings whom they will probably know on a personal basis. This relationship can in any case be very valuable in ironing out problems on timing, procedures or documentation before they become major obstacles. The brokers will, if necessary, discuss with the exchange the mechanics of share registration and initial delivery of share certificates, dealing and settlement.

The role of sponsor extends beyond the approval of the prospectus. The sponsor is expected to guide the directors of the newly public company on compliance with the listing agreement and takeover code (in markets where one exists) with which an experienced market practitioner can be expected to be more familiar, at least in the early days. In this connection, the sponsor may vet any public announcements by the company particularly the announcement of results which both the sponsor and underwriter will be concerned to ensure are fully consistent with the prospectus. In some markets, the underwriter will act as sponsor rather than the broker.

(d) Funding of applications and 'market making'

Many of the applications for an issue will come from clients of the brokers close to the issue. The brokers form a view on the likely level of subscriptions and may advise their clients to apply for more shares than they ultimately want, to allow for a scaling-down of applications. Such clients will require short-term finance which the brokers, in conjunction with their bankers, are well placed to supply. Where there is a commission payable to brokers on successful applications, it will be to the interest of individual brokers to have as many applications submitted by their clients as possible. The ability to provide finance is an important incentive to clients in this respect.

Brokers may also act as 'market-makers' after the shares begin to trade. Investors' knowledge that a leading broker will be actively involved in the after-market gives investors increased confidence in applying for shares. Trading conditions for newly-listed shares can be difficult if they are left entirely to their own devices to 'sink or swim' after the initial interest generated by the prospectus dies away.

(vi) Valuers

Recent valuations of major fixed assets may in some instances be required by regulation. They may be desirable in any case to provide full information to the market or to highlight the strengths of an asset-rich company.

In the case of a property company, the report of the valuer is likely to be the portion of the document which sets the tone for the whole issue.

The reputation and standing of the valuer is vital. The valuer should be recognised as a leader in his profession. There should be no question of his independence from the company. When the properties concerned are located in different countries, it is advantageous to use an international firm or one with strong international affiliations to ensure a consistent approach to valuation is adopted.

Other assets which are regularly revalued include ships, mines and quarries. Plant and equipment can also be revalued, especially in cases like the construction groups or manufacturers where plant and equipment form a significant proportion of total assets. Techniques also exist for valuing intangible assets such as brand names or newspaper titles, essentially on the basis of the revenue they are expected to generate. In choosing valuers for other fixed assets, the same general criteria will apply as for property revaluations. It must be recognised, however, that there may be some disagreement on the basis of valuation and its validity where a revaluation is carried out on a category of asset which is not regularly bought and sold in the open market.

(vii) Public relations consultants

It has become usual to engage a firm of public relations consultants to co-ordinate the publicity arrangements for a flotation. The merits of a company going public are not always obvious from reading the dry prose of a prospectus and not all investors have the patience to read it in any case. Further channels of communication are needed. The role of the PR consultants can stretch from sowing the original seeds of interest in the months before the prospectus to an intensive media operation at the time of going public. A press conference to announce the issue can be very effective in obtaining coverage which the availability of a certain amount of food and drink does nothing to hinder. At a more nuts and bolts level, the prospectus will usually be summarised in one or more newspapers and advice is needed on the effectiveness of various alternative advertising strategies.

Care must be taken that nothing is released by the PR consultants which implies the flotation has been approved before it actually has, which would create difficulties with the regulatory authorities. In addition, nothing must be said which goes beyond what can be substantiated in the prospectus. The profit forecast or the asset backing of a company are particularly sensitive; a loose comment on these aspects can result in extreme cases in the postponement or even cancellation of the listing, unless the prospectus can be altered to accommodate what has been said. Great discipline is required, particularly in interviews, where the interviewee may be tempted to go beyond the limitations of a 'boring' but strictly verified prospectus and the interviewer may be angling for a 'scoop'.

(viii) Other professionals involved

Other professionals include:

(a) Receiving bankers

The application forms with the cheques attached will normally be delivered to a bank specialising in receiving and checking such documents.

The bank chosen may be the clearing bank of the group or may be recommended by the merchant bank. Banks who specialise in this role have numerous branches capable of receiving applications and pools of experienced staff who can be drafted in to help at short notice in the event of a high level of applications.

The bank may also act as a temporary registrar for an initial period.

(b) Registrars

After applications have been received (and the cheques detached), they will be passed to a registration company. It is their responsibility to tally the applications, analyse the applications by size and carry out the procedure decided on for allocation. They will then draw up the first register of members and send out certificates for the securities being issued.

It is unlikely that a private group will have any existing contact with a registration company. Such companies are often affiliated with firms of accountants or with banks. The company will normally act on their recommendation in choice of registrar.

(c) Printers

Although the role of the printer may not seem glamorous, their help with eleventh-hour changes to the documents is often vital. Their efficiency in updating and circulating the many proofs required is also a considerable factor in the smooth running of the operation. There is usually little time to spare between agreeing the text of the final proof of the prospectus and distributing the large quantities needed to the various locations to be available when the issue opens. A printer specialising in this kind of work is essential. Normally the choice will be one the merchant bank knows well and can rely on to 'pull out the stops' if a crisis arises.

II EXPENSES

There are three main types of expenses which are incurred in going public—the time of the company's own executives, the charges of the professional firms and taxes and fees paid to the authorities.

(i) The company's own costs

This element is often ignored because it is rarely separately calculated. Companies which do go through the exercise of costing in retrospect the time expended by their own executives may well be appalled at the result. The amount is likely to be higher than any of the professional charges, excluding underwriting.

As well as direct costs there are opportunity costs. The preparation of a prospectus requires heavy involvement on the part of senior management who are likely to be the major generators of new business. Even day-to-day management may suffer under the voracious capacity of the prospectus to absorb time.

(ii) Professionals

The major amounts payable to the various professional firms are as follows:

(a) Merchant banks

Underwriting fees vary widely from market to market, being perhaps most expensive in the US where fees for underwriting and marketing a medium-sized issue are about 5–6% and for a small initial public offering can go as high as 10%. In the UK and markets influenced by the UK, underwriting fees tend to be about $2\frac{1}{2}$% of the amount raised. The total fee will be split into two. A management fee will be retained by the lead merchant bank(s) as their reward for bringing the company to market, putting their name to the prospectus and underwriting and managing the issue. The remainder of the fee will be passed on to the underwriting or selling syndicate, for their risk in taking sub-underwriting or their efforts in selling.

On the whole, there seems to be little competition among institutions on the fee structure. Underwriting fees suggested by merchant banks for similar types of issues are not likely to vary sharply in a particular market. The major participants in the market probably know each other well enough to avoid a price war.

From the company's point of view, though the expense of underwriting is important, it is greatly outweighed by whether the issue can be underwritten at all. Bargaining takes place at the outset when the promoters may be ill-informed about the flotation process, although a well-briefed company may hold a 'beauty contest' between rival underwriters. Promoters preoccupied about the overall success of the issue in the later stages are in a poor position to argue hard about the precise underwriting expense.

Underwriting and selling fees may be paid directly as such, or may be built into a spread between the price at which securities are acquired from the company or the vendor shareholders and the price at which they are sold to the market, depending on the type of issue being made.

In addition to underwriting fees, the merchant bank will charge a financial advisory or documentation fee to cover the work involved on the structure of the issue and in drafting the prospectus. This fee will be a flat charge, rather than a percentage as in the case of underwriting and selling. Except in the case of a small issue, the merchant bank's major reward will come from underwriting fees. Merchant banks would rather reduce the advisory/documentation fee than disturb a relatively fixed underwriting fee structure.

(b) Accountants and lawyers

The fees of the merchant bankers will not vary significantly with the amount of work done. The accountants and lawyers on the other hand will charge primarily on a time spent basis. Most accountants and lawyers have a system of weighting a particular job by urgency and complexity. Flotations tend to score heavily on both counts. However, the final bill will principally depend on the number of man hours absorbed in the work required.

(c) Stockbrokers

The stockbrokers will be paid a fee (perhaps $\frac{1}{4}$% of the amount of the issue) directly by the company or by the merchant bank out of their overall underwriting fee for their involvement in putting together the sub-underwriting syndicate. They will also charge a flat fee for their processing work as regards the stock exchange. In some markets, a brokerage fee (say 1%) is payable by applicants in respect of successful applications. This is built into the price of the issue and is not therefore paid directly by the company.

The principal reward for a broker in being associated with a flotation may come later, from commissions when market dealings begin. The broker sponsoring the launch of a company is likely to be seen as a leader in the market for the securities of that company and would hope to gain a lion's share of the trading. Trading can be particularly heavy in the first few days as 'stags' aim to take profits and other investors seek to 'top up' their allocations.

(d) Valuers

Valuers may be members of an association which publishes fixed fees for its members. In the context of a flotation, it may prove possible to negotiate a fee separately from the standard rate.

(e) Public relations

The public relations consultants will base their charges for a campaign mainly on estimated time involved. They may also charge a fee based on the cost of advertising placed.

(f) Receiving bankers, registrars and printers

A minimum charge will be levied to cover set-up costs and other fixed expenses. The overall costs incurred will depend on variable factors such as the number of applications received, shares allotted and prospectuses printed.

(iii) Taxes and listing fees

Two principal taxes are likely to be incurred:

(a) Capital duty

Capital duty may arise when the authorised share capital of a company is increased or when new shares are issued. The tax is usually based on a percentage (perhaps $\frac{1}{2}\%$) of the amount involved. If authorised share capital is used as the basis, it will be calculated on the face amount of the increase. If the tax is based on the issued share capital, it is likely to include any premium at which the shares are issued over par value.

If no acquisitions are made for shares and existing shares are sold via an offer for sale, no capital duty will be payable.

If a new company is set up to act as the holding company for the group and acquires its subsidiaries by an exchange of shares, capital duty will be payable in effect not only on any new shares issued at the time of the flotation but on the entire value of the group as reorganised for going public. There is a substantial cost saving if an existing company controlling as many of the interests to be floated as possible is suitable for use as the new listed company. Any reorganisation of the group should be designed with an eye to minimising the capital duty impact.

If it is acceptable to the relevant stock exchange for the holding company to be incorporated in a low tax jurisdiction, such as Bermuda or the Cayman Islands, a significant sum can be saved.

(b) Transfer duty

Transfer duty can arise in two ways. In the first instance it can arise upon the reorganisation of the group when assets or businesses are transferred to the new holding company. Transfer tax may be incurred whatever form of payment the holding company uses. Different rates may apply, however, on assets and shares so that it may be advantageous for example to transfer the share capital of a company which holds an asset rather than transfer the asset itself. Various tax avoidance schemes are available (depending on the jurisdiction involved) to limit the extent to which transfer duty may be incurred. Such schemes tend to be subject to periodic attack by tax authorities and changes of legislation.

The second area where transfer duty is involved is if existing shares are sold. In this case both the vendors and the purchasers will be obliged to pay transfer duty at the relevant rate, based on the issue price.

The payment of some tax is almost inevitable. A new issue does not involve transfer duty but will probably incur capital duty, an offer for sale of existing shares vice versa. The use of renounceable certificates may help in some jurisdictions. A corporate reorganisation prior to flotation may also trigger transfer duty and capital duty if a share exchange is used.

(c) Listing fees

The stock exchange will charge an initial listing fee, normally on a scale varying with the market value (at the issue price) of the entire class of capital for which a listing is granted. Thereafter, a lower annual fee is payable by all listed companies.

(iv) Estimate of expenses

One of the first documents the underwriter will produce is the estimate of expenses to be incurred under the headings listed in paragraphs (ii) and (iii) above. An example of an estimate for an assumed issue of say $100 million is as follows:

List of estimated expenses for an assumed issue of $100 million:

	$000
Underwriting fee (based 2½% on $100 million offer)	2,500
Financial advisory fees	500
Accountancy	1,000
Legal fees	
—to Company	700
—to Underwriters	500
Stockbrokers	250
Valuation	200
Advertising and publicity	500
Receiving bank	200
Registrar	200
Printing	500
Capital duty and transfer duty	750
Listing fee	200
Contingency	500
Total	8,500
As percentage of proceeds	8.5%

(v) Offsets to expenses

If the issue is over-subscribed, there may be a considerable amount of funds available for placing in the money markets until the over-subscription moneys are returned. The money cannot be returned until the basis of allotment is arrived at and refund cheques are prepared and posted out which may take a number of days. It is customary for the interest earned on over-subscriptions to be retained by the company to defray the expenses of the issue. It is not unknown for a heavy over-subscription at a period of high interest rates to result in expenses being covered and an overall profit being made. Although there may be a suspicion in investors' minds that return of over-subscription moneys is delayed deliberately, the merchant and receiving banks are sensitive to possible criticism and do not themselves benefit from delay.

It is sometimes suggested that an attempt should be made to pay the interest back to unsuccessful applicants. Their funds generate the interest in the first place and they perhaps deserve a consolation prize for not achieving their desired investment. In some jurisdictions, the basis of allotment is decided before cheques are cashed, which allows cheques to be returned to wholly unsuccessful applicants without being cashed.

(vi) Who pays?

If the whole issue is devoted to raising new funds for the company, all the expenses incurred are payable by the company. If the prospectus involves solely the sale of existing shares, the underwriting costs will be borne by the holders of those shares. There is some flexibility in who bears the remaining costs, with the majority normally borne by the company on the grounds that the company benefits from obtaining listed status.

Where a new issue and an offer for sale are combined, the underwriting fees are shared in the same proportion as the proceeds. The administrative expenses involved in gaining the listing (such as printing and advertising costs and professional fees) may be borne wholly by the company going public, on the grounds mentioned above, or they may be split in the same proportion as the proceeds of the issue. Any transfer duty payable on the offer for sale shares is borne by the shareholders who sell those shares. The capital duty on new shares issued to the public will be borne entirely by the company.

CONCLUSIONS

The composition of the team of people involved in the issue is central to its success and the way the team is chosen is therefore a critical factor. Expertise is required but personal factors are also important in what is often a long drawn-out process. This chapter has reviewed who is involved, how they are chosen and what their rule is.

The merchant bank will present an estimate of expenses at an early stage and suggest how these can be controlled. The availability of funds from the flotation, including possible interest on over-subscriptions, makes the payment of expenses a little less painful. Some expenses will be incurred whether or not the issue proceeds. Underwriting fees are based on a percentage of funds raised and therefore vary with the size of the issue. Other fees are largely fixed, based on time spent with a loading for complexity and urgency.

CHAPTER 6

Components of a prospectus, timetable and list of documents

The major administrative task in a flotation is the production of a prospectus document. While the precise contents of a prospectus vary from market to market, there tend to be 'building blocks' in common. In 'I Main components of a prospectus' below, the main components of these building blocks are summarised. Some components are critical and set the tone for the issue. Others may be laborious to draft or verify but rarely affect the overall outcome. Relative importance is not determined by the order in which they appear in the prospectus or the amount of text they are accorded.

In 'II Timetable and document list' below, the time required to put together the prospectus is considered and a sample checklist of documents is given. Certain items, such as the accountant's report, provide basic information for other parts and so must be completed first. The timetable and list of documents together form the blueprint for the issue and allow progress and procedures to be monitored and controlled.

I MAIN COMPONENTS OF A PROSPECTUS

The main components of a prospectus (based broadly on UK legislation) in the order which they generally appear are set out below, with brief comments on their importance.

(i) Description of the share capital of the company

The authorised and issued share capital is set out as it will be immediately following the flotation, taking account of any capital reorganisation to be carried out for the purpose of listing. If the flotation is by way of new issue, the description of the share capital should include the effect of the issue of the new shares. The impact of any options outstanding, the exercise of any warrants and the conversion of convertible securities should also be disclosed.

(ii) Statement of the indebtedness of the group including contingent liabilities, guarantees and commitments

Information on indebtedness has to be obtained independently from the banks concerned and this information takes time to collect and verify. Preparations should be made so that the figures are as current as possible, normally as at a date no more than a month before the date of the prospectus.

There is no one 'correct' level of borrowing. An apparently high level of gearing may deter some potential investors but assurances on the adequacy of working capital are given elsewhere in the document and one of the purposes of going public may be to reduce borrowings.

(iii) Directors of the company and a list of the other parties (chiefly professional firms) involved in the issue

This part is straightforward descriptive material, although it would be a mistake to under-estimate participants' sensitivity to even the most basic information presented about themselves. Directors can object to their age, address or nationality being disclosed; professional firms jealously guard their position on a page or even the typeface in which their name appears. Written consent must be obtained from any professional firm whose opinion is given or who are quoted as experts for the use of their name in the form and context in which it is included. Care must be taken throughout the prospectus that names of third parties are not mentioned without their knowledge and approval.

(iv) History and business of the group, including background industry information and an explanation of the main commercial factors governing its operations and future prospects

It may be helpful to provide a summary of the relevant characteristics of the industry or sector(s) in which the group operates. Technology, production methods, distribution channels and barriers to entry may be important factors not necessarily familiar to the general investor.

In order to give investors a general appreciation of how the group has evolved, there will be a few paragraphs prepared by the company's executives and edited by professional advisers which will summarise the origins of the business and its development to the present day, highlighting the most significant events.

The potted history is followed by a lengthy descriptive section, covering the various activities, countries, products and business conditions which are relevant to the operations of the company and its subsidiaries. A chart or 'family tree' of the corporate structure may help the potential investor understand the position more readily. The chart can show the holding company and its major subsidiaries, giving percentage ownership, place of incorporation and principal activities and other relevant information.

Different product lines and divisions should be explained and a geographical analysis of production, sales and operating profit may be given. Commercial aspects such as retail network, agencies and distributorships, brand names, franchises, licences, patents and research and development capabilities should be discussed depending on the type of business. Critical relationships with suppliers and customers should be mentioned. For example, could the supply of key components restrict output? Are they dual-sourced? Do sales to any individual customers represent a significant percentage of output of the group as a whole or of an individual product line or division? Have significant bad debts been incurred?

This section provides the directors of the company with their main opportunity to get across the spirit and traditions of the company. Although the wording used, as is the case with the whole prospectus, is subject to strict legal scrutiny this section tends to be less dry than the remainder. A little pride in achievement is allowed to show through.

(v) Directors, management and staff

Details should be given of the experience and areas of responsibility of the directors, distinguishing between executive and non-executive. Investors will also be interested to know something of senior management below the director level and be assured of the depth and professionalism of the management team. Excessive influence by one individual could have a negative impact. The separation of the roles of chairman and chief executive may be considered desirable. Underwriters will wish to see an experienced and independent-minded finance director in place. A professional company secretary will handle the record-keeping which may have been informally done before. Where directors are also major shareholders, their commitment to the company may be unquestioned. However, service contracts should be drawn up for all executive directors for a period of say two to three years particularly in service industries, such as advertising, where the investor is reliant on people and their expertise, without the comfort of a substantial net asset base. Any profit-participation or share-incentive scheme in operation or planned should be mentioned.

Information on other employees may also be relevant particularly for groups with large labour forces. Some comment on labour relations may be helpful. Remarkably, all companies going public seem to have excellent relations with their staff and workforce, although this may of course be plausible in a growing company.

(vi) Track record

(a) Profits

The audited results and other financial information for a certain period, commonly three to five years, will be set out in the accountant's report, which is reproduced in full in an appendix to the prospectus. The results included in the report should cover a period ending not later than six months before the date of the prospectus. The report will include such notes as the auditors feel necessary to explain the figures in an objective way.

In the body of the prospectus, the directors of the company may wish to add their own comments and explanation of the past trend or of any special circumstances which might distort a particular year's figures. Significant changes in turnover and profits from year to year and the main reasons for them will be explained, together with an analysis of margins and other relevant factors. As well as giving background information, it is essential to anticipate any perception of weakness derived from the past record which could cast doubt on the quality and recurrent nature of past profits and so of profits in the future.

(b) Dividends

There is little reason for a private company to be concerned about consistency of dividend payments or indeed, depending on the tax position and requirements of the shareholders, about dividend payments at all. Consequently, the past record of dividends, which is included in the accountant's report, may be of little guidance to future policy. On occasions, particularly where a new issue of shares is being made but the reason for flotation is not primarily to raise new capital (but for example to increase the company's public profile) the directors may resolve to pay a substantial dividend to existing shareholders prior to flotation. This reduces the company's net assets, but may not affect the price of the issue if the company is being valued by reference to a forecast of earnings. Consequently, existing shareholders will maximise their return by paying out sufficient of the company's accumulated retained earnings to reduce net assets to the level just acceptable to the market. A similar effect could be achieved by the shareholders selling a proportion of their existing shares (rather than the company making a new issue); however, some shareholders feel that while they are entitled to a dividend out of past profits, they do not wish to be seen as sellers of their shares.

(vii) Profit and dividend forecast

(a) Profits

A formal forecast of profits, while not a prospectus requirement, is highly desirable in normal circumstances. The forecast does not usually go beyond the end of the current financial period. Forecasts for periods which have not yet started are regarded as too tentative to be verified to prospectus standards.

Where a company is being valued on an earnings basis, the forecast of profits is arguably the single most important item in the prospectus. It is by reference to the forecast of profits, not by the historical record, that the issue price will be set, although the past record is relevant to judging the reasonableness of the profit forecast and the underlying rate of growth.

The main assumptions on which the profit forecast is based are set out in an appendix to the prospectus and reviewed by the underwriters. The reporting accountants will also review the accounting bases and calculations for the forecast. The figure will be made up of a certain number of months actual results based on unaudited management accounts, and a forecast for the remainder of the period. Usually the directors will not offer background commentary on the forecast itself; this is one of the most sensitive parts of the document as it constitutes a firm promise for the future. Some cushion (say at least 5–10%) should be allowed in the forecast. Other things being equal, the cushion will be greater the earlier in the year the forecast is made. For some businessess with a large seasonal factor (eg toys, retailing), a forecast may not be possible until the results for the peak season are known. The legal consequences of a forecast being 'missed' are too severe for the directors or the other professionals involved to contemplate this possibility.

(b) Dividends

Depending on the time of year when the company is floated, the first year's dividend payments may well be less than if the company had been a public company throughout the relevant financial year. The directors must therefore spell out not only their immediate intentions for the first period, but also how this may be validly scaled up for a full year's payment.

The amount of dividend to be paid will depend on a number of factors including the company's own need to retain funds for future growth. Very often a market will have fairly specific expectations of a dividend yield appropriate to a company in a particular sector in a particular market. Occasionally there is a 'target' yield in a market irrespective of the type of company.

The directors will wish to maintain future dividends at no less than the initial level. A dividend cut is widely interpreted as evidence of management failure, even in cyclical industries. The most common measure to assess whether a dividend can be maintained is the number of times it is covered by earnings. Some particularly stable component of earnings, such as rentals receivable under long-term leases or interest on bonds, may be weighted more heavily. A dividend cover of two times (ie paying out half earnings as dividends) may be considered comfortable in most circumstances.

(viii) Working capital

The forecast of profit forms the basis of a forecast of cash flow which the company will prepare in support of a statement required to be included in the prospectus that the group being floated has sufficient working capital for its present requirements. Conventionally, this statement is expected to cover a period of at least one year from the date of the prospectus. As this will be longer than the period covered by the profit forecast, further projections are needed. The directors of the company will normally ask the reporting accountants to review these projections also and give them a 'letter of comfort' that they have been prepared correctly and on a reasonable basis. This letter is not published. In this part of the prospectus, a few words may represent several weeks of investigation and analysis.

(ix) Balance sheet, asset valuations and adjusted net assets

The latest audited balance sheet of the company and the group with supporting notes will form part of the accountant's report. The date of the balance sheet should be the final date covered by the accountant's report and, as noted above, should be not more than six months before the date of the prospectus. Directors may feel some commentary on the balance sheet and planned capital expenditure is helpful.

If a group is made up primarily of asset-intensive businesses such as property or shipping, it may be required and in any case be desirable to show up-to-date valuations of its major assets carried out by an independent professionally qualified valuer. Freehold and long leasehold properties are the items most frequently revalued. Plant and equipment may also be revalued. On occasion, more exotic valuations of brand names and other intangible assets may be carried out, although it is not clear what credibility they carry with investors. If the valuations show significant differences from book value (either surpluses or deficits) an adjusted statement of net assets incorporating the valuations should be shown in this section. Any significant tax consequences of disposals at the valuation figures should also be shown. Other adjustments might include accrued profits (less any dividends) since the balance sheet date and any surplus on listed investments.

It is not necessary for the valuations actually to be written into the books of the companies concerned. If they are, tax problems may arise and the charge for depreciation may increase, reducing reported profits.

(x) Use of proceeds

If existing shares are being sold to raise money for shareholders, no proceeds are received by the company. However, if new money is going into the company the reasons why it is being raised and the uses to which it will be put should be spelt out. This is a highly sensitive part of the prospectus. The uses stated should be regarded as commitments rather than just possibilities. If it later turns out that the proceeds have been used for different purposes, shareholders may rightly claim that they subscribed on a false basis. Consequently, contractual or other firm arrangements are desirable to back up the statements made in this section.

(xi) Future prospects

It is helpful and legitimate to give potential investors a general idea of the prospects for the company beyond the relatively short period covered by the formal profit forecast. Some discussion of prospects leads on naturally from the forecast, and from the use of proceeds section if new funds are being raised. Areas which may be covered include fresh products in the pipeline, new markets to be opened up and capital investment plans. There is an obvious danger in revealing commercially sensitive details prematurely; on the other hand, investors often prefer the lure of future excitements to past achievements. Hopeful descriptions of developments which may not come to pass, however, will be vigorously screened out by the lawyers.

(xii) Appendices

There will also be a number of appendices to the prospectus. These typically consist of:

(a) Accountant's report on the group

The accountant's report forms one of the main building blocks of the prospectus. Once the companies forming the basis of the flotation have been selected, it is the first significant piece of work to be put in hand. The requirement (if applicable) that the accountant's report should be prepared up to a date not more than six months before the date of the prospectus is one of the key limitations on timing.

The report will explain how the financial information on the companies in the group has been compiled, whether all such information has been audited and who the auditors have been. It will list details of the companies reported on and summarise the accounting policies adopted. Policies on such items as depreciation, goodwill, associated companies, stocks, investments, leases and foreign currency transactions may be particularly relevant. If the companies have not all been members of the group throughout the period covered by the report, combined figures will be presented, prepared as if the group structure at the date of flotation had been in place during such period. If a company joins the group after the final date covered by the report, it may be reported on separately, or alternatively incorporated in the report. Depending on whether the company is profitable or not, this treatment may have an impact on the 'track record' of the group as presented in the accountant's report. The profit and loss accounts for past periods, commonly 3 to 5 years, will be shown together with notes. The notes will cover such items as the definition of turnover, what deductions, including the amount of interest, are made from trading profits and how taxation is calculated. A statement of net assets of the company and of the group at the final date covered by the report and, depending on requirements, for a number of years past will also be given, again with all relevant notes. These notes will cover such items as fixed assets, the treatment of associates and investments, stocks and the maturity of debts. Statements of sources and uses of funds may also be included.

The formal report is addressed to the directors of the company to be floated and to the merchant bank. It is normally produced in draft form as soon as possible to highlight any potential snags in the flotation. At the same time, the accountants may be carrying out a more detailed investigation into the group for a 'long form' report, which is not for publication. Depending on the complexity of the group, the report for inclusion in the prospectus may take up to, say, three months to finalise.

(b) Summary of professional valuations

In the case of asset intensive businesses, such as property or shipping, the asset valuation is the key to the whole prospectus. For such companies, independent professional valuations are required by law or stock exchange regulations and the feasibility of the flotation and the pricing will depend principally on the valuation. In the case of other types of company, the directors or the underwriters may in any event decide that it would be desirable to show the financial position of the group taking into account revaluation of assets. In these cases, letters from the valuers giving the basis of their valuation and a summary of the results of their valuations will be set out in an appendix. In the case of a property company, relevant details of site and development areas, tenure, planning permissions and tenants' leases will be given, depending on the nature of the property. Developments should be valued on an 'existing state' basis, and not as if they had been completed.

Other fixed assets besides property and ships can be revalued. However, the most acceptable basis of valuation is 'open market', so it is important that it can be demonstrated that such a market exists. There may well be an international market for widely used construction equipment, for example, but not for specialised production machinery. If there is no active market, the basis of valuation becomes theoretical and may not carry credibility with investors. Brand names undoubtedly have a value but whether it can be quantified tangibly to the satisfaction of investors is another matter.

(c) Reports on profit forecast

Assuming a profit forecast is made, the bases and assumptions underlying the forecast will be set out. If the forecast relates to a financial period which has already started, some months' results (audited or unaudited) will already be available and this should be stated. The accountants will confirm that the forecast has been prepared consistently with the accounting policies normally adopted by the group and summarised in the accountant's report. They will also check the calculations of the forecast have been carried out correctly and that the forecast has been properly compiled on the basis of the assumptions made by the directors.

The underwriters will discuss with the directors of the company whether the basis and assumptions used for the forecast are realistic and comprehensive. The assumptions should relate principally to factors beyond the directors' control, such as changes in political, legal or economic conditions in the countries where the group operates. Economic conditions might include tax, interest and foreign exchange rates. Factors which are within the directors' control and fall within the province of prudent management should not be included. Assumptions of a circular nature, for example, that a certain profit will be made, should also be excluded. As a general rule, the fewer the assumptions, the greater confidence investors will tend to have in a forecast. Assumptions are widely regarded as a 'let out' for the directors. Following these discussions, the underwriters will write to the company to confirm that in their opinion the forecast has been prepared after due and careful enquiry.

The letters from the auditors and the underwriters covering these points will be included in the appendix. The letters always state that despite the involvement of the professional firms the forecast is the sole responsibility of the directors of the company. This can make them feel rather lonely.

It may be argued that the assumptions listed in this appendix are virtually meaningless. They may be couched in sweeping terms and therefore unlikely to be fulfilled in all respects. They also tend to deal more with general conditions or trends in the economy, such as interest, taxation and exchange rates, than with specific commercial factors which have more meaning to a reader and a much more immediate effect on the company's business. It is countered that the most critical commercial factors cannot be set out without giving too much away to competitors.

(d) Statutory and general information

This appendix is prepared chiefly by the lawyers and deals with legal and regulatory points not already covered elsewhere in the prospectus. The main headings are likely to include the following:

—Details of incorporation of the company and share capital history including any reorganisation carried out in anticipation of the flotation.

—A list of the company's subsidiaries and associated companies giving share capital, date of incorporation and percentage owned by the group, unless this information has already been presented in the accountant's report.

—Arrangements for underwriting including circumstances in which the underwriting contract could be cancelled, for example because of a material adverse change in market conditions. Details of the holdings of the major existing shareholders (together with undertakings by them not to sell shares for a given period, say six months) are also set out in this section.

—Expenses of the issue.

—Disclosure of interests. This is a wide ranging section and is basically intended to cover details of shareholders' or directors' interests which might have some bearing on an investor's decision to invest. Obvious points include who the major shareholders are and the extent of their shareholding, whether any directors are selling shares, any service contracts the directors have and whether they are parties to any other contracts with the group. A number of other factors may be relevant, depending on the circumstances of the case. A rather cynical definition of what is material for disclosure is anything which one of the promoters does not wish to disclose. Some statement of the controlling shareholders' future business dealings with the group may be relevant at this point.

—Summary of relevant provisions of new articles of association. A company going public will adopt new articles of association which are available in full for public inspection. Relevant sections will be summarised in the prospectus. These will include clauses regarding voting and dividend rights of shares, procedures for changing the share capital and for transfer and issue of shares, any restrictions on the company's ability to borrow money and a summary of the directors' powers.

—If relevant, a summary of any warrants being issued on listing and of any share option scheme being introduced. Rights being given to the directors to issue or repurchase any securities of the group will also be noted.

—Material contracts entered into by the company and its subsidiaries over say the two years before the date of the prospectus. Some contracts may be sensitive from a commercial or other viewpoint; however, contracts entered into in the ordinary course of business are normally excluded. What is and is not a material contract is often the subject of one of the more lively debates to take place during the preparation of a prospectus.

Copies of the full documentation referred to or summarised in this appendix will be available for inspection during the period of the flotation at the offices of the company's lawyers.

(xiii) Procedures for application

It is easy to lose sight of the fact that the main objective in the preparation of a prospectus is to facilitate applications. The procedures for application should be spelt out in as clear a manner as possible, even if they are fairly technical. These procedures will be covered both in the body of the prospectus and on a separate application form. Applications from residents in jurisdictions where the prospectus has not been filed with the relevant authorities may not be accepted. Details of which countries such restrictions apply to will be given. The prospectus will cover procedures for applying for shares and the timetable for declaring results, posting out share certificates and the start of trading.

The application form will contain details of the minimum and other numbers of shares which may be applied for. If trading in the shares takes place in certain fixed amounts or board lots, the minimum application will be for one board lot and thereafter applications have to be for multiples of board lots. A table may be included to help in calculations of the amount of money which will be required for each application. Procedures for cashing cheques and returning amounts in respect of wholly or partially unsuccessful applications will also be set out.

This section of the prospectus and the wording of the application form are highly standardised and familiar to professional investors. They can cause confusion for small investors or for people who do not regularly apply for new issues. If there is time, the receiving bankers or registrars will contact applicants who have submitted invalid applications to obtain clarification and make corrections.

II TIMETABLE AND DOCUMENT LIST

The precise period needed to prepare and publish a prospectus will vary with the regulations and practice of the particular markets being tapped and the circumstances of the company going public. The only general rule seems to be that it takes longer than expected. In constructing a timetable it is as well to build in some slack for unexpected delays and problems. The main stages are as follows:

(i) Decision to proceed

A degree of indecision is inevitable since it is not until the executives concerned have a detailed appreciation of the costs and the work involved that they can take a final decision on whether a flotation is worthwhile. Very often it is not immediately clear which elements in a complex collection of businesses and assets should be included in the package for flotation. Groups contemplating flotation are often in a strongly expansionary and acquisitive stage of their development, so that the task of identifying the businesses to form the public group can seem like hitting a moving target. At a reasonable period before the flotation, a 'close season' must be declared on new acquisitions of significant size.

Management has to assess the risk of time and money being spent only for the flotation to be cancelled for market reasons which may have nothing to do with the company itself or the wish of the promoters to proceed. One method of limiting costs is to make any reorganisation conditional on a listing being obtained.

(ii) Commissioning the accountant's report

A decision on the elements to be floated must be taken before the accountants can be instructed to produce their report. It may prove desirable for the report to be carried out by or in conjunction with a firm which may not be familiar with the group. This will add to the time the report takes to complete. In addition, as accounts will not previously have been published, it is likely that some additional accounting work will be required beyond the programme which was previously followed.

In some jurisdictions, the stock exchange may require the audited accounts shown in the prospectus to be no more than six months old at the date of the prospectus. Since it normally takes two to three months to prepare an accountant's report, this leaves a window of, say, three months between the time the report is completed and the deadline. This assumes that the accountants are instructed soon after the close of the financial period in question. If discussions about the elements to be floated delay the instructions to the accountants, the window will become even narrower.

Owing to the frequent experience of delays, it is desirable to build in contingency plans for a special audit to be conducted if the six months' stock exchange limitation on the age of the audited figures (or other time limit) runs out. If the company has relatively simple operations, such as a property company with a portfolio of a few large investment properties, a further audit may only take a matter of two or three weeks. In a major manufacturing or retailing concern, the requirement for a physical stock check among other factors may mean that elaborate preparations will have to be made if a further audit is needed.

(iii) Profit forecast

Where a profit forecast is to be included in the prospectus, the pressures on management run in the other direction. Directors would prefer to have actual results 'under their belt' for as much of the period to be forecast as possible. Where there is difficulty in forecasting to prospectus standards early in the financial year, a special audit may have to be performed at, say, the interim stage and the prospectus itself dated towards the end of the year. In that case, eight or nine months' management accounts would be available, making the task of forecasting the remainder of the year less hazardous.

(iv) Legal work, valuations and general drafting

While the accounting work is underway, it will be necessary for the lawyers to be instructed so that the basic legal work can be completed at approximately the same time as the accountant's report becomes available. If a valuation of assets is to be undertaken this work should also proceed in parallel. During this time, the underwriter will begin to put together the first draft prospectus and to discuss with the company any difficult or sensitive areas as they are discovered.

Altogether it is rare for a prospectus to be published less than four months after the first major planning meeting. A typical timetable for a flotation based on the four-month period is set out below. Executives involved in the processs normally query the amount of time allowed at first, only to find that in the event they have to scramble to meet the deadlines.

Note. 'I' means 'Impact Day', the first day on which the detailed terms of the issue are made known to the market and to the press. This is earlier than the date of the prospectus and considerably earlier than the start of trading in the shares on the stock market.

Date (in days)		*Event*
I − 120		First planning meeting held. Decision taken to proceed in principle. Merchant bank appointed. Estimated expenses discussed.
I − 110	(i)	Package of companies/businesses assets to be floated decided on.
	(ii)	Accountants instructed and begin work.
	(iii)	Lawyers instructed and begin work.
	(iv)	Detailed timetable and list of responsibilities circulated to those involved.
	(v)	Public relations campaign discussed.
I − 90	(i)	Progress and possible problems reviewed with accountants.
	(ii)	Property/other valuers instructed if appropriate.
I − 60	(i)	Draft audited accounts for the latest period and draft accountant's report available.
	(ii)	Work commences on profit and cash flow forecasts.
	(iii)	Basis of issue reviewed by company and underwriter.
I − 50	(i)	Draft profit forecast and asset valuations available.
	(ii)	Outline typewritten proof circulated to parties involved in the issue.
	(iii)	Drafting and other work progresses. First typeset proof produced.
I − 40	(i)	Drafts of application form, share certificate, underwriting agreement and other documentation available.
	(ii)	Receiving bankers, registrars and printers appointed.
	(iii)	Draft documentation submitted to stock exchange (and other relevant authorities) for review.

I − 30	(i)	Record date for borrowings and disclosures.
	(ii)	Discussions between regulatory authorities and advisers as required.
I − 20	(i)	Further proofs circulated to advisers and other parties involved, discussed and sent for re-proofing.
	(ii)	Confirm flotation date with stock exchange.
	(iii)	Lawyers commence verification meetings.
	(iv)	Launch publicity decided.
	(v)	Pricing tentatively set.
I − 10		Final proof prepared and circulated to all relevant parties. Final comments obtained. Pricing decided.
I − 6		Formal meeting held with stock exchange for listing.
I − 1	(i)	Board meeting to approve prospectus and related documents and ratify price.
	(ii)	Underwriting proofs available.
IMPACT DAY	(i)	Presentation of issue to potential sub-underwriters/investors.
	(ii)	Sub-underwritng letters sent out.
	(iii)	Bulk printing ordered.
	(iv)	Underwriting agreement signed.
I + 4		Prospectus signed and legal formalities complied with. Press conference held.
I + 5		Prospectus advertised and distributed to the public. First day for receipt of applications.
I + 9		Last day for receipt of applications. Application lists open and close.
I + 10	(i)	Cheques cleared.
	(ii)	Basis of allocation discussed.
I + 13	(i)	Press announcement of results and basis of allocation.
	(ii)	Underwriters' liability (if any) crystallised.
	(iii)	Stock exchange grants listing.
	(iv)	Letters of regret and refund cheques posted.
I + 20	(i)	Documents of title posted.
	(ii)	Funds released to company/vendors.
	(iii)	Listing becomes unconditional.
I + 23 (say)		First day of dealings.

The details of the above timetable will vary according to local regulations. In particular, the arrangements for dealings and settlement differ from market to market.

Very rarely does the original timetable for a flotation remain intact—indeed numerous revisions are the rule. On completion, the participants may look back at the original target dates ruefully indeed. Nevertheless, the timetable (however often revised) is the basic tool for co-ordinating and monitoring the progress of a flotation. To assist in this process, a checklist of documents is drawn up, with responsibilities assigned to the various parties involved in the flotation. This checklist should tie in with the timetable and vice versa, so that all relevant parties are aware who is responsible for producing what and when it is required. A sample list of documents and the parties who are primarily responsible for each item is set out below:

SAMPLE LIST OF DOCUMENTS

Document	Primary responsibility
1. Documents included in the prospectus	
1.1 Summary of the new issue	Underwriter
1.2 Expected timetable	Underwriter
1.3 Statement of indebtedness	Company/ Reporting accountants
1.4 Preliminary informaton	Lawyers
1.5 Particulars of the group	Underwriter/ Company
1.6 Accountants' report	Reporting accountants
1.7 Property valuation	Valuer
1.8 Profit/dividend forecast	Company/ Reporting accountants
1.9 Letters in respect of directors' profit forecast	Reporting accountants/ Underwriters
1.10 Memorandum of association and bye-laws of company	Lawyers
1.11 Warrant particulars	Lawyers
1.12 Summary of share option scheme	Lawyers
1.13 Statutory and general information	All parties
1.14 Application forms	Registrar
1.15 Procedure for application	Company/ Lawyers/ Underwriter/ Registrar

Document	Primary responsibility
2. Supporting documents for the prospectus	
2.1 Certificate of incorporation of the new holding company	Lawyers
2.2 Underwriting agreement	Lawyers
2.3 Sub-underwriting letters	Underwriters/ Lawyers
2.4 Rules of share option scheme	Lawyers
2.5 Warrant deed poll	Lawyers
2.6 Audited accounts of company	Reporting accountants
2.7 Statement of working capital	Company/ Reporting accountants
2.8 Statement of adjusted consolidated net assets	Company/ Reporting accountants
2.9 Estimates of expenses	Company/ Underwriter
2.10 Statements of interest from all parties	All parties
2.11 Directors' responsibility statements and power of atttorney, and statements of interest	Company
2.12 Material contracts	Company/ Lawyers
2.13 Written consents from underwriters, reporting accountants and property valuer	All relevant parties
2.14 Verification notes	Lawyers
2.15 Listing application	Underwriter
2.16 Listing agreement	Company
2.17 Corporate reorganisation documents	Company/ Lawyers
3. Press announcements/publications in respect of:-	
3.1 Summary of prospectus	Underwriter
3.2 Results of applications and basis of allotment	Underwriter

Document	Primary responsibility
4. Board minutes	
4.1 Board minutes to approve prospectus documentation and any accompanying changes to corporate and capital structure	Company/ Lawyers
4.2 Board minutes to approve basis of allotment and related press announcements	Company/ Lawyers
5. Other documents	
5.1 Account opening form(s) with receiving banker(s) and receiving bankers agreement	Company/ Receiving bankers
5.2 Application form for employees	Registrar/ Lawyers
5.3 Share and warrant certificates	Registrar/ Lawyers
5.4 Envelopes for refund cheques	Registrar

CHAPTER 7

How to judge timing and pricing

The launch of a new public company on the stock market is a delicate operation which requires favourable conditions for a successful outcome. Two of the most important elements are timing and pricing. A listing which is otherwise sound can fail if the timing is poorly judged. Even if all other circumstances are auspicious, the market is not likely to accept an issue which is over-priced.

I TIMING

The art of timing has been likened to astrology. The object is to divine when three factors which may only be approximately related to each other will swing into alignment. These are:

(i)   market cycles;
(ii) fashions in sectors; and
(iii) fortunes of the particular company.

(i) Market cycles

Stock markets tend to run in cycles of some years' duration. Periods of time when, on average, prices are increasing are called 'bull' markets, while periods when they are in decline are dubbed 'bear' markets.

Flotations are likely to be concentrated in the later phases of a bull market, particularly when the level of market trading is also high.

It is fairly obvious that companies would seek to issue new shares, or existing shareholders seek to dispose of some part of their holdings, when prices are high. It is less obvious why investors also tend to be more receptive to flotations during a bull market. They might be expected to consider prices expensive and to be suspicious that existing shareholders were trying to off-load their shares at the peak of the market.

While some such feelings do no doubt exist, they seem to be outweighed by a mood of buoyant optimism which a bull market tends to bring with it. Investors are feeling confident and confidence spawns a willingness to experiment with new companies. Profits on existing holdings may be viewed as a bonus, available for trying something new. Finance tends to be more readily available from brokers or bankers. There may also be a shortage of sellers of shares in the more familiar companies. In these conditions, a pool of funds seems to be attracted to a series of new issues. As one closes, the over-subscriptions tend to be rolled into the next one.

It is important for those planning a flotation to catch the market while it is in a receptive mood. In smaller markets, the duration of this atmosphere may be quite brief. There tends to be a 'window of opportunity' which can close as quickly as it opens. If conditions change, it may be a question not simply of adjusting the terms of the issue but of re-evaluating whether the issue can be undertaken at all.

(ii) Fashions in sectors

In addition to generally favourable market conditions, the success of a flotation is dependent on investors' current view of the sector in which a company is located. Sector may be defined as a specific industry, such as chemicals, or by a characteristic, such as 'high tech' or by a function, such as distribution.

The market can be fickle as regards which sectors it finds attractive. Previously favoured sectors can go rapidly out of style. Sometimes changes in basic economic conditions lie behind the market movements. For example, a drop in inflation, which can assist the industrial sector, may not suit property or financial shares. At other times, trends may reflect media attention or other ephemeral factors.

In view of the butterfly existence of a sector's popularity, it may be necessary to accelerate launch plans. However, the first company in a new sector to go public often plays a pioneering role, awakening investor interest and smoothing the path for others to follow. The pricing of the first issue is likely to be conservative. It may be more advantageous for the company going public to be a close follower rather than a leader.

Some sectors may be so depressed that it is unlikely that a flotation on any reasonable terms would be acceptable to investors. If an industry like shipping or steel is caught in the throes of a long-term crisis, even a good company in the sector may beat on the door to no avail.

(iii) Fortunes of the particular company

The final element in timing of a flotation is to identify a period when an upswing in a company's own fortunes coincides with its sector being in fashion and the market being in a bullish phase. The ideal time in the development of the company is when it can show a solid history of past performance and when a strong current year's profit can be forecast so as to achieve an attractive price for existing shareholders.

From a market point of view, there should be still the prospect of growth after the current year is completed. Markets are alert to an owner selling out a company in the peak year of its performance. The multiple at which the issue is pitched may prove misleading if earnings are reduced in the following years.

A balance should be struck between obtaining the best price for existing shareholders and leaving something for the market to go for. It may be argued that an enthusiastic response to the issue is, in any case, in the existing shareholders' interests if it results in a well-spread shareholder base with appetite for further investment and a good level of trading. This should prove of greater benefit to the company and its shareholders than engineering a one-time killing. Assuming the original shareholders retain the majority of their holdings, they should be more concerned with the market value of their remaining shares than with achieving the highest possible issue price. If a flotation gets off to a bad start, the resulting market disappointment may take a considerable time to overcome.

II PRICING

The pricing of a new issue must be approached from both a theoretical and practical angle. It is necessary to build up from fundamentals an assessment of what the price 'ought to be' within a reasonable range. However, it must be recognised that over-sophistication can be dangerous. Discrepancies are inevitable between the theoretical basis and the realities of the market-place. In practice, investors have a choice between shares in the new company and existing shares. Pricing must be set with a keen eye on the alternative opportunities open to investors.

(i) Fundamental analysis

The starting point is to determine the appropriate basis for analysis. Care must be taken that valuation is not based on an assumption of a willing buyer/willing seller for the whole company, which will incorporate a premium for control. Value must be considered from the point of view of the buyer of a small number of shares in the market.

The principles of valuation which may be used are discussed in Part 1 of this book and some of them are quite elaborate. However, companies are principally valued for stock market purposes by reference to their future earnings and their net asset backing.

(a) Multiple of earnings (price earnings ratio)

Pricing by reference to a multiple of earnings (the price earnings ratio) is the most common method of valuing a company's shares for flotation. This method is particularly suitable for young expanding companies (the type which seek to go public) which have growing earnings but not necessarily a large asset base. Valuing such companies by way of earnings provides an attractive price for existing shareholders (often far in excess of what they put into the company) while being acceptable to new investors.

Forecast earnings.   As discussed above, the prospectus document for a new issue will normally include a forecast of earnings for the current year. For example, if the company has a 31st December year end and the prospectus is published in June, the forecast would be for the year ending 31st December of that year, in other words looking about six months ahead. Although not always required by regulations, it is normally in the interests of all concerned to prepare a forecast not only to give investors up-to-date information but to secure a better price for the existing shareholders. Forecast earnings should be showing some growth over achieved figures.

The forecast must be prepared with great care as it is often the single most important figure in the document. An element of 'cushion' is normally incorporated since there are substantial penalties for the directors and the professionals involved if the profit forecast is 'missed'; on the other hand, a lower profit forecast translates to a lower price, so that too much conservatism also carries a cost.

Although an analysis of historical figures by type of activity is usually given in the prospectus, this is rarely done with the forecast which is presented as one figure. It may therefore include, as well as trading profits from the group's main businesses, other elements such as interest and foreign exchange income, sales of minor assets or dealing profits. In addition, the size or basis of the taxation charge or any minority interests may not be disclosed. Sometimes, the profit forecast takes no account of the contribution made by any new capital being raised; sometimes the profits are reconstructed as if the new funds had been available throughout the period. Care must be taken by the company to ensure that the elements included are representative of the group's recurring operations. Investors for their part should be prepared to cast a sceptical eye over the figures presented.

Earnings forecasts for inclusion in a prospectus rarely cover a period of more than one year, so that short-term factors predominate. However, in considering price, the merchant bank should ask for, and will normally have access to, earnings projections for some longer period depending on the company's own planning process and the nature of the industry. Such forecasts are used mainly to assess the quality of the company's earnings and are not published.

Earnings per share.   Total earnings are divided by shares in issue to arrive at earnings per share, a calculation which depends on how many shares are considered to be in issue. Sometimes, shares will have been issued during the year but before the date of the prospectus; in the case of a new issue, a significant number of shares will be issued shortly after the date of the prospectus. This factor means that the number of shares in issue at the year end will significantly exceed both the number in issue at the start of the year and the average number of shares (weighted by time in issue). In the prospectus, the figure shown for earnings per share will be based on the weighted average number of shares in issue which is the standard accounting treatment.

EXAMPLE

Effect on earnings per share and price earnings ratio of using the weighted average number of issued shares:

1.   Share capital

		Shares in issue (million shares)	Porportion of year in issue	Weighted average shares in issue (million shares)
(i)	In issue at 1st January	100	12/12	100
(ii)	Issued at 31st March as consideration for assets	20	9/12	15
(iii)	Issued at 30th September as new issue	40	3/12	10
		160		125

2. Forecast earnings for calendar year $50 million

3. Earnings per share (EPS)
    –   Based on weighted average shares in issue $0.40
    –   Based on shares in issue at year end $0.3125

4. Price earnings ratio (at assumed issue price of $5)
    –   Based on EPS $0.40   12.5 times
    –   Based on EPS $0.3125   16.0 times

5. Growth in earnings required in following year to prevent EPS falling from weighted average EPS level   28%

Using the weighted average number of shares in issue means that profits will have to grow in absolute terms in the following year simply for earnings per share to remain the same. This may indeed be realistic since new capital is being raised but it begs the question as to whether the new capital can be employed as productively as the old. Consequently, the use of the proceeds of the new issue will be very important. This factor does not apply if existing shares are being sold by the original shareholders without new capital being raised.

Multiple. The major factors determining the multiple to be applied to the earnings per share include:

Market and sector multiples. Multiples vary quite widely from country to country, although part of the difference may be attributed to different accounting practices and tax rates. Multiples will also vary by sector depending on the market's perception of the attractions of the sector.

Growth prospects. Other things being equal, the faster the earnings of a company are likely to grow, the higher the multiple of current earnings it will attract. If a company's earnings are expected to grow by 40% next year, a current multiple of 20 times is equivalent to a prospective multiple of 14.3 times, whereas with only a 10% expected growth rate, the prospective multiple would be 18.2 times.

Risk. The multiple applied to a given level of earnings can be used to adjust for risk. The risk may be of volatility of earnings (which is likely to be the case in a small growing company), commercial risk – perhaps the company is in a highly competitive or unproven field – and financial risk in terms of its indebtedness levels. A company with a volatile earnings record, in a competitive field with a highly geared balance sheet would be accorded a lower multiple than a stable company with an established name and no borrowings. Nevertheless, the former type of company may still carry a high multiple (particularly if its earnings are low in absolute terms) if its growth prospects are very exciting.

(b) Related methods

The projections which form the basis of earnings forecasts can be adapted to produce forecasts of cash flow to the company or to the shareholders in the form of dividends. Valuations can therefore also be carried out on the basis of discounted cash flow or dividends. Specific projections are rarely available beyond say three years, after which the usual expedient is to assume a constant growth rate. It should be appreciated, however, that, ignoring any differences in tax effects, valuations by reference to earnings, cash flow or dividends are all variations on the same theme. Any material differences in the results of valuations of the same company based on these three factors must be due to a difference in the assumptions underlying the calculations.

The main factors determining the multiple to be applied to the forecast earnings are expected future growth and financial and commercial risk. If cash flows are used then the discount rate will be set principally to reflect risk. The estimate of growth will be built into the cash flows themselves. As a matter of mathematics, if cash flows are not assumed to increase, then an identical valuation will be produced by using a discount rate which is the reciprocal of the price earnings ratio. For example, if cash flows are assumed not to grow and to continue indefinitely, a price earnings ratio of 8 and a discount rate of $12\frac{1}{2}\%$ will produce the same valuation.

If dividends are used, the discount rate will again be set by risk factors. However, it is very likely that cash flows to the company will be substantially higher than cash flows to the shareholders, i.e. dividends paid. Consequently the discount rate will have to be significantly lower if a valuation based on dividends is to be in the same range as one based on the company's cash flow. One justification for a lower discount rate is that the retention of earnings should produce higher growth.

(c) Effect of dividends

The level of dividends which may be paid is determined by the level of earnings and cash flow. Preferences of markets and individual investors vary widely as regards dividends and are strongly influenced by such factors as how dividend receipts are treated for tax purposes. Few markets would expect a growing and newly listed company to pay out more than half its earnings as dividends. However, investors may have a target dividend yield in mind which may therefore act as a constraint on pricing.

EXAMPLE

A company is willing to pay out 45% of its earnings as dividend. The market expects a dividend yield of 7% for this type of company.

Dividend yield required	7%
Maximum percentage of earnings company is prepared to pay as dividend	45%
Maximum 'earnings yield' at which issue can be priced	15.5% (7% ÷ 0.45)
Maximum price earnings ratio at which issue can be priced	6.5 times (1 ÷ 0.155)

For the purpose of a flotation, it seems unhelpful to base a valuation on dividends. The dividend yield on a share is likely to form only part of the investors' returns, the remaining and sometimes more significant contribution coming from capital gains in the market value.

(d) Net asset basis

An asset-intensive company, such as those in the property or shipping sectors, may be most usefully priced by reference to the valuation of those assets less liabilities. The valuations should be carried out by an independent professional valuer whose standing will carry weight in the market. On a theoretical basis, it is possible to argue that the value should include a premium over asset value to reflect the skill involved in putting together a portfolio, arranging finance and presenting a convenient package for an investor.

In practice, the price in the market often reflects a discount from the underlying asset value. This is most easily observed in the case of investment trusts whose assets consist of other listed shares and where the market value of the portfolio is regularly calculated and published. Despite the liquidity of these investments and the fact that the prices of the shares owned by the trust may already reflect a discount from their own underlying net asset value, the price of the shares in the investment trust usually reflects a further discount from the total market price of its portfolio, say, in the range of 10 to 15%. The reason for this phenomenon is not entirely clear; it may reflect an investor preference for being as close to the actual asset as possible. While this effect is most easily calculable in the case of investment trusts, it seems likely that it applies generally to companies valued in the market on a net asset basis. The discount at which asset-intensive companies frequently stand to net assets may be a reason for fewer such companies going public. Existing shareholders place some importance on obtaining a premium over net assets (and certainly a premium over their cost) when they float and may be reluctant to proceed if they cannot do so.

The level of gearing will also be relevant. The growth of companies which are capital intensive is likely to be significantly dependent on the skill with which loan finance is deployed. The ideal level of gearing is one which reflects management's ability to use borrowings to increase shareholders' returns while not approaching levels which could impose financial strain and cramp the company's commercial freedom.

(e) Composite

It is possible to analyse a group into businesses which are best valued on an earnings basis and those which are best valued on an assets basis and then add the two. However, this method is more appropriate in the context of a takeover, where the acquiror has direct access to the company's assets, than to a flotation, where an investor does not.

(f) Use of warrants

The shares being offered in a flotation may be offered together with warrants to subscribe for further shares on a basis of say one warrant for every five shares. The proportion of warrants which can be attached may be governed by regulations and the company will in any case wish to limit the extent of future dilution. The exercise price for the warrants should be set at a premium (say at least 10%) to the price of the flotation. The use of warrants may add speculative appeal to the issue and the company may view the cost of giving a warrant to new subscribers as more apparent than real.

In pricing an issue based on net assets, warrants may prove helpful in 'bridging the gap' between the net asset value, which the existing shareholders emphasise, and the discount to net assets which the market may expect. The issue of warrants has no immediate effect on the balance sheet of the company and the market value of the package of shares plus warrants may stand at net asset value where shares alone could not.

(ii) Realities of the market

No matter what valuation may be placed on a company by a theoretical exercise, if investors can purchase what they regard as a comparable company at a cheaper price they will do so and ignore the new issue. For this reason, the price at which a company is floated is influenced at least as much by the ratings of existing listed companies which are considered to be comparable as by the theoretical valuation exercise. In addition, discreet soundings will be taken by the merchant bank and the stockbroker among their market contacts to establish what the market feels is a reasonable price range for the flotation.

(a) Comparable companies

Considerable time and effort will be spent in selecting the companies which can be legitimately used as the basis of comparison for setting the appropriate multiple of earnings (or, less frequently, discount to net assets) to be applied to the company to be listed.

A price earnings multiple is essentially an artificial thing, created by dividing the market price, an observable fact, by the reported earnings per share which may be open to some interpretation but are nevertheless calculated on generally accepted principles. Dividing one by the other often produces a seductively plausible figure, such as 8.39 times. It only remains plausible, however, as long as nothing untoward happens to either of its parents. A loss-making company has a market price but no price earnings multiple. Anything which changes the market price or the reported earnings per share will also change the price earnings multiple.

If a new company fits neatly into a clearly defined sector, the average multiple for that sector may be taken. However, a *sector average* is precisely that and may be biased by the rating of a few very large companies. A newly listed company is likely to be at the smaller end of the scale so that an average rating too heavily affected by big companies may be misleading.

Special factors may affect the multiples of individual companies in the sector. A price may be depressed after a disappointing recent announcement or be 'frothy' owing to possible takeover prospects. A company which has very low profits may appear to have a very high multiple; however, this may be better interpreted as the market's expectation of a recovery in earnings to a more normal level. Companies which are not comparable for one of these reasons, although they may be in the same market sector, should be discarded to leave a more relevant list.

Care must be taken not to confuse *forecast* with *historic* multiples. Usually a company going public will be forecasting strong growth for the current year and the pricing will be based on that forecast. Similar information is unlikely to be available on comparable companies, which may well be valued on the basis of results for the year past. If growth is expected in the sector, the historic multiple will be higher than one based on a forecast and an adjustment will be needed.

Once a valid comparison has been established it will usually be necessary to apply a small *discount* to the standard. The discount is to overcome the inertia factor and persuade potential investors to take the risk of investing in a new company rather than one which may be more familiar to them.

(b) Market soundings

There is usually sufficient grounds for disagreement on what is or is not a comparable company that even pricing on the basis of comparables has a degree of subjectivity. The merchant bank and stockbroker will therefore take soundings from their own colleagues and from close associates in the market to see whether an appropriate consensus can be identified on what the pricing should be. The identity of the company may be disguised which confuses the issue somewhat but worthwhile reactions can be obtained. These opinions are of course themselves formed partly by fundamentals and comparables but will also include an element of personal interpretation and market feel.

In different markets, investors place different degrees of reliance on the factors underlying a valuation. In some markets, for example, investors prefer shares to be fully backed by net assets despite the fact that they are most appropriately valued by reference to earnings. The regulatory authorities may impose, officially or unofficially, certain guidelines such as a maximum price earnings ratio, a minimum discount of the share price to net assets, and a minimum dividend yield.

Part of the significance of the sounding-out process is that the people contacted will later be approached as sub-underwriters and possible subscribers for the issue.

(iii) Tender method of pricing

(a) Procedures

Rather than fixing the price in advance, it is possible to specify a minimum price and call for tenders. Under this procedure, the applicants themselves choose the price at which they wish to apply, subject to a minimum set by the company being floated. After applications have been received, a 'striking price' is fixed which generally is the price per share which realises the desired amount of money for the issue or sale of the fewest number of shares. Since it is conceivable that one applicant could tender for the whole issue at the highest price, factors such as spread of shareholders will also be taken into account. In this manner, the pricing decision is chiefly determined by the forces of supply and demand prevailing over a short period of time.

(b) Advantages

The tender method may appeal where the issue is not very large and there are no obviously comparable companies on which to base the price. A typical example might be a company with a new technology which is the first of its kind to be listed on the stock market. Existing shareholders may feel that pricing will be pitched too cautiously. The lack of similar listed companies means that underwriters are in uncharted waters. If the issue is small and a large over-subscription is expected after sounding out investor interest, vendors may feel they have little to risk and everything to gain by calling for tenders.

(c) Disadvantages and effect on 'stagging'

The tender method of fixing price is not always welcomed by potential investors who find a fixed price less complicated and more easily evaluated. It may also be considered that tenders reduce or eliminate stagging profits. Stagging is a term used for subscriptions by speculators often in excess of the holding they actually desire (in the expectation that applications will be scaled down) and with the object of selling at a profit as soon as trading begins.

(iv) Role of the stags

The success of issues in some markets may be heavily dependent on the activities of the stags. A market view develops on whether an issue is conservatively priced, in which case it will be heavily over-subscribed, or slightly over-priced in which case the level of subscription may be very low indeed.

If the issue is priced at such a level that stags do not believe a profit is obtainable, arguments about the fundamental attractions of the company as an investment tend to fall on deaf ears. Even investors who believe such arguments may take the view that an under-subscription is likely. This will result in a weak opening price, caused partly by selling from underwriters keen to limit losses on commitments they have been obliged to take up. If investors see a likelihood of obtaining shares in the market at a discount to the issue price, no amount of cajoling them to support the issue is likely to succeed. Some prospect of capital gain is in any case needed to compensate applicants for having funds locked into the issuing procedures rather than keeping the flexibility to make purchases on market terms when trading begins.

CHAPTER 8

Marketing, underwriting, applications and the start of trading

As the time for the publication of the prospectus draws near, a detailed programme leading to the launch of the company must be organised. A marketing campaign will be undertaken with various aspects as set out below in Section I. Section II deals with the formal process of underwriting, both the underwriting agreement and the sub-underwriting arrangements. Section III covers the procedures for application, how investors' applications are dealt with and, assuming an over-subscription, how the basis of allotment is determined. This at least has the consolation of being a problem of success. Section IV covers the early days of trading which should hopefully be a celebration after the months of preparation. But as to what exactly constitutes the 'success' of an issue, there is some measure of debate.

I MARKETING

(i) General publicity

The objective of the publicity campaign is to increase the investing public's awareness of the company and its attractions as an investment. The more familiar the public are with the name of the company, the more comfortable they are likely to be with holding its shares as an investment. In some cases, for example a company with a famous brand name or a well-known retail chain, the name itself will have already been extensively advertised and this is a distinct advantage. However, the publicity may need to be redirected from the company's customers towards the investment community, from the glossy magazines towards the inky financial press.

As a general rule, companies seeking an initial listing are not likely to be well known before flotation and carefully orchestrated promotional efforts will be needed. This may be done in various ways over the months before the launch. The promoters may engage the services of a public relations firm specialising in financial matters. A corporate advertising campaign may be undertaken. New products or services being launched by the company may be publicised more widely than usual. Opportunities will be taken to bring senior executives of the company to the attention of the public through speaking engagements and other public appearances. Profiles in the newspapers and interviews on radio or television will be engineered. If the company has a significant anniversary, moves its head office or opens a new branch, this may be made the occasion for more visible celebrations than would normally be the case.

(ii) 'Road show'

As well as general publicity, the underwriters and brokers to the issue may approach target investors with a detailed presentation of the company in advance of the issue. This can be quite a snappy affair, accompanied by charts, slides, sometimes a company film and other visual effects. This presentation may be given in a number of financial centres and has become irreverently known as a 'road show'.

(iii) Advertising

At the time of publication, depending on the regulations of the market concerned, the issue and applications procedures are likely to be advertised in a number of publications specialising in financial matters. In addition, there will be editorial comment on the company and merits of the issue. It would be entirely natural if those publications in which the issue is advertised consider that the flotation is a newsworthy event.

(iv) Radio and TV

The use of radio and television for publicity purposes carries some potential dangers. It may not be possible to give all relevant details in the short time available and in an interview it is difficult to stick to a carefully prepared script. Off-the-cuff remarks may lead to information being presented or implied which has not been fully checked. If such information is given by the company's management or its advisers, it must either be fully substantiated or be publicly withdrawn. This causes embarrassment for the individuals concerned and may damage the chances of a successful issue or cause a significant delay.

(v) Press conference

Coverage of the flotation is encouraged by holding a pre-launch press conference with plenty of time for a question and answer session. Senior executives of the company should be available to lend authenticity to the rehearsed presentations of the advisers.

Information which is presented to the press must be extracted from the prospectus and be fully consistent with it. Care must be taken when answering questions and entering into discussions that no additional information is released. Suggestions that the prospectus figures are deliberately conservative may be tempting to a management frustrated by lawyers' verification procedures but would be fatal to the issue.

(iv) Company visit

It may prove helpful for management to organise a visit to the headquarters of the company or selected facilities for key institutional investors and brokers.

Managers may feel like tour guides shepherding a group of confused tourists but the effort is worthwhile in helping potential investors to understand the business. In addition, a visit affords the opportunity for informal discussion which can build up investors' confidence while allowing the company and its advisers to gauge the level of support for the issue.

(vii) Brokers' circulars

Based on the visit and perhaps selected extracts from the draft prospectus, the broker to the issue and other interested brokers will have sufficient information to put together a circular on the company if they consider it appropriate. They are unlikely to take the trouble to circularise clients with a negative reaction which generates no potential business so there is a reasonable chance that their recommendations will be positive.

(viii) Publicity within the company

Under stock exchange rules, a certain percentage of an issue (say 10%) may be reserved for priority applications from the company's employees. Management may take steps to publicise the procedures for application within the company. Some directors have felt so strongly that employees should be encouraged to participate that they have made arrangements either personally or with the company's bankers for finance to be available to allow employees to take up their allocations. However, this can misfire if, despite all good intentions, the shares of the company subsequently fall below the issue price.

(ix) Special offers

Companies offering a consumer product or service may give shareholders some special concession or discount. This may serve as an incentive for investors not only to apply for shares but to remain as long-term holders. Product loyalty may be increased by having customers as shareholders. Although sometimes dismissed as gimmicky, this tactic appears to be highly effective where the product or service is a suitable one. The basis of any offer requires careful consideration, as the expense can be substantial, not only of the concession itself but of maintaining an increased share register.

As the level of investor awareness of an issue grows, a general view is likely to emerge as to whether the issue will be a success or a failure. This tends to be very much a self-feeding process. If applicants feel the issue will be over-subscribed, they will be inclined to increase their level of applications in anticipation of receiving less than the number of shares they apply for. On the other hand, if an issue is thought likely to be under-subscribed, investors may hesitate to apply at all, not necessarily because they dislike the company, but in anticipation of being able to buy the shares at a cheaper price after dealings start in the market. A good share is even better if it can be purchased at a discount.

II   UNDERWRITING

(i)   Underwriting agreement

The underwriting agreement is the agreement by which the underwriter agrees to subscribe or buy (or procure subscribers or buyers for) any of the shares being offered in the flotation which are not taken up by investors at the agreed price. The other parties to this agreement are usually the company itself and its directors and major shareholders. If there is more than one underwriter, the obligations of the underwriters will be several, and not joint and several.

Fees payable to the underwriters will be set out in the agreement. The underwriters will usually ask for and obtain warranties from the company, its executive directors and major existing shareholders that all the information set out in the prospectus is correct and complete. The warranties also cover profit and cash flow forecasts, the accounts and the tax position. Major shareholders will undertake not to sell or transfer their shares for a minimum period after the flotation (say six months) and the company will agree not to make any significant public announcement for a similar period without consulting the underwriters.

The underwriters' obligations are subject to conditions. Some of these are mainly procedural, such as the stock exchange granting listing for the shares and the flotation going ahead on the agreed timetable. However, the underwriters will also seek the protection of a force majeure clause which allows them to withdraw from the issue in the event of any material adverse change in political, economic or market conditions of a kind which would jeopardise the success of the issue. This is intended to protect the underwriters against catastrophic changes but if widely drafted can turn the underwriting agreement into a one-way option in favour of the underwriters.

Some managements regard the underwriting agreement as the key document in the flotation process. After it is signed, the company can more or less relax as the raising of the relevant funds is guaranteed whatever the level of subscriptions. This attitude tends to make underwriters nervous and they may respond by seeking some under-pricing of the issue as a protection from having to take up shares. As the underwriter may well also be acting as the company's financial adviser, there may be an element of conflict in the advice given by the underwriter as regards setting the issue price.

(ii)   Sub-underwriting

Shortly before or just after signature of the underwriting agreement, the lead underwriter will normally offer the major part of the issue for sub-underwriting in the market. The numbers of sub-underwriters approached will vary but may exceed 100 in a large issue.

In some markets, the sub-underwriting syndicate is organised directly by the lead underwriter, which is usually an investment or merchant bank. In other markets a stockbroker will serve as the intermediary to contact the sub-underwriters. One of the functions of the stockbroker to the company is to sound out in advance of the pricing of the issue the level of investment interest in the shares. Based on this research, the stockbroker will have already identified institutions who have expressed some intention to subscribe and therefore are a logical choice for sub-underwriting.

The sub-underwriting syndicate is normally comprised of other merchant banks, stockbrokers, investment and unit trusts, fund managers and other professionals in the market. These institutions may be investors themselves or may be partly, or wholly, intermediaries, passing on portions of their allocation to their own clients. In this way the risk of the issue being unfavourably received is widely spread through the market. Even if there is a disappointing level of public response, there will through the sub-underwriting syndicate be a reasonable spread of shareholders.

The company itself and its management is not usually involved in the sub-underwriting process. Indeed, often they may be entirely unaware who the sub-underwriters are. The promoters may of course express a desire for certain institutions or major investors to be included and these wishes would be taken into account by the lead underwriter.

Sub-underwriters receive a fee based on the money amount of risk they have assumed. The level of this fee depends on market practice and the length of time of exposure, but is commonly in the region of $1\frac{1}{4}$ to $1\frac{1}{2}\%$. If they pass the risk on to their own clients they would keep some portion of the fee for themselves and re-allow the remainder to their clients. The split is standardised as institutions prefer to avoid criticism which might arise if different tiers of sub-underwriting commissions were circulating in the market.

(iii) Timing of signature

If the lead underwriter has sufficient financial muscle and is confident enough about the company, market conditions and the reception of the issue, it may commit itself to sign the underwriting contract for the issue before it has formal replies from the institutions invited to sub-underwrite. A more cautious approach is to await the reaction of sub-underwriters before entering into a formal underwriting commitment although, of course, a withdrawal at this stage would be deeply embarrassing to the institution involved, is likely to enrage the client and would be widely known in the market. The promoters obviously prefer a firm underwriting commitment before any approach is made to sub-underwriters with the inevitable publicity leak. Sometimes a lead underwriter will encourage a certain vagueness about the precise stage an issue has reached during this sensitive period.

(iv) Over-subscription

If the issue is fully subscribed, the sub-underwriters are released from their obligation to subscribe and are paid their fee. They do not normally receive any preferential allotment of shares, and if they apply, are treated on an equal footing with all other applicants. In special circumstances, particularly where the issue is very large and may be difficult for the market to absorb, sub-underwriters may be offered the incentive of being permitted some preferential allotment.

(v) Under-subscription

If the issue is under-subscribed, sub-underwriters will be called upon to subscribe for the shortfall pro rata to their commitments. Arrangements will have been put in place by the merchant bank to ensure that any applications generated by the sub-underwriter would be counted against their commitment should they be called upon.

(vi) Weaknesses of sub-underwriting system

The system of sub-underwriting has some inherent weaknesses. In a successful issue, sub-underwriters (except as noted above) are not preferred to any other applicant. Consequently they cannot 'protect' their clients' position, that is, guarantee them any allotment. This acts as a disincentive to develop a distribution network as compared to a system where investment banks know they have a certain number of shares available to sell to their customers.

If the issue is under-subscribed, the opening market price is likely to be weak and the sub-underwriters are not going to be thanked by their clients for 'stuffing' them with over-priced shares. If sub-underwriters retain the risk on their own book, the loss on a single unsuccessful issue can wipe out the fees received from ten successful ones. Only the capital profits from obtaining a preferred position in good issues can compensate for the losses incurred in bad ones.

The sub-underwriting system described above is based on UK practice or practice in markets based on the UK model. In the US, the underwriting syndicate functions much more effectively as a selling syndicate. Applications are generated by dealers who are granted concessions on price and reallowances rather than relying on a more direct appeal to retail investors. A preliminary prospectus is widely circulated as the basis for 'book building', a practice also being adopted in the UK in some instances.

It would seem that the US system has some advantages in encouraging a professional approach to the marketing and distribution of new issues. It may however mean that subscriptions to 'hot' new issues of smaller companies are reserved to preferred clients of the selling syndicate and shares may be difficult to obtain for the general public.

III   APPLICATIONS

(i) Procedures for application

The procedure for application should be kept as simple as possible. Even minor complications can cause confusion and make the difference between whether a wavering subscriber applies or not.

The application procedures will be set out fully in the prospectus and again on the application form. The investor states the number of shares he is applying for and attaches a cheque for the cost of the investment. The total amount will be made up of the price for the shares, plus any associated costs such as taxes and brokerage. There is normally a minimum size for applications. In markets where a board lot system of trading is used, the minimum application will be for one board lot. Applications for greater than the minimum may be in some specified multiple of the minimum in which case the application form will include a table showing the amount payable for the number of the shares which may be applied for.

Practice varies as to whether all cheques accompanying application forms are presented for payment. Whenever an issue is under-subscribed, all cheques will be presented. In the case of a heavy over-subscription requiring a ballot, in some markets the ballot is held before cheques are cashed so that the applicants who are wholly unsuccessful are not out of funds. This procedure also greatly decreases the number of refund cheques which need to be prepared and despatched. A reserve list is required in case cheques accompanying successful applications are dishonoured.

Applications from the public must normally be made within a few days of the publication of a prospectus. After the deadline for receipt of applications, the application list actually opens and closes in a very short period, sometimes only a few minutes. Technically speaking, a company has the right to extend the offer period, but to do so can invite suspicion that the response to the issue has been 'managed' after the event.

Applications must be delivered to the receiving bank. This bank designates certain of its branches to process applications, which may be sent by post. Many, however, are delivered by hand close to the deadline to give applicants the chance to assess market reaction to the issue. Applications once made will be irrevocable during the period of issue.

(ii) Allocation

If the issue is under-subscribed no problem of allocation arises. Valid applications will be allotted in full. Application forms will be passed on to the registrar by the receiving banker for drawing up the first register of members.

If the issue is over-subscribed, a decision will have to be made on the basis of allocation. Applications may first be screened to eliminate multiple applications, that is, one person or group putting in many small applications in the hope of receiving more favourable treatment than if they had submitted one large one. In some jurisdictions, this practice is illegal.

Following this screening, the registrar will classify the applications by size, showing the number of applications and amount of money in each category. This classification will then be reviewed by the company and the merchant bank with a view to producing an equitable basis of allocation, bearing in mind any preference the company may have for the profile of its shareholder base.

It is generally thought desirable to have a wide base of shareholders and for a preference to be given to the smaller applications. On the other hand, the success of an issue may be primarily due to a relatively few very large applicants.

It is important that such people, who tie up considerable amounts of their funds, should not feel unfairly treated.

It is not possible to scale down applications if the scaling down will result in an allotment of less than the minimum application set out in the prospectus. Consequently, depending on the size of any over-subscription, a ballot may have to be held (normally done by computer) to determine allocation to the smaller applicants. A person who is successful in the ballot will be allotted his application in full if it is for the minimum amount. Other applicants for the minimum size will not be allotted any shares.

Once an application reaches a size where a percentage scaling down will result in a holding of more than the minimum amount, this procedure is usually adopted. Consequently, if an issue is say ten times subscribed, applicants above a certain fairly small size can expect to receive approximately 10% of the shares for which they applied.

Under listing regulations, it is often permissible to reserve 10% of the issue for employees of the company. Employee application forms will be coloured differently and are handled separately from other applications, usually by the company secretary. Amounts for which an individual employee may apply may be set by the directors on the basis of length of service and seniority.

(iii) Applications and allotment under the tender method

Applicants state the number of shares they wish to apply for and fill in the price per share they are prepared to pay. The company may state or have in mind the minimum amount it wishes to raise. The maximum number of shares to be issued or sold is also stated. Once the applications have been received, a price will be fixed, called the 'striking price', at which sufficient applications have been received to cover at least the amount intended to be raised.

The striking price will not necessarily be the highest price at which sufficient applications are received to cover the target amount. Factors such as number and distribution of shareholdings will also be taken into account because of the need to establish a satisfactory market in the shares.

Applicants who tender at below the striking price receive no shares and their cheques are returned to them.

All the shares will be sold or issued at the striking price. Applicants who tender at or above the striking price may be subject to a ballot or may be scaled down. In some issues, applicants at prices above the striking price are favoured. The application form may also allow applicants to apply at whatever striking price is set, leaving the actual price blank at the time of application.

If the issue is underwritten, it will be underwritten at the minimum price for the issue stated by the company.

IV   START OF TRADING

(i) Register and share certificates

Once the basis of allocation has been decided, the first register of the holders of the securities just listed can be produced. If a large number of share certificates are involved, this process may take, say, one week. In some countries, trading starts immediately after the basis of allotment is announced for deferred settlement. Temporary documents of title may be issued which can be renounced to a third party when the holding is sold without the payment of transfer duties. Some markets settle trades through a central clearing system without delivery of physical certificates. It seems likely that most markets will in due course adopt such systems as turnover increases and as the systems themselves prove their reliability.

If trading is on the basis of immediate settlement, dealings in the securities are not permitted before all shareholders are expected to have received their share certificates. Several trading days are allowed for receipt after the registrar can certify that certificates have been despatched. Large shareholders may prefer to collect their share certificates direct from the registrar.

(ii) 'Grey market'

Because of the considerable gap in time between the publication of the prospectus and the commencement of official trading, there sometimes is an informal market in anticipation of official trading which is referred to as the 'grey market'. Trading in the grey market may begin even before the issue has closed with prices obtainable being widely although unofficially reported. If the grey market price is above the issue price, this may be a factor contributing to the over-subscription of an issue. This process is open to some abuse.

Grey market trading is often on a verbal basis only and by definition is not conducted through the stock exchange, with the safeguard of its regulations and procedures. Participants in the grey market may therefore be exposed to increased risk of transactions being dishonoured or not settled promptly. Such dealings are legally enforceable, as any contract would be, but resort to the law is unwelcome to most dealers.

(iii) 'Stagging'

A number of investors may well have subscribed for an issue in the belief that the issue price has been set conservatively so that an immediate dealing profit will be available. Stags apply for more shares than they actually want (often borrowing a high proportion of the funds required from banks or brokers), on the assumption that the issue will be over-subscribed and their applications will be scaled down. This process is referred to as 'stagging'. Stags are normally very short-term holders and will seek to sell out either in the grey market (without knowing their precise allocation) or in the official market as soon as trading commences.

Large applicants who have been scaled down may be seeking to top up their allocations. Many institutions set a minimum value for their holdings in order to control the cost of monitoring them. The clash of the stags aiming to realise a profit and the institutions looking to build up their holdings can make for an active two-way market in the shares on the opening. After say the first two weeks of trading, levels of turnover will normally fall.

It is interesting to compare the register of shareholders of a company at its first annual general meeting as a public company with the initial register compiled by the registrars after the flotation. The number of shareholders sometimes halves in this period.

(iv) Attitude of existing shareholders

If the controlling shareholder of the company has been a buyer, the shareholding base of the company will have contracted although the price may benefit. If only the minimum number of shares has been issued or sold to the public to qualify for a listing under the stock exchange rules, even small purchases by directors or major shareholders (who do not qualify as 'the public') would jeopardise the company's newly won listed status. It is standard procedure for the merchant bank to ask for assurances that the promoters and other major existing shareholders will not sell their holdings into the market for a period of, say, six months after the flotation. Where the original shareholders, whose base cost for the shares may be very low compared to the issue price, do unload their holdings into the market, the price of the shares may be depressed for a considerable time.

(v) Over-allotments and stabilisation

In certain markets, the underwriters of an issue may be granted options by the company being floated to purchase additional shares to cover over-allotments, if any. Such options may amount to 7.5–10% of the size of the issue and are exercisable for a relatively short period from the date of the prospectus, say one month. The options in effect allow the underwriter, if there is sufficient demand, to allot more shares than are being offered in the knowledge that they can cover the short position created by buying shares in the market or, failing that, by obtaining them from the company. This ensures that should the price fall below the issue price on the start of trading, there will be at least one firm buyer in the market and the share price will be supported to a degree. Such market activity by the underwriter is called 'stabilisation'. Disarmingly, prospectuses for such issues carry a specific warning that the underwriter may effect transactions which stabilise or maintain the market price of the shares 'at levels above those which might otherwise prevail on the open market'.

WHAT IS 'SUCCESS'?

Opinions vary on what constitutes the success of an issue judged by the level of subscriptions and the price at which the shares start trading. One complicating factor is that the relationship between the issue price and the trading price is not always obvious. An over-priced, and consequently under-subscribed, issue can result in a market price lower than the issue price, a setback from which it usually takes some time to recover. An apparent under-pricing can stimulate investor interest and demand to the extent that the market price may exceed the level it would have reached if the issue had been pitched higher. The different points of views include:

Management. Professional managers may feel they have done the best deal for the company (as opposed to the new shareholders) if the flotation price is high enough to eliminate any significant premium when trading starts. They may also feel that the underwriters should earn their fee by underwriting at a price which carries some risk of under-subscription. The issue is essentially completed from the company's point of view when it is underwritten and the company (or vendor shareholders) are sure of getting their money.

Underwriters and subscribers. Underwriters like to see a 'cushion' for their underwriting risk and view a successful issue principally as one which is oversubscribed. The managing underwriter in particular must balance this understandable desire for a safety margin with the possible annoyance of his client (and loss of future business) if the issue is too cautiously priced. Subscribers are attracted by an issue price which leaves 'something to go for' and would look for say at least a 10%–15% premium when trading starts in order to cover their expenses and risk.

Existing shareholders. Vendor shareholders dislike high stagging profits which represent 'money left on the table' by themselves. However, particularly in the case of a new issue where no existing shares are sold, the promoters may measure their own prestige against the level of subscriptions and the premium on trading. If they have encouraged friends and associates to subscribe, a discount at the opening is embarrassing to them. Since the market price determines the value of their shareholding (and they are likely still to be the biggest shareholders), the market price should concern them more than the issue price. As noted above, the relationship between the two is not always straightforward.

The success of an issue should be judged by long-term as well as short-term criteria. The level of subscriptions is important for all concerned and the opening of trading is hectic, glamorous and often leaves a lasting impression. However, after the 'captains and the kings' of the broking and investment banking world depart, the company is largely on its own and it is the longer-term price performance (measured against say the market index) which is of most relevance to the majority of shareholders.

Part 3

Alternatives and additions

– Alternatives to full flotation
– Additions to equity capital

Introduction

The first two chapters of Part 3 of this book deal with shell companies and other alternative methods of gaining a listing. The second two chapters deal with raising further equity capital once an initial listing has been achieved.

The need for a 'Plan B' is a constant theme of management gurus and this is certainly true of flotations, areas where the best laid plans have a tendency to go awry up to the last minute.

Shell companies (backdoor listings/reverse takeovers) (see ch 9 below)

This chapter examines the merits of obtaining control of an already listed company as an alternative to a full flotation. The factors involved in the decision are analysed under five headings: the speed of the operation, the degree of control of the circumstances, the type of assets which can be used, the cost and the ability to raise funds and achieve adequate marketability. The procedures for acquiring and consolidating control are described. The stages are: identification of a suitable shell company and negotiations with the present controlling party, acquiring control through a sale and purchase agreement, documentation/approvals, the making of a general offer (if required) and the placing out or other marketing of shares.

The regulatory attitude to shell companies can be ambivalent – on the one hand, a dormant company is reactivated and its existing shareholders benefit, on the other hand problems may arise subsequently and future shareholders be put at risk. However, it seems likely that there will be a continuing place for shell companies as one means of obtaining a listing.

Alternative markets, alternative methods (see ch 10 below)

This chapter looks at various alternative strategies as regards listings. Listing on a market other than the company's 'home' market is an ambitious target for most companies but may become more common as equity markets grow increasingly international. What type of company might be suitable, the reasons for considering an overseas listings and how to assess different markets are discussed. Secondary listings overseas are also considered.

Another method of creating a new listing is by a demerger or spin-off. The steps involved are described, including the methods by which shares in the new company are distributed. Listing is then obtained by way of introduction. The possible advantages of carrying out a demerger are also considered.

There are other occasions on which a listing by introduction may be used, such as following a placing or series of placings or a share exchange, for example as part of a move of domicile. Other types of issues discussed are bonus issues, share/scrip dividends, options and debt/equity swaps.

Rights issues (see ch 11 below)

Once a listing has been obtained, capital can be raised more simply by subsequent issues. Issues which are first offered to existing shareholders are said to be made by way of 'rights'. Issues of further ordinary shares of a listed company for cash are often required by law, the company's articles or stock exchange regulations to be made by rights. Other types of security, including shares of other companies, may be offered by way of rights on occasions.

Rights issues have proved a reliable means of raising further equity. They are pitched at a discount to the market price 'ex rights' and aimed at 'the converted', ie investors who have already bought shares in the company. In these circumstances, management could, but rarely does, decide to dispense with underwriting and instead increase the discount at which the issue is priced. There is a lively debate on whether rights issues are the most efficient way of raising further equity.

Documentation and expenses are considerably less for a rights issue than for the initial flotation. The timetable has to allow for a period of trading in the rights 'nil paid'. It is this feature of being able to trade in the 'nil paid' rights which distinguishes rights issues from the types of issues described in the following chapter.

Open offers and placings (see ch 12 below)

As an alternative to a rights issue, further equity issues for cash may be made by way of open offer or by way of placing. The procedures for an open offer are described with the arrangements for trading, pricing, timing and shareholders' approval. Similar considerations apply in the case of placings.

The main point of contention is whether shareholders receive a pro rata allotment as part of the procedures and whether they have the ability to sell their 'nil paid' entitlements in the market. While arrangements can be made for shareholders to participate in open offers (in fact they usually do) and in placings on some occasions, neither open offers nor placings give shareholders any right to sell entitlements in the market. On the other hand, open offers and placings offer greater flexibility and speed for the company in raising new equity. A table comparing the different aspects of rights issues, open offers and placings is set out at the end of the chapter.

CHAPTER 9

Shell companies (backdoor listings/reverse takeovers)

As discussed in Part 2 of this book, obtaining a listing through a full-scale flotation (initial public offering) is a demanding process with numerous obstacles to be overcome. It is uncertain of success up to the moment of announcement and underwriting. 'There must be an easier way' is the cry often heard from an impatient or frustrated management. Certainly, any alternative method which cuts through the delay and uncertainty is worth serious consideration. Why not buy an already listed company?

A listing may indeed be purchased by gaining control of a company which already has a listing, often referred to as a 'shell company' (not to be confused with a 'shelf' company which is a newly formed, unlisted company). Obtaining a listing via a shell company is also called a 'backdoor listing' or 'reverse takeover'. The factors involved and the advantages and disadvantages of this method are summarised in the table below and discussed in Section I of this chapter.

Control is obtained either (i) by a purchase of a major block of existing shares, usually by negotiation with an existing controlling shareholder, or (ii) by reaching agreement with the company and its shareholders for the issue of a large number of new shares in exchange for assets being sold to the company or for cash. The procedures involved are set out in Section II of this chapter.

I FACTORS INVOLVED WHEN CONSIDERING A 'SHELL'

The factors involved in the decision whether to obtain a listing by way of a shell company and the attendant advantages and disadvantages may be summarised as follows:

Factor	Advantages	Disadvantages
(i) Speed	Immediate impact. If full information can be announced, any suspension of trading should be brief.	Identifying a suitable shell and negotiating with vendors for control is time consuming and uncertain.
(ii) Control of circumstances	Greater flexibility in timing, procedures and pricing.	'Skeletons in the closet' and incomplete warranties.
(iii) Types of assets to be injected	Greater chance of listing for certain assets/businesses.	Authorities are tending to insist on a 'level playing field' as regards regulatory aspects.

Factor	Advantages	Disadvantages
(iv) Cost	Some costs are reduced.	Premium over net assets payable.
(v) Raising funds/ marketability	Placing can be made to sympathetic placees at a favourable price.	Controlling a shell company does not of itself raise equity or increase marketability.

(i) Speed

(a) Advantages – immediate impact

Although the procedures for a shell company operation may take several months to work through, the impact is felt as soon as a full announcement of the terms of the proposals can be made, providing that a suspension of trading is not necessary or can be kept to a short period.

Practice varies in different markets as to the length of time it may be necessary (if at all) to suspend trading in the shares of a shell company at the time proposals are announced. However, provided that the intentions of the parties and the eventual financial position of the company can be clearly and fully stated at the outset, any suspension in the trading of the shares should be brief. The shares of the shell company are likely to be re-rated in the market almost immediately, on the basis that the transaction will proceed. Although all the transactions involved may not be completed for a number of months, the controlling shareholders already have a listed vehicle which reflects what is intended. This is not the case with a full-scale flotation where trading in the shares cannot begin until the end of the whole operation.

(b) Disadvantages – difficulty of obtaining control of a suitable shell

Negotiating for control of a shell company can tax the patience of the most persistent suitor. Although there are usually existing major shareholders with whom negotiations can be conducted, they are often unable or unwilling to make final decisions on the sale of a controlling stake. If they are under financial pressure, a sale may not necessarily give them any free cash and the decision may rest with their bankers rather than themselves. If they are not under financial pressure, the prospect of someone wishing to buy their dormant company may be the very factor which convinces them to keep it. Changes in market conditions may also affect the price which is demanded for control, so that pinning down the final terms proves elusive.

(ii) Control of circumstances

(a) Advantages – greater flexibility in timing, procedures and pricing

The procedure for a full-scale flotation is relatively rigid and lengthy. Because of rules calling for audited accounts not more than a certain number of months old (often six months) and documentary and regulatory requirements, there may only be a limited number of months in a year for a company to go public. Bunching of issues is likely as a consensus emerges on favourable conditions and timing. An issue can easily be crowded out. Market conditions which are beyond the control of the company may delay the launch. Complications in the legal or accounting work may also force a delay. Once a delay has occurred it may be several months before the procedure can be completed or even restarted. If the mood breaks, the new issue market can be virtually closed and the chance lost.

With a shell company, the timing, procedures and pricing are more flexible. Once control of the shell has been obtained, assets can be injected to suit regulatory requirements at convenient occasions, although a vote of independent shareholders is likely to be required. There is no deadline for accounts. No flotation price has to be set and sometimes no funds are raised. There is no highly publicised under- or over-subscription.

(b) Disadvantages – skeletons in the closet, incomplete warranties

While the purchaser can control present procedures, he cannot control problems which have already happened. The reason that a shell company has become a shell may be traced to something that has gone badly wrong in the past. Large losses may have been incurred, the aftermath of which may include law suits or other events which taint the name of the company. As accounts may have not always been efficiently kept, there is the danger of unrecorded or undisclosed liabilities and other claims and contingencies. These are all the more likely to surface once potential claimants realise that a new party has made a financial commitment to the company or injected new assets or capital, which it will wish to preserve.

A purchaser may be able to protect himself through the terms of a sale-and-purchase contract. However, the vendors may argue that, as the company is public, the basis of the transaction is the same as any market purchase of listed shares and resist additional documentation, particularly giving warranties. Although this argument has some theoretical merit, a shell company is by definition a 'failed' public company and retains some of the character of a private company, where warranties would be given on a purchase. Its major shareholders will certainly know more of its affairs than the average shareholder of a public company. The giving of limited warranties is a fair compromise.

(iii) Type of assets to be injected

(a) Advantages – greater chance of listing for certain assets/businesses

It has, on occasion, arguably proved possible to obtain listings via a shell company for assets or businesses which would not meet all the criteria for a full-scale flotation or which might not for the moment prove attractive to investors. For example, a business which has only been in existence for a relatively short time might not have a sufficient track record to form the basis of a standard flotation. It might therefore be rejected by the authorities as the basis for a flotation but nevertheless be acceptable as an acquisition by an already listed company. A property development might take some years to come to fruition and until it did there would be no prospects of dividends. A special situation might be too speculative for investors in general. Sometimes a particular market sector, say property, is simply out of fashion. Fearing an under-subscription, the promoters may be reluctant to proceed whereas in the context of a shell company the risk may be more manageable.

(b) Disadvantages – 'level playing field' concept

The attitude of regulators has tended towards insisting on a 'level playing field' as between flotations and shell companies. In other words, if the regulatory requirements for a full prospectus could not be satisfied, an attempt to achieve the same result through a shell company will meet with a jaundiced eye. As a response to this approach, purchasers look for 'shell' companies with assets or businesses compatible with the planned injections. This allows the transaction to be presented as an expansion rather than a transformation.

There would appear to be some inconsistency on this point. The attitude of the regulatory authorities in different jurisdictions varies and, within markets, has changed from time to time and case to case. One view might be that anything done to improve the prospects of dormant listed companies is good and should be encouraged. If the company remains inactive and is eventually de-listed, the public shareholders will be penalised. A contrary view holds that such benefits are outweighed by the potential dangers of allowing a listing for businesses which might not otherwise be able to achieve this status. If a business is not suitable for listing on its own, what is the logic for allowing it to be listed via a shell?

(iv) Cost

(a) Advantages – some costs are reduced

The legal and accounting work involved in a shell company operation tends to be less than for a full flotation. Underwriting and listing fees may be reduced or eliminated. The company may have significant authorised but unissued share capital (saving capital duty in some jurisdictions) or tax losses which may be utilised, although this will need to be confirmed after specialist tax advice.

(b) Disadvantages – premium over net assets payable

Although some of the costs associated with the production of a full-scale prospectus will be avoided or reduced, a premium over the net asset value will normally be required by the shareholders relinquishing control, reflecting among other factors the convenience of a shell company and the possible cost saving. A premium at the upper end of the market range can render a shell company operation more expensive than a flotation. The premium is likely to be calculated as an absolute amount (up to US$5 million in some markets) rather than as a percentage of net assets.

Some purchasers have in mind that although they are buying less than 100% of the share capital, they are in effect gaining control of all the assets, and in some shell companies those assets may be highly liquid. In such a case, a purchaser may attribute a value to the leverage which control of the company gives him and justify the premium in that way.

(v) Raising funds/marketability

(a) Advantages

The incoming shareholders may acquire more new shares than they wish to retain, or are allowed to retain under stock exchange liquidity rules. In this case, they will 'place down' through a broker. While the placees must not be associates of the incoming shareholders, nevertheless the broker should still be able to place the shares in what they regard as safe, or at least sympathetic hands. It may be possible to give such professional investors a more detailed presentation of the company's prospects than could be included in a prospectus issued to the general public. Consequently, a higher price may be achievable for such a placing than would be possible on flotation.

(b) Disadvantages

An important result of a flotation once it is underwritten is the guarantee of funds to the company or its existing shareholders. No funds are raised through the simple purchase of a shell company or by the injection of assets. The raising of new equity must be tackled separately.

A full-scale prospectus achieves a very high degree of visibility and, if successful, a large shareholding base for the newly floated group. A shell company is not likely to have many existing shareholders (perhaps a few hundred or less) and almost no marketability. If a general offer is required to all shareholders after the acquisition of control, the position may be worsened in the first instance owing to acceptances of the offer. A subsequent placing may not achieve as wide a spread of shareholders as a flotation.

II PROCEDURE

The procedure for obtaining a listing by way of a shell company may be summarised as follows:

(i) Identification and negotiations

Identify a suitable shell company and negotiate terms with the board and/or controlling shareholders. Very often they are the same body of people.

(ii) Control is acquired by sale and purchase agreement covering:

(a) purchase of a substantial block of shares (normally over 50%);

(b) sale to the company of assets or businesses in exchange for the issue of new shares;

(c) a combination of (a) and (b).

(iii) Documentation/approvals

The steps set out in (ii) above will normally require information to be provided to shareholders via a circular and approval at a shareholders' meeting. The circular and other procedures will be agreed with the relevant stock exchange and any period of suspension of trading discussed.

(iv) General offer

Once control has been acquired, it may be required or be desirable to make a comparable offer to all shareholders.

(v) Placing out or other marketing of shares

Obtaining control, injecting assets and making a general offer can result in a very low percentage of share capital being left in the hands of the public. Steps may be needed to widen the shareholding base.

(i) Identification and negotiations

A suitable shell company will have the following characteristics:

(a) Size

The company is being sought for its listing and not for its existing business or assets. It may therefore have a low level of issued share capital and assets. On the other hand, the attitude of regulatory authorities towards very small companies acquiring major assets or businesses is hardening. Consequently, a company with existing assets/businesses which are simple to understand and conservatively run can serve as a shell company, although it may not appear to be one. If the company has a large authorised share capital, this may save capital duty at a later stage (depending on local taxation rules), when further issues of shares are made.

(b) Simplicity

The assets of the group should be as straightforward as possible, for example, holdings of cash, marketable securities or investment properties. If the company or any of its subsidiaries operate active businesses, can they be easily understood and evaluated by the purchaser? Are there lawsuits, disputes with bankers or creditors or other actual or contingent liabilities?

(c) *Availability*

It is highly desirable that there should be one existing controlling shareholder who can be approached as regards a possible transaction and who can give a commitment before any public announcement is needed. It is also an advantage if this controlling shareholder is a substantial party whose integrity can be relied upon and from whom, subject to negotiation, worthwhile warranties about the financial position of the shell company can be obtained.

(ii) Acquiring control/sale and purchase agreement

(a) *Sale and purchase agreement*

The purchaser will attempt to obtain control by signing a full sale and purchase agreement with the controlling shareholders of the shell company or the company itself. The agreement will cover a number of aspects:

– information being provided to the purchaser regarding the assets and liabilities and the overall financial position of the company; the purchaser will undertake to keep such information confidential and return it if the purchase does not proceed;

– the price and the terms of payment. The most common basis is a negotiated premium over net asset value, after an up-to-date assessment of significant assets and liabilities;

– the conditions of the purchase, eg the completion of satisfactory due diligence and maintenance of listing;

– the warranties given by the vendors, eg that the company's accounts are correct and complete, that all information supplied to the purchaser is accurate, that there has been no material adverse change in the financial position of the company since the date of the accounts, that the company has sufficient working capital, that it has good title to its assets and there are no undisclosed liabilities, litigation or contracts or commitments of significant size and that all relevant terms of service of employees have been disclosed;

– that in the period to completion, the existing management will do nothing outside the normal course of business; and

– completion procedures will be set out so that the purchaser can take immediate full control of the company, its bank accounts and other assets.

If it is proposed that the shell company purchase assets from the incoming shareholder, information as set out above would be requested by the company for examination by its own management and advisers. The purchaser is usually willing to provide and warrant this type of information as it is the purchaser who will control and manage the company after the acquisition.

The vendors on the other hand will seek to limit the information supplied and warranties given. Even where it is agreed that warranties will be included in the contract, the vendor will try to negotiate a maximum claim (say, no more than the consideration received) and a minimum claim to avoid disputes on amounts which are not material. A time limit (say, one year) may be set during which claims under the warranties can be made.

An alternative approach is to provide all the information requested and allow time for due diligence but to give no warranties on the grounds that the purchaser has had the chance to ask for information and check it.

(b) Assets to be injected/repurchased

The assets to be injected should be identified by the new controlling shareholder before he acquires control of a shell. The practice of acquiring a shell and then thinking of what to put in it frequently has unfortunate results.

The suitability of the assets or business to be injected should be assessed against the desired position of the company after it has made the acquisitions. The factors to be considered include asset backing, earnings and dividend paying ability. The fundamentals of the enlarged group should be attractive to the investing public.

If assets are purchased from the new controlling shareholders by the company at around this time, particularly for cash, care must be taken not to infringe any applicable regulations preventing the company giving assistance in the purchase of its own shares. If there may be a problem in this area, the party taking control should be able to demonstrate that they could finance the acquisition without any subsequent transaction with the company.

On occasions, a controlling shareholder may be willing to sell a company but may wish to retain certain of its assets, perhaps a prized property or a long-held family business. In these circumstances, the controlling shareholder may buy these assets out, using part of the funds received from selling the shares in the company to complete the purchase. It is unusual for negotiations to succeed if the major shareholder has to pay more for assets purchased than he receives for selling his shares.

On other occasions, it may be the purchaser who is unwilling to go ahead unless certain assets are taken out. If negotiations are stalled because it proves impossible to reach agreement on valuation of assets, one solution is for the assets in question to be purchased from the company by the existing shareholders. The value is then established by the purchase price.

(iii) Documentation/approvals

(a) Circular to shareholders

The above transactions will require relevant information to be sent to shareholders. Accountants reports on businesses being acquired or sold may be required and independent professional valuations of properties are desirable.

(b) Independent financial advice and shareholders' vote

Acquisitions of assets from the incoming shareholders and sales of assets to the outgoing shareholders will normally require vetting by independent financial advisers. Independent shareholders will have to approve the transactions at an extraordinary general meeting of the company to be convened for that purpose.

(c) Stock exchange approvals

A major concern of the incoming shareholders will be to ensure that trading in the shares of the company is not suspended or suspended only for a short time. Usually, there is a period of intense negotiation with the stock exchange and other regulatory bodies to determine whether a suspension is required. The attitude of the authorities will be influenced by the extent to which full information can be made available to shareholders and the market in a timely fashion.

(iv) General offer

(a) Obligation to make general offer

Control of a public company is defined differently in different markets. If control of a company is obtained, or if a substantial block of shares is purchased and a subsequent issue of shares gives one party a controlling position, a general offer may be required to be made to the remaining shareholders. The offer, if required, will be in cash or with a cash alternative at the highest price paid for the shares. The offer documentation is likely to emphasise information on the new controlling shareholder and his intentions for the future direction of the company.

(b) Attitude of minorities

On the face of it, the offer is likely to be attractive to minority shareholders. They may be influenced by the decision of the major shareholder to sell and follow his example. In the past, they may have been 'locked in' by lack of trading in the shares and wish to take the opportunity to dispose of their investment. In order to obtain control of the shell company, the purchaser is likely to have paid a premium over net assets. The offer price will therefore be at a premium to the net asset value.

The new shareholder must guard against possible de-listing (and therefore total frustration of his plans) if the offer is overwhelmingly accepted. Careful attention to the assets to be injected and to marketing plans for the shares is therefore needed.

(c) 'Whitewash'

The existing controlling shareholder of a shell company may agree not to sell his shares but instead to allow control to pass by way of injection into the company of assets to be paid for by the issue of new shares. In this case, the requirement for a general offer (if any) may be waived by the relevant authorities provided that the issue of new shares has been approved by the shareholders of the shell company in general meeting. Any shareholders with a conflict of interest must not vote. Such approval is referred to as a 'whitewash'.

(v) Placing out or other marketing of shares

Purchasing control of a shell company achieves a listing but does nothing of itself to improve marketability or raise funds. Improvements in marketability and fund-raising must be undertaken as a separate exercise by the new controlling shareholders. Methods used are as follows:

(a) Placing through brokers

The new controlling shareholders may seek to develop their links with the broking community. They may provide background information for circulars on the new group and its prospects. It is in a broker's interest to circulate clients if the circular provokes sufficient market interest to generate commission on purchase and sales of the shares. Sometimes the new controlling shareholders will undertake to make lines of shares available to the market to ensure that the interest aroused can be satisfied in reasonable size without an immediate price rise and tightening of the market.

(b) Rights issue

After obtaining control, a rights issue may be announced on relatively attractive terms. To facilitate a broadening of the shareholder base, the new controlling shareholder may elect not to take up some or all of his rights. Shares will be available for placing in the market or for other shareholders through excess application forms (if permitted by stock exchange rules) or alternatively they may be taken up by underwriting institutions. If the company's plans are favourably received by the market, new shareholders can be expected to buy so as to be eligible for the rights issue.

(c) Further acquisitions

The shareholding base may be widened by acquisition of further assets or companies from third parties for new shares. If the vendors do not wish to retain the shares it may be possible to arrange a vendor placing through a merchant bank or stockbroker.

In general terms, whether these measures will succeed will be heavily dependent on the quality of assets injected into the shell company and the reputation of the new shareholders.

CONCLUSION

As discussed above, any feasible alternative to a full-scale flotation is worth considering. The names for such methods, however, are unappealing and imply the second rate. 'Shell companies' suggest something insubstantial or hollow, perhaps not reliable; 'backdoor listings' or 'reverse takeovers' invoke images of underhand or covert dealings, if not downright perversity.

But is this necessarily so? On the face of it, the revival and expansion of moribund public companies should be a good thing. It cleans up the position of some of the less worthy public companies; long suffering shareholders can benefit handsomely from accepting the general offer, which is normally part of the process, or enjoying the ride with a more ambitious incoming management. Is there any harm in this?

Regulatory authorities seem instinctively suspicious of incoming parties who may not, as they see it, be willing to undergo the full rigours of the prospectus procedures and vetting by underwriters. Some conspicuous corporate collapses have involved groups which have obtained their listing via shell companies, causing embarrassment to the market.

It may be difficult to protect the interests of both the original shareholders and shareholders who are attracted at a later stage. However, to take away the listing of a shell company chiefly penalises the very shareholders regulators try to protect and seems a 'nuclear option' – too drastic a sanction. Consequently, most markets aim to build sufficient safeguards into the reactivation process to avoid abuse while stopping short of a veto. This has had the effect of shifting purchasers' perception of what a shell company is towards larger companies with sometimes significant businesses and assets. Perhaps in due course the use of the more neutral 'listed vehicle' will render the term 'shell company' obsolete.

CHAPTER 10

Alternative markets, alternative methods

As the equity markets become increasingly international, it is sometimes possible for a company to consider going public outside its home base and select a market which it considers offers the most advantageous terms. How to assess whether this is a possibility and the reasons for considering it are discussed in Section I below. This section also deals with secondary listings, where a company which is already listed in one country seeks an additional listing in another.

A central part of obtaining a listing is ensuring that sufficient shares are in public hands so that there is a fair market in those shares. In a flotation, this is achieved by selling to the public an agreed percentage of the issued share capital of the company being floated. In addition to the agreed percentage, stock exchange rules normally specify that there should be a minimum number of individual shareholders of the company.

In a demerger or spin-off, the spread of shareholdings in public hands is achieved not by marketing but by a distribution of shares. This technique can only be used by an already listed company which distributes shares in a third company (usually its subsidiary) to its existing shareholders. The listing of the third company is then said to be obtained via an 'introduction'. A secondary listing (referred to above) is also obtained by introduction, with little or no marketing taking place as in the case where a new holding company is formed and its shares issued in exchange for shares of an already listed company. Demergers and other listings by introduction are discussed in Section II of this chapter.

Listings may also be sought in a variety of other circumstances which are summarised in section III of this chapter.

I ALTERNATIVE MARKETS

For most companies going public, the obvious and perhaps the only choice of market is one of the main stock markets in the country where the company is incorporated, which is normally the same country where the directors and shareholders are resident and the company carries on its principal business. However, certain countries in which holding companies are domiciled chiefly for tax purposes, such as Bermuda and the Cayman Islands, do not have a stock market. Once a company is not to be listed in the same market where it is incorporated, why should the directors not consider various international markets? The possibility is not open to all companies. To qualify, a company must be able to satisfy certain basic criteria:

(i) Criteria

(a) Size

A company needs to be of sufficient size to attract international interest. While it is hard to set definite figures for say assets or profits, it is likely that the company would have to be significantly larger than the minimum size criterion in a domestic market.

(b) Business

The company will need some significant business connection with the country where the listing is to take place. For this reason, a group with an international spread of business is more suitable. For example, manufacturing operations may be carried out in the Far East and marketing and distribution in North America or Europe. It may be as logical to list the company where its customers are as where its manufacturing base is situated.

(c) Country of incorporation

Some markets do not allow foreign domiciled companies to be listed on a domestic stock exchange. However, most major international markets are prepared to accept a 'neutral' country of domicile such as Bermuda. The more international the spread of the group's business, the more it is natural for the holding company of the group to be incorporated in a tax efficient jurisdiction, as long as its system of company law is considered satisfactory by international standards.

(ii) Reasons for listing overseas

A listing on an overseas stock exchange is likely to be a more complex operation, other things being equal, than listing on a domestic exchange. Why should a company incur the additional risk and expense? Some of the potential benefits are:

(a) Ratings

Different markets tend to rate sectors and companies within them at different multiples. There is also a distinction between markets as regards the price earnings multiples at which companies may go public. In particular, the North American markets seem prepared to place a higher rating on unfamiliar 'growth' companies than the Far East markets, which have suffered from 'boom and bust' cycles. Consequently, an Asian growth company may be able to float at a higher price earnings ratio in the USA than in say Hong Kong.

(b) Prestige and publicity

Companies may regard a listing on the more traditional markets of the USA or Europe as more prestigious than their home market. If they are well known domestically in any event, an overseas listing may raise their profile internationally.

(c) Attracting international institutions

Institutional investors are not familiar with all markets or may limit their participation to 'blue chips'. If a company wishes to attract international institutional shareholders, it may have to go to their home markets in the first instance.

(iii) Assessment of markets

The attractiveness of the different international equity markets may be assessed by the following features:

(a) Pricing

As mentioned above, the overall rating is a key attraction. In addition to the price earnings ratio at which the market stands, the rating of individual companies and the levels at which flotations can be undertaken should also be considered. In less developed markets, it has been argued that flotations tend to be systematically under-priced so as to ensure success. A fairly narrow pricing range for flotations may emerge, almost disregarding the quality of the individual company or the sector it is in. In more mature markets, the failure of a flotation is less likely to affect overall confidence and so may be considered a less sensitive matter. In that case, there may be a greater readiness among underwriters to price up to the general market level.

(b) Degree of regulation

This is something of a two-edged sword. There must be a sufficient level of regulation and supervision by the exchange under the listing rules and by law to promote investor confidence while still allowing the company to operate efficiently – eg make further issues of shares and undertake acquisitions – without undue delay or excessive (and expensive) documentation.

(c) Volume of trading and other market factors

The volume of trading in the market is an important attraction – generally speaking, the higher, the better. Along with volume goes transparency and the efficiency of trading and the quality of information which is available to shareholders on a regular basis.

(d) Costs

There are likely to be some additional costs in listing overseas. As well as the initial cost, the continuing expense of compliance with the listing rules and company law must be taken into account. One of the heaviest expenses may be in bringing the accounts of the company into line with accountng principles generally accepted in the country of listing.

(iv) Secondary listings overseas

(a) Timing and benefits

To list a company for the first time on an overseas stock exchange may seem too complex and ambitious to many managements, even of companies with international operations. However, once the company has become established as a public listed company and the directors are comfortable with the procedures for compliance with the regulations, they may be inclined to seek an overseas listing as a second stage. The benefits are mainly in terms of publicity as the majority of trading tends to take place where the primary listing is located, which also takes the lead on establishing the market price levels.

(b) Documentation

Most stock exchanges are prepared to waive some of the documentation requirements provided the company's primary listing is on a stock exchange which is recognised by the exchange on which the secondary listing is planned. Nevertheless, a prospectus will still have to be produced to provide investors in the relevant market with full information. As noted above, bringing accounting conventions into line may be the most difficult requirement to fulfil.

II DEMERGER/SPIN-OFF

In a demerger/spin-off, a company which is already listed establishes a separate vehicle for a part of its assets or business and then distributes the shares in that vehicle to its own shareholders, creating an independent listed group.

(i) Procedure

The steps involved in a demerger/spin-off are as follows:

(a) Separation

The business or assets which are to be spun off must first be put into a separate subsidiary, if they are not already held in this form. This achieves legal separation from the parent company. However, there may be substantial inter-company borrowings or other financial dealings which must be unwound or put on an arm's length basis. Care must be taken that the company is strong enough financially to survive on its own. Management must also be independent. Transitional arrangements may be needed for such matters as shared computer facilities, insurance and employee benefits.

(b) Distribution

The shares of the subsidiary are distributed pro rata to the shareholders of the holding company. The shareholders do not pay any consideration for the shares they receive but may be liable for transfer duty when they are registered in their name. The receipt of the new shares is not likely to be taxed as income in the hands of shareholders. On a subsequent sale, however, tax liability is likely to be incurred.

The articles of the holding company may not always provide for this kind of distribution. If they do not, or if the relevant clauses are ambiguous, a shareholders' meeting will be needed to authorise the distribution. It may be desirable in any case.

The distribution, like any dividend, requires sufficient distributable reserves to be available. The amount of reserves needed is equal to the book value of the shares to be distributed.

(c) Reduction of capital

If sufficient reserves are not available or if the distribution would absorb so much of the reserves that future cash dividends would be prejudiced, it is possible to proceed by way of a reduction of capital. This requires a meeting of shareholders and legal confirmation. It is facilitated if the holding company has no creditors or if the creditors can be safeguarded in some way, for example, by a bank guarantee.

(d) Sale by rights

It is possible to mitigate the impact on distributable reserves by offering the shares of the subsidiary for purchase by the shareholders of the holding company by way of rights rather than distributing them without payment. This is not a popular method, perhaps because it appears to shareholders that they are being asked to buy something which they already (if indirectly) own. However, shareholders still benefit if the shares are offered at a substantial discount to their real worth, while the proceeds received by the company may serve to keep the decrease in distributable reserves, referred to above, to manageable proportions.

(e) Obtaining a listing

A listing for the company is applied for on the basis that there is already a sufficiently wide spread of shareholders and no separate marketing exercise is required. A company which has been spun off from a larger group will have initially the same shareholders as that already listed group. The spread of shareholders must therefore by definition be adequate to obtain a listing for the shares of the newly spun-off company by way of introduction.

Despite the fact that there may be no sales of shares undertaken, the requirements to provide information to the market must still be fulfilled and a full prospectus document produced.

(f) Market price of the shares

One of the uncertainties of this type of operation is the price at which the shares will initially trade. As there has been no pricing or underwriting and no previous trading, the price can only be estimated by reference to the financial information published about the company and by comparison with similar listed companies. The group undertaking the spin-off will not normally hazard any indication of the likely price at which trading will commence.

(ii) Reasons for carrying out a demerger/spin-off

(a) Rationalisation of group structure

A demerger may be carried out by a conglomerate or other group which concludes part of its business is so different in commercial or financial needs that it should be managed and owned outside the group. Sometimes the technique is used when the financial future of a member of the group is uncertain. A spin-off may be preferable to jeopardising the whole group by supporting the company or incurring the odium of having a subsidiary go bankrupt. Rather than the business being sold to an unrelated party, which may in any case be unrealistic at a reasonable price, ownership is transferred to the shareholders of the parent company via a spin-off.

(b) Increase in market value

After the demerger, shareholders will have two distinct investments, one being their original holding and the other a proportionate holding in the newly spun-off company. This gives them greater flexibility and may, by appealing to different investor preferences, increase the combined market value of the two holdings over the market value of the original one. The attractions of the newly spun-off company might have been buried in the complexities or problems of the parent group and so not given full weight; or the demerged company may be in a 'glamour' sector and on its own can attract a premium rating from investors who wish to have an investment wholly in that sector. Sceptics might of course query why the company became part of the original group in the first place.

(c) Creating a separate listing

A spin-off is a useful technique for a group which wants to create a listed vehicle for some specific purpose, such as starting a new line of business or investing in more speculative situations than its normal activities. Instead of buying a shell company, it may create one by setting up a subsidiary, putting some appropriate assets or business into it and then distributing the shares to its own shareholders. The alternative would be to buy a shell company, but the spin-off avoids the need to identify a suitable shell and paying a premium for control.

(d) Defence tactic

If a takeover is threatened, a spin-off may be used as a defence tactic to increase the market value of a group, put a 'crown jewel' beyond the reach of an aggressor or simply muddy the waters. This is discussed in more detail in Part 4 of this book.

III   LISTINGS AND ISSUES IN OTHER CIRCUMSTANCES

(i) Listing by introduction

Various other methods may be adopted to achieve a sufficiently wide spread of shareholders for a company to be granted a listing via an introduction without any further marketing of shares.

(a) Private sales and private placements

Well-established businesses may become public companies and achieve a considerable spread of shareholders through private sales and placements at various times without actually becoming listed. Application for listing may be made subsequently with or without a further distribution or marketing of shares. A prospectus document will be required to be produced in support of the application to the stock exchange for listing.

(b) Share exchange by scheme or offer

A new company may be incorporated to take over an existing listed company via a share exchange. This may be undertaken, for example, in order to change the domicile of the holding company of a group. The shareholders of say a Hong Kong company may be offered shares in a Bermuda or Cayman Islands company in exchange for their existing holdings. The new company will have the same shareholders as the previously listed company, which will become a subsidiary of the new holding company. The new company will obtain a listing by introduction.

A share exchange may be desirable in circumstances where it is not possible to be certain of the financial position of a shell company. Rather than using the shell as the holding company, a new holding company is put on top of the shell. The advantage of this structure is that any assets or businesses to be injected can be controlled by the new holding company or through a separate subsidiary rather than by the shell. The financial damage of any claims can then be limited to the shell company and kept isolated from the rest of the new listed group.

(ii) Bonus issues

(a) Basis

A bonus (or capitalisation) issue does not involve any payment by shareholders. The issue is effected by transferring amounts from share premium account and/or reserves and applying them in paying up further issued share capital. As with a rights issue, the size of a bonus issue is expressed in relation to an existing shareholding (for example one-for-ten). In theory, the bonus issue should make no difference at all to the market value of an investor's total holding. If the price prior to a one-for-ten bonus is $1 per share, ex bonus it should adjust to $0.91 as follows:

	Shares in issue	*Value*
Before bonus	10	10
Bonus issue	1	nil
After bonus	11	10
Market value of one share		0.91

Following adjustment, the market value of eleven shares will be identical to the previous market value of ten shares.

(b) Reasons for bonus issues

There are a number of reasons why bonus issues have a degree of popularity. Some directors feel that issued share capital should be kept roughly in line with net worth. As retained profits and other reserves grow a proportion is capitalised via bonus issues. This has the effect that they cannot be paid out as cash dividends. In some markets, shareholders pay at least as much attention to the level of bonus issue as to cash dividends and are pleased to see the number of shares they hold increase.

(c) 'Announcement effect'

Despite the fact that the value of shareholders' investments should be unchanged after the issue, it appears that in some markets there may not always be a full adjustment. This may be partly due to investors' fondness for bonus issues. However, it seems likely that the announcement of a bonus issue is taken as the directors' expression of confidence in satisfactory future growth. This impression will be strengthened if the announcement of a bonus is accompanied by a statement that the directors expect that cash dividends on the enlarged share capital can be maintained at the same per share figure. In such circumstances, experience suggests that share prices may recover towards the 'cum bonus' price quite rapidly.

(iii) Share/scrip dividend

(a) Mechanics

A company may offer its shareholders new shares as an alternative to receiving a cash dividend. The new shares will be paid up from the amount of cash dividend the shareholder foregoes. The articles of association of a company do not always permit shares to be issued in this way. A change to the articles may be required therefore if a company wishes to introduce such a scheme.

(b) Issue price of shares

If a company operates a share dividend scheme, shareholders are allowed to choose whether to receive their dividend in the form of new shares, in cash or a mixture of the two. The price at which the new shares are issued is normally based on the average market price for a period ending a few days before the shareholder must make his decision.

(c) Advantages

Companies have found share dividend schemes a useful way of conserving cash while maintaining an attractive level of dividend. For some shareholders, there may be tax advantages in receiving their dividend by way of shares, which may not be counted as income until sold, rather than in cash. Major shareholders may find such an arrangement a convenient way of keeping their holdings topped up. In a rising market, shareholders will make a gain by taking shares rather than the fixed cash amount.

(iv) Options

A company may grant options over unissued shares as part of a share incentive scheme for employees. Such a scheme may well be limited to the more senior employees who are considered to have some influence on the results of the company. The options are usually issued at a fixed price based on the market price at the time the options are granted. The scheme should be approved by shareholders and is normally limited to a relatively small percentage (say 10%) of the current issued share capital of the company.

(v) Debt/equity swaps

At times of financial stress, it may be possible for a company to use an issue of shares to cancel a liability. This, however, requires that the creditor in question is prepared to see the ranking of his claim decrease in return for the chance of future growth by becoming a shareholder. The effect on the balance sheet of cancelling debt in exchange for equity can be very dramatic as liabilities decrease at the same time as net worth increases. For this reason, a cancellation of debt in return for new preference or ordinary shares is a common feature in difficult corporate debt restructurings.

CONCLUSIONS

This chapter has considered alternatives in the area of listings and issues. Seeking a listing in an overseas market either initially, or more commonly, as a secondary listing in addition to a listing in a 'home market', is an alternative which is becoming feasible for an imaginative management. Demergers have grown fashionable as the appeal of the conglomerate as a form of group corporate organisation has waned. Listings and issues in other contexts have also been discussed to illustrate the diversity of occasions on which such transactions can be undertaken. It seems likely that the diversity already apparent in this area will continue to increase in future.

CHAPTER 11

Rights issues

Once a listing has been obtained, a company may raise further capital by issuing securities without such extensive documentation as is required for the initial listing. As information is published about public companies, investors are considered to be aware of it or to be able to inform themselves if they wish. Existing registered shareholders of a company will receive regular information about its fortunes, including the interim and final accounts.

What is a rights issue?

As a general rule existing shareholders have a prior claim (or pre-emptive right) to distributions made by the company. This right may be based on law, the articles of the company, stock exchange regulations or market practice. It may be argued that issues of new shares or equity-linked securities, particularly on terms which reflect a discount to the market price, affect this right and consequently should be offered first to existing shareholders. Issues made in this way are termed 'rights issues'.

Basis for rights issues and exceptions

In the UK, issues of new shares for cash (except where shareholders have agreed otherwise) have by law to be made by way or rights. In countries where market practice is influenced by the UK, this requirement may be founded on stock exchange regulations rather than law and be subject to certain quite common exceptions. For example, it may be possible to issue a limited percentage of a company's issued share capital, say up to 20%, to outside investors for cash without participation by existing shareholders, provided shareholders have previously agreed in general meeting to waive their rights or give directors a mandate to issue shares to third parties. In the US, it is common to find the articles of association of a company permit shares to be offered for cash to outside investors via public offerings. In such circumstances, rights issues are a rarity. Shares are sold through a lead manager and syndicate. After preliminary marketing, the issue may be priced, underwritten and sold in the course of a day.

Arguments in favour

There are two main arguments in favour of the rights issue procedure. First, it provides a shareholder with a means of ensuring that his percentage holding in the company is not diluted, at least not by issues of new shares for cash. Second, he receives the benefit of any discount in the price at which the new shares are issued compared to the prevailing market price.

Existing shareholders are a very logical source of new equity for the company as they have already made a deliberate decision to invest in it. On the other hand, it may be argued that a public offering of shares is a quicker and simpler procedure, allows more direct participation by major institutions and consequently is a more efficient way of raising further equity.

The basis and technical aspects of rights issues are considered in Section I. Pricing and underwriting are covered in Section II and timing and costs in Section III.

I BASIS AND TECHNICAL ASPECTS

(i) Size

(a) Basis

The basis of the rights issue is expressed as the number of new shares (or other securities) a shareholder is entitled to subscribe for in relation to an existing holding. A one-for-four rights issue is an issue where a shareholder can subscribe for one new share for every four shares he currently holds. In a one-for-four issue, a holder of 1,000 shares could subscribe for 250 new shares, making his total holding 1,250 shares.

(b) Amount to be raised

The basis of the issue is governed by the amount it is desired to raise. A standard amount to raise by way of rights would be approximately 20% of the company's current market capitalisation, which is found by multiplying the number of shares currently in issue by the market price. Except in special circumstances, larger issues might be considered to make unreasonably heavy calls on shareholders to increase their investment. Allowing for a normal discount on pricing, to raise 20% of the market capitalisation requires an issue of, say, one-for-four or three-for-ten, that is existing shareholders will be offered three new shares at the rights issue price for every ten shares that they currently hold.

(c) Partly paid formula

If the issue is a relatively large one, a partly paid formula may be used. Shareholders may be asked to pay, for example, 50% on acceptance and the balance some months later. The final date is usually before the end of the company's financial year to prevent partly paid shares appearing in the balance sheet. During the time that they are partly paid, the shares will be separately traded. Registered shareholders who do not pay the second instalment on the due date are liable to forfeit their shares and could, in theory, be sued by the company for the balance outstanding.

(ii) Type of security

(a) Ordinary shares

The most common type of rights issue is a further issue of ordinary shares ranking equally in all respects with the existing ordinary shares. The equal ranking is required to avoid confusion in trading in the shares which would arise if ordinary shares with different entitlements were in the market. In fact, it is unlikely that the stock exchange will allow dealings at all unless the new shares when fully paid rank equally with the existing shares.

(b) How to deal with dividends

A likely area of difficulty is as regards dividend payments. If the money raised by the issue is received after the end of (or part way through) a financial period but before the record date for the dividend for that period it is not obvious whether the new shares should rank for this dividend. To reduce this problem, a rights issue may be announced simultaneously with final or interim results so that the record dates for the dividend and the rights issue coincide. In this case, only the existing shares rank for the dividend in respect of the period just ended but both existing and new shares rank for all subsequent distributions. A final dividend, which requires approval by shareholders and may therefore cause delay, is sometimes replaced by a special interim dividend in this context as the directors can pay an interim dividend without reference to shareholders.

(c) Other kinds of rights issues

While new ordinary shares are the securities most frequently issued by way of rights, other kinds of securities may be employed. The security will gain a listing because it is issued by a company whose shares are themselves listed and will be held, if everything goes smoothly, by approximately the same investors as the ordinary shares. On occasion, preference shares, deferred or preferred shares and unsecured or convertible unsecured loan stock are used instead of or in addition to ordinary shares. It is possible to make a rights offering of shares in another company, if a suitable block of investments is held by the company making the rights offer.

(iii) Fractions and odd lots

The use of a round number for the basis of an issue (such as three-for-ten) will reduce the number of fractions of a share which arise on a rights issue. As it is not possible to allot a fraction of a share, the fractions which would arise are aggregated and the resulting shares sold for the benefit of the company. This involves a small penalty to the shareholder.

A further inconvenience may arise in markets where a board lot system of trading is used. Investors will tend to hold their shares in complete board lots. The basis of the rights issue will almost certainly result in an odd lot being issued to them which may have to be sold at a discount to market price. To minimise losses, the company may make special arrangements with designated stock-brokers to facilitate trading in odd lots for a limited period of time. On occasions, a company may offer shareholders new shares sufficient to 'top up' their holding to the nearest board lot.

(iv) Documentation

The documentation for rights issues is considerably simpler than for a flotation. The reason is that shares are being offered to existing shareholders in an existing listed company. It can therefore be assumed that the potential subscribers are already reasonably well-informed about the company. The documents which shareholders receive in connection with a rights issue are:

(a) Preliminary circular (if required)

If there is insufficient authorised share capital, a preliminary circular will be needed with a notice of extraordinary general meeting to gain shareholders' approval for an appropriate increase in authorised share capital. This circular will repeat the press announcement of the issue which will include the basis, the amount to be raised, the record date for the issue, the main purpose of raising the money, any conditions of the issue and the underwriting arrangements.

(b) Explanatory circular

The explanatory circular is intended to provide shareholders with the technical details of the issue and sufficient financial and other information to make an informed judgment on the merits of the issue. The technical details include the terms and conditions of the issue and the procedures for acceptance and payment and for trading in the nil paid rights.

The financial information includes the most recent audited results and balance sheet and any interim results. It also includes a statement of indebtedness at a recent date (by convention, not more than a month before the date of the document), a statement that working capital is sufficient for the company's present requirements and a statement of the prospects for the current financial year. Depending on how early it is in the year (among other factors), the statement of prospects may include a formal forecast of profits and dividends for the year. If a formal profit forecast is made it is normally reported on by the auditors of the company and the underwriters of the issue.

Other information will include a description of the use of the proceeds and the contribution which projects to be funded by the issue will make to the future of the company. If a business is being bought with the proceeds, an accountant's report on that business is normally required. A revaluation of the group's properties may be undertaken to give shareholders an up-to-date picture of the net asset backing for the issue.

A statutory and general section covers relevant disclosure of interests by the directors of the company. It also contains details of material contracts, substantial shareholdings, expenses, litigation and underwriting arrangements, including any force majeure provisions

(c) Provisional allotment letter

This sets out how many shares have been provisionally allotted to the share-holder to whom it is addressed. The shares are said to be provisionally allotted because allotment is subject to the payment of the rights issue price per share. The form also describes the procedures and timing for paying the amount due, for selling the rights and for splitting them, if the shareholder wants to subscribe for some and sell the remainder. The provisional allotment letter serves as the document of title for trading in the rights shares before the amount due is paid. The opportunity to trade in 'nil paid' rights is the main factor which distinguishes rights issues from open offers and placings, which are dealt with in the next chapter.

(d) Excess application form

In some markets, shareholders will receive a form which allows them to subscribe for additional shares over and above those which they have been provisionally allotted. If some shareholders do not take up their rights, these shares will be allotted to shareholders who make excess applications prior to any call being made on the underwriters. In some markets, this procedure is considered to penalise shareholders who do not either take up or sell their rights and is not permitted. In such markets, rights not taken up are aggregated and sold in the market if possible, with the proceeds being distributed to the shareholders whose rights they were.

(e) Registration

In most jurisdictions, rights issue documents (including provisional allotment letters, excess application forms and written consents from experts for the use of their names) must be filed with the relevant regulatory authorites before their despatch.

(v) Accounting aspects

(a) Earnings per share

In the short term, a rights issue priced at a discount to market will, like any issue at a discount, tend to reduce the earnings per share. In the long term, the effect on earnings per share will depend on the use to which the new capital is put. Unless the company needs new equity simply for survival, it is unlikely that the directors would invest funds raised via a rights issue in projects which were not expected ultimately to increase the earnings per share, as adjusted. Following a rights issue, the prior years' earnings per share will be adjusted downwards by a factor $\frac{A}{B}$ where:

> A is the theoretical 'ex rights' price (see below)
>
> and B is the actual 'cum rights' price on the last day before the shares are traded ex rights.

Consequently, if the earnings per share for the previous year had been $1 and the theoretical ex rights price (A) was $9.50 and the share price in the market on the last day of trading cum rights (B) was $10, the factor $\frac{A}{B}$ would be 0.950 and the prior year's earnings per share would be adjusted to $0.950. In the short term, the company may be taking advantage of favourable market conditions and have no immediate use for the funds. At the time of the issue, the increase in earnings attributable to the issue is normally calculated by assuming the funds are used to repay debt (reducing the interest charge) or are put on deposit.

Earnings per share for a year in which a rights issue has been made are based on actual earnings for that year divided by the weighted average number of shares in issue (not the actual number in issue at the year end). The weighted average takes into account two factors: first that the rights shares have only been in issue for a proportion of the year; and second that there is a 'bonus' element in the rights issue. An example is as follows:

EXAMPLE

A company has 100 million shares in issue with a market price of $10 and announces a 1-for-four rights issue at $7.50 per share at the time of releasing its results for the previous year. The theoretical ex rights price is $9.50, calculated by adding one new share at $7.50 to the value of 4 existing shares at $10 and dividing the total ($47.50) by 5 (ie 1 new share plus 4 existing shares). The rights issue closes on 31st May. The company's actual earnings for the year in question turn out to be $120 million.

The calculation of the weighted average number of shares in issue for that year would be:

		000 shares
(i)	Shares in issue from the close of the rights issue (31st May) to the year end (31st December):	
	$125 \text{ million} \times \frac{7}{12}$	72,917
(ii)	Shares in issue up to the close of the rights issue, increased to reflect the bonus element in the rights issue (Note: this adjustment is the reciprocal of the adjustment to prior years' earnings per share noted above):	
	$100 \text{ million} \times \frac{B}{A} \times \frac{5}{12}$	43,861
		116,778
	Earnings per share	$1.03

(b) Assets per share

While a rights issue is likely to decrease earnings per share in the short term, assets per share may actually rise. A company which is valued principally by reference to earnings and which does not have a large net asset base might well be in this position. In the example noted above, if the net assets of the company before the rights issue were $600 million, net assets per share would increase after the rights issue, as follows:

	Net assets ($000)	Shares in issue (000)	Net assets per share ($)
Before rights issue	600,000	100,000	6.00
Rights issue	187,500	25,000	
Expenses of rights issue (say 5%)	(9,375)	—	
	778,125	125,000	6.23

On the other hand, if a company is valued principally by reference to its net asset value, the market price normally reflects a discount to such value. If a rights issue is pitched at a further discount to the market value, dilution in the the net asset backing is inevitable.

II   MARKET ASPECTS: PRICING, UNDERWRITING AND TRADING

(i) Pricing

(a) Discount to market

Unlike setting the price for an initial flotation, the pricing of a conventionally-sized rights issue owes little to fundamental analysis or the rating of comparable companies. The pricing of a rights issue is based on the market price of the shares of the company at the time of the issue, adjusted for the expected effect of issuing new shares at below market price.

Shareholders must be given a reasonable incentive to buy the new shares, their alternative being to buy existing shares from the market, not in a merely comparable company but in the company itself. Consequently, a rights issue must be made at a discount to the market price. A fairly standard discount can be observed in most markets, required for the issue to be underwritten by a merchant bank or other financial institution. This institution will wish to spread its risk to sub-underwriters who will in turn look to the discount to protect them from market fluctuations. The amount of discount which is necessary to attract market support depends on the volatility of the market concerned and the length of time during which the sub-underwriters will be exposed. The standard discount varies from about 15% to about 25% on the 'ex rights' price.

(b) Calculation of 'ex rights' price and discount

An adjustment to the prevailing market price has to be made to reflect the fall which will occur (other things being equal) owing to the issue of new shares at a discount to the market price. In addition, most rights issues are made in conjunction with the final or interim announcement when a cash dividend will be paid and possibly also a bonus issue made. In most cases, the new rights shares will not rank for the dividend or bonus issue as these relate to a financial period which has already finished. Taking all these factors into account, the apparent discount between the market price before the issue and the issue price is not as great as it appears. An example of how to calculate the ex rights price and the discount at which the issue is pitched is as follows:

EXAMPLE

A company's current share price is $5. Its financial year coincides with the calendar year. With the announcement of its result for the past year, the company declares a final dividend of 30 cents and bonus issue of one share for every ten shares held. It also announces a rights issue of three new shares for every ten shares held at a price of $3 per share. The new rights shares do not rank for the final cash dividend or the bonus issue. The bonus shares do not rank for the cash dividend or the rights issue. The method of calculation of the ex rights price and rights issue discount is as follows:

Ex dividend adjustment:

Current market price per share	$5.00
Less final dividend per share	0.30
	$4.70

Ex bonus adjustment:
10 existing shares at $4.70 per share plus 1 free
share results in a weighted average price of $4.27
                                                ($47 divided by 11)

Ex rights adjustment:

	No of shares	Market value ($)
10 existing shares ex dividend and ex bonus at $4.27 per share	10	42.70
3 new rights shares at $3.00 per share	3	9.00
	13	51.70

Ex rights price: $3.98
                                        ($51.70 divided by 13)

Rights issue discount is:
1—(rights price divided by price ex dividend, bonus and rights)
1—(3 ÷ 3.98)   24.6%

This compares with an 'apparent' discount of 40% based on the $3 rights price and the $5 market price before the announcement of the results and the rights issue.

(c) Longer-term impact on price

The level to which the market price settles will depend not only on the terms of the rights issue but on the results and the tone of the announcement itself which accompany it. The announcement of the issue of a significant number of new shares at a discount to market price tends to have a depressing effect. However, if the company appears to be doing well and a good profit and dividend forecast is made, shareholders will naturally be encouraged to invest more money. If the reasons for making the issue carry the promise of growth to come, this may meet a better response than if funds are required, for example, to reduce a high level of borrowings. The share price may actually rise owing to the 'announcement effects' and the belief that the rights issue is a sign of an aggressive management and an exciting future.

(ii) Underwriting

(a) Underwriting vs 'deep discount'

Although rights issues are usually underwritten, there is no absolute requirement for underwriting. An alternative strategy is for a company to make an issue at a 'deep discount', offering shares to its shareholders at such an attractive price that the risk of an alert shareholder not taking up his rights is virtually nil. Even if some shareholders do not respond, their rights can be easily placed in the market or will be taken up by other shareholders through excess applications, where this is the market practice.

The main advantage of a deeply discounted issue is that it enables the company to avoid paying underwriting fees. A possible disadvantage is that the drop in the market price occasioned by the rights issue will be a good deal steeper than it would have been with a conventional issue. It may be argued that the drop in share price after a deeply discounted issue may in some way affect confidence among investors who do not understand the procedure or who are not following the company closely, but notice the share price drop.

(b) Attitude of management

In practice, directors seem reluctant to abandon the comfort of an underwriting. This may be in part due to the unfamiliarity of management with the procedures involved as equity issues for the average company are an infrequent occurrence. They will therefore seek the guidance of a merchant bank at an early stage and the merchant bank will have an overall financial advisory role as well as being the underwriter. Unless they have severe doubts about the attractions of the company's shares, it is likely that the merchant bank will steer the company in the direction of an underwritten issue. They may well believe this is the best way to ensure that the company achieves its objectives. In addition, the transaction will be potentially much more profitable for themselves.

Some managements are reluctant to adopt the deep discount method as they consider it results in shares being issued too cheaply. However, it may be argued that provided the existing shareholders take up the issue, the price at which the issue is made is not relevant. Any benefit in the price will go to existing shareholders pro rata to their shareholdings and therefore their interests are not harmed. Conceptually, a rights issue at a deep discount could be considered as partly a conventional rights issue and partly a bonus issue combined into one.

(c) Commonsense approach

It is possible that these arguments may be too academic for a practical management's taste. A commonsense view is that the company should issue the shares as close to the market price as possible. This often leads to a spirited argument on price with management deaf to underwriters' pleas that a high discount is irrelevant to shareholders and that the issue should not be priced too finely.

In some sense, a low discount must be of value to shareholders. If the shares are not taken up, the underwriters will have to subscribe for them at a higher price. They will therefore have to contribute more money to the company, or the same money for less shares, than they would have if the discount had been higher.

(iii) Trading

(a) Market sensitivity

In the case of an initial flotation, a leak of information is not market sensitive as no securities of the company are yet traded. A rights issue on the other hand (assuming the company is already listed) is likely to affect the price of the shares and therefore elaborate security precautions are taken. These may include the use of code names and drafting meetings held on neutral ground.

(b) Trading in 'nil paid' rights

Rights issues provide that the rights themselves are tradable 'nil paid', that is before any payment of the amount due has been made. As noted above, the ability to trade 'nil paid' is the major distinguishing feature of rights issues, as opposed to open offers and placings. The rights will have a value reflecting the difference between the market price of the shares 'ex rights' and the rights issue price. In the example given above on the calculation of the ex rights price and discount, the theoretical value of the rights would be $0.98 per nil paid share, that is the difference between the ex rights price ($3.98) and the price of the rights issue ($3). This enables shareholders who do not wish to subscribe for more shares to sell their rights and thus recoup any loss in value after the shares are traded ex rights. One possible market strategy is for a shareholder to sell sufficient of his rights to enable him to subscribe for the remainder.

Dealings in the market in the rights 'nil paid' are likely to be very active owing to adjustments of shareholders' desired holdings and to the activities of speculators who may be attracted by the geared nature of the investment. The price of the rights will vary much more in percentage terms than the price of the underlying shares. Thus, in our example, if the share price increases by 10% from $3.98 to $4.38, the 'nil paid' price would appreciate by 41% from $0.98 to $1.38. A major indicator of whether or not an issue will be fully subscribed is the level of activity in trading in the rights and whether a reasonable premium exists up to the close of trading.

Problems can arise in trading nil paid rights where the rights issue is conditional, for example where a force majeure clause would enable an underwriter to withdraw, thus causing the issue to collapse. Purchasers of such rights would find themselves holding valueless paper. However, in circumstances where a force majeure clause is invoked, it is unlikely that the rights would have any value in any event.

(c) Attitude of substantial shareholders

It is important to find out the attitude of any substantial shareholder in advance. A major shareholder not taking up his rights may sour the whole issue unless a good reason can be given. One possible reason is to allow scope to widen the spread of shareholders.

If a major shareholder sells his rights continually in the market, this is likely to depress the price of the 'nil paid' rights and jeopardise the success of the issue. It is preferable for the merchant bank or stockbroker managing the issue to be instructed to place the shareholder's rights in an organised way as soon as possible after trading commences.

III   TIMING AND COSTS

(i) Overall factors

(a) High share price/opportunism

The number of rights issues made is closely correlated to the level and turnover of the stock market. Directors prefer to make issues when the market price of the company's shares is high, perhaps considering that this is in some sense 'cheap money' for the company. This may lead to criticism of management for opportunism, but shareholders may also be more inclined to support their company with fresh capital when the share price has been going up. They may therefore be happy to subscribe for new shares even at prices which are historically high.

(b) 'No umbrella when it rains'

It is a common experience that funds may not necessarily be required by a company at a time which coincides with the peak of the market. However, a management may be well-advised to adopt a long-term view of the amount of new equity which is desirable and take advantage of periods of market strength to raise funds smoothly. If a company delays until it has an urgent requirement for new equity, there is a danger that the market mood may have changed. There may be a reluctance on investors' part to provide funds when they are really needed as the need may be perceived as a sign of weakness. The market prefers to feel it is backing winners, even when they have no real need of additional capital, than nursing lame ducks back to health.

(ii) Timetable

The detailed timing of a rights issue will vary with local market procedures. It is usual to give shareholders a fairly long period (say 2/3 weeks) to decide whether to subscribe for the new shares and to make their own funding arrangements, if necessary. This period also allows a reasonable opportunity for trading in the nil paid rights.

(a) Record date

The starting point for an issue is to establish the shareholders who are entitled to receive it. This involves a record date being announced. Sufficient time should be allowed for shareholders who have not held their shares in registered form to make the necessary arrangements to receive the benefit of the issue.

(b) Need to increase authorised share capital

If there is insufficient authorised share capital to allow for the rights issue, an extraordinary general meeting of the company will be required to agree to an increase. Depending on the articles of association of the company, the period of notice required for the meeting may cause some delay to the timetable. It is important that no trading in the rights shares takes place before the meeting. If for some reason the increase in authorised share capital was turned down, the issue could not proceed and any dealings would have been on a false basis.

A sample rights issue timetable for which an increase in authorised share capital is required is set out below. The precise timing will vary by as much as three weeks depending on the practice in different markets.

Note. I means 'Impact Day', the first day on which the detailed terms of the issue are made known to the market and the press.

Date (days)

I − 30	(i) Decide in principle to proceed and whether profit forecast will be made.
	(ii) Instruct merchant bank, accountants and lawyers.
	(iii) Begin drafting rights issue documents.
	(iv) Record date for indebtedness.
By I − 10	(i) Financial position of company reviewed and basis of issue decided.
	(ii) Printed proof of rights issue documents prepared, circulated and discussed.
	(iii) Record date for issue (depending on local dealing rules).
I − 7	Further proofs and drafting meetings as required.
I	(i) Board meeting to approve issue. Underwriting agreement signed.
	(ii) Press announcement released.
	(iii) Sub-underwriting completed.
	(iv) Print order given.

Date (days)

I + 1	Posting of explanatory circular with notice of meeting.
I + 15	Extraordinary general meeting held.
I + 16	Posting of provisional allotment letter and, where appropriate, form of application for excess shares.
I + 19	Dealings in rights shares (nil paid) commence.
I + 30	Last day for acceptance and payment for rights shares.
I + 31	Underwriters and sub-underwriters informed of their liability (if any).
I + 38	New share certificates/refund cheques for unsuccessful excess applications despatched.

The dealing arrangements for the rights shares nil paid and fully paid will vary with local market practice as regards dealing and settlement and whether renounceable temporary documents of title are used.

(iii) Costs

The costs of a rights issue are substantially less than for a new flotation owing to the lesser degree of investigation and documentation required and the simpler procedures.

(a) Underwriting

The major expense is for underwriting, assuming the issue is made at a conventional discount. Most markets have fairly standard rates for underwriting which seem resistant to competitive pressures. The rates range from about 2% to about 4% of the amount raised by the issue. They may be increased by say $\frac{1}{2}$% if a new class of security (such as preference shares or loan stock) is used. If the timetable of the issue involves a longer exposure than standard, for example because of the need to hold an extraordinary general meeting, an additional fee of say $\frac{1}{8}$% per week may be payable.

(b) Capital duty

As new securities are being issued, it is likely that there will be capital duty at the rates prevailing in the relevant market.

(c) Professional fees

The other main expenses will be for accounting and legal work, based principally on time spent. The charges of the registrars and receiving bankers and for the printing and distribution of the documents will depend on variable factors such as the number of shareholders.

The average costs of rights issues depend on size. Some costs (principally professional fees) are largely fixed but the underwriting fees (and capital duty, if applicable) are variable. In addition, smaller issues may be perceived as more risky and consequently the percentage underwriting charge may be increased. On average the cost may range from a minimum of $3\frac{1}{2}\%$ of the funds raised for a large issue by a well-known company to about 7% of the funds raised or more for a speculative, rarely traded concern.

CONCLUSIONS

There has been a lively debate on whether rights issues are the most appropriate way for listed companies to raise further equity capital. Supporters point to the protections which rights issues give to existing shareholders against dilution of their percentage holding and of the value of their shares. Some of these supporters however tend to benefit from what has been called an underwriting cartel, while management may chafe at the restrictions and longer timetable which the rights issue procedures impose.

Rights issues have proved a reliable source of new equity funds for already listed companies. Shareholders who have already decided to buy shares in a company are likely to agree to increase their investment by a reasonable amount when offered further shares at a discount to the market price. Management may, however, be well advised to approach shareholders when the company is doing well rather than waiting until funds are urgently needed.

Rights issues require a circular to shareholders to inform them of the terms of the issue and update them about the affairs of the company. They also allow a fairly long gestation period for shareholders to trade in their rights and decide whether to invest. For these reasons, offering new shares direct to institutions and other investors may be a more streamlined way of raising new equity. Methods of issuing new equity which do not involve existing shareholders are discussed in the next chapter.

CHAPTER 12

Open offers and placings

In the previous chapter, the raising of further equity capital by way of rights issue was discussed. In addition to rights issues, companies frequently employ open offers and placings to achieve the same end. In this chapter, the procedures for making open offers and placings are described and the differences between these techniques and rights issues are highlighted and discussed.

Placings are also used when a holder of a large block of existing shares wishes to reduce or dispose of his holding in one transaction rather than by a series of sales in the market. A single transaction allows him to be certain of the amount realised. From the point of view of the company and the other shareholders, it is desirable to avoid a constant 'tap' of shares on to the market which is likely to depress the share price.

I OPEN OFFERS

(i) What is an open offer?

As in the case of a rights issue, an open offer is an offer to existing shareholders of a company to subscribe for or to purchase securities. However, the offer is not made to shareholders specifically pro rata to their existing shareholding (eg 1-for-4). Instead, shareholders may apply for any number of securities they wish subject to the stated total number available under the offer. Shareholders are usually guaranteed a certain minimum entitlement (see below). As with rights issues, the offer is normally of ordinary shares of the company, but other types of security or assets are occasionally used.

(ii) Procedures and documentation

The procedures involved in an open offer are broadly similar to a rights issue. The main difference is that instead of receiving a provisional allotment letter, shareholders are sent an application form to apply for the number of new shares they wish.

Shareholders will have a certain assured or guaranteed entitlement, which by convention is approximately the same as their provisional allotment would have been if the issue had been made by way of rights.

As an example, if a company with 100 million shares in issue wished to make an open offer of 26 million new shares in order to raise a certain amount, the assured entitlement for shareholders might be set at say 1-for-4. If the company wished to be more precise, it could set the entitlement at 26-for-100, but it would not be obliged to do so.

Other documentation in terms of circulars, underwriting and disclosure is the same as for a rights issue. The documents require registration with the relevant authorities as is the case for a rights issue.

(iii) Trading

The most significant difference between an open offer and a rights issue is that the application form which shareholders receive under the open offer procedure is personal, and not transferable. Consequently, it cannot be bought and sold in the market and there is no method of trading in the nil paid entitlements. This means that the open offer is more of a shotgun approach – shareholders can either apply or not, but if they do not they are likely to be diluted.

The open offer procedure is sometimes criticised on these grounds. The shareholder who would like to take up his entitlement but does not have funds to do so has no means of realising the value inherent in the offer. Unlike a rights issue, he cannot sell in the market either to compensate himself for the 'ex offer' effect or to raise sufficient funds to take up a portion of his entitlement. Both these options are available to him under the rights issue procedure.

Management on the other hand may perceive an advantage in the lack of trading. In a rights issue, the price of the nil paid rights sometimes comes under pressure as shareholders who dislike the call for further funds 'dump' their rights in the market at whatever price they can get. This may have a knock-on effect on the price of the shares, damaging confidence and jeopardising the success of the offer. If shareholders have a choice only between taking up their entitlements and letting them lapse, they may be more inclined to 'put up and shut up'.

(iv) Pricing

Because shareholders do not have the option of trading their nil paid entitlements, the price at which an open offer is made is more sensitive than a rights issue. Management usually tries to keep the discount narrow, although a 10–20% discount to the ex-offer price is likely to be required to attract underwriting on a commercial basis. Even if the pricing is relatively tight at the time the open offer is announced, shareholders are not protected against a subsequent rise in share price if the offer is well received. If such a rise does occur, shareholders have no choice but to take up their entitlements if they want to avoid dilution.

(v) Timing

The time required to complete the documentation for an open offer is broadly similar to a rights issue. However, one of the reasons for the 2/3 week acceptance period for rights is to allow sufficient time for shareholders to have a reasonable opportunity to deal in their rights nil paid. This constraint does not apply to open offers and consequently it would be possible to have a shorter acceptance period. As a practical matter, stock exchange authorities may not wish to be seen to discriminate in favour of the open offer method by allowing a shorter timetable than for rights.

(vi) Shareholders' approval

As an open offer does not ensure pro rata entitlements and there is no ability to trade in the market, this procedure is usually made subject to prior approval by shareholders in general meeting.

II   PLACINGS

(i) Nature of a placing

Existing shareholders are not normally given the opportunity to participate in a placing; instead the shares are sold direct to third parties. The term 'placing' implies that the securities being placed are not offered generally to the public but rather to a group of selected investors. If such investors are professionals and already knowledgeable about the company, the need to register issue document-ation with the authorities is usually avoided. Placings are normally organised by merchant banks or stockbrokers, or the two acting in combination. Depending on the size of the placing, a syndicate of 'placees' may be formed with institutions ranked by the size of their participation.

(ii) Placement in advance of listing

Placings may be made with the investment funds of merchant banks or other venture capitalists at an early stage in a company's development, before the shares are actively traded or a listing is obtained. This type of transaction is referred to as a private placement, meaning that there will be no attempt at this stage to interest the general public in the shares. The investors will be principally major clients of the merchant bank or other institution organising the private placement. Companies which accept an injection of capital from such sources should recognise that they will come under considerable pressure from their new shareholders to go public as soon as practicable. Such investors look to achieve a degree of marketability for their investment within, say, three to five years.

A placing or a series of placings can serve to establish a wide enough spread of shareholders to apply for a listing via an introduction. A placing can also be used as the method of marketing the shares at the time when a company goes public. In some countries, stock exchange authorities frown on this practice, as it favours selected clients of the underwriters and stockbrokers. Public investors may not have a genuine opportunity to get in 'at the ground floor'.

(iii) Placing with clawback

In this format, a placing differs little from an open offer. Presentationally, instead of shareholders having an assured entitlement and underwriters taking up any shares not applied for, the sequence is reversed. The shares are placed with investors in the first instance, on terms that if any shareholders wish to take up their proportional entitlement, such shares will be 'clawed back' from the placees. Existing shareholders' position is consequently protected.

For this procedure to be practicable, the placees must be prepared to be flexible in the amount of shares they receive. Most placees would prefer to know with certainty how many shares they will take; however, the clawback mechanism makes this difficult to predict. Placees may feel they are on a hiding to nothing – if the issue proves attractive, the level of clawback will be high; if it is not, the issue will remain with the placees.

For the company, this mechanism has attractions. The issue is safely placed and yet shareholders still have a chance to participate. There is no under- or over-subscription announcement, as is the case with a rights issue or an open offer.

(iv) Placing under a mandate from shareholders

Even in jurisdictions where the rights issue method is favoured, it is normally possible for the directors to receive a mandate from shareholders in general meeting to issue shares up to a certain level, say 10% or 20% of the current issued share capital.

This gives management great flexibility to take advantage of strong market conditions when they arise. Documentation for an issue of this type usually consists of a simple subscription or underwriting agreement, a set of board minutes and a press announcement, all of which can be finalised in a day. If new shares are involved, issue and completion are normally subject only to a listing for the shares being granted by the stock exchange authorities, which might take perhaps one week. This efficient procedure allows the placing to be priced very close to market, while the market risks which can overtake the longer rights issue timetable are virtually eliminated.

If there is a substantial shareholder, the procedure can be streamlined still further. The shares can be sold for immediate settlement by the substantial holder who agrees to use the proceeds to subscribe for new shares. The company will normally pay or refund all the expenses of the exercise in such circumstances. The substantial shareholder may on occasions subscribe for more shares than it sells so as to maintain its percentage holding in the enlarged share capital.

A placing of this type is limited in the amount of funds which can be raised and in most circumstances there is no opportunity for existing shareholders to participate. Nevertheless, it is a useful avenue for the company owing to its high degree of certainty and very short timetable.

(v) Vendor placing

While it may suit the company to pay for shares or assets by means of a new issue of its own securities, it may not necessarily be convenient or acceptable to the vendors to retain the shares which they receive. In these circumstances, a vendor placing may be arranged as an integral part of the transaction. In a vendor placing, the shares issued to the vendors of the assets are immediately placed on to third parties who have been lined up by the company or its financial advisers in advance. The third parties will normally be institutions who are already shareholders of the company or who through existing contacts with stockbrokers or merchant banks are known to be receptive to taking a significant investment. As is the case with a normal placing, timing can be very rapid. A vendor placing would normally be underwritten or carried out on a fully committed basis since it is unlikely that the vendors will accept any other terms in such circumstances.

(vi) Timing

(a) Speed

The great advantage of placings is speed. Because of the sophistication of the participants (normally institutions and other major investors), a placing can be carried out very quickly. It may be completed within one trading day or even a few hours. This assumes that some preparatory sounding out will have been done by the organisers of the placing. Such preparations can be carried out without committing the company to the placing or making any public announcement.

(b) Flexibility

One of the advantages of a placing is that a company and its advisers are not locked into a particular timetable. Timing can be adjusted to correspond to the state of the market. The company and its advisers can await favourable conditions to launch the operation.

(c) Favourable market conditions

Placings are most common in periods of strong institutional demand for securities. These tend to coincide with periods of high market activity overall. In such conditions, the ability to pick up a substantial block of securities at a fixed price may be valuable to institutions. The alternative is to carry out a programme of market purchases over a short period of time which may have the effect of pushing up the price against the purchaser.

(vii) **Pricing and market reaction**

(a) Narrow discount

If the securities to be placed are already listed, pricing is set at a discount to the prevailing market price on the assumption that the placees would have the alternative of buying the shares in the open market. In normal circumstances, a discount of 10% to the market price (or less) will be sufficient. Because of the short time taken to complete a placing, the discount is not required to cushion a long period of exposure as in the case of a rights issue, where shareholders may be given three weeks to make up their minds. In circumstances where there is a strong institutional demand for the shares, the placing price may be very near the market price. In difficult conditions, a higher discount may have to be offered.

The advisers handling the placing will also take into account the level of market trading in the shares and the recent price movements. A sharp rise in the price of the securities to be placed shortly before the placing operation may be viewed with some scepticism.

(b) Keeping the market informed

Placings can give rise to some confusion in the market. Companies and their advisers may be reluctant to announce a placing until it has been successfully completed in case any problems are encountered and the placing is called off. This may have the effect that rumours arise concerning a market operation being underway about which clarification from the company is delayed. In addition, some participants in the market will have been offered shares and will be aware of the situation whereas others will not. In the case of a placing of existing shares, there may not be an obligation to make an announcement at all which can lead to a prolonged period of doubt as to what has actually happened. Management of companies in which a placing is occurring with their knowledge should keep in mind the confusion which may arise and try to minimise it to the extent possible.

(viii) **Costs**

The costs for a placing are in general lower than for a rights issue or open offer, particularly if no substantial documentation is required.

The placing may be underwritten, in which case normal underwriting fees will apply. Alternatively, the placing may be handled on a best efforts basis in which case a brokerage or placing fee of say around 1–2% of the value of the securities would be charged.

The discount to the market price at which a placing is made will be considerably less than for a comparable rights issue, say 10% against 25%. However, whether this in some sense saves money for the company (in the case where new capital is being raised) is arguable. In a rights issue the benefit of the discount goes to the existing owners of the company whereas in a placing this benefit, although smaller, goes to third parties.

CONCLUSIONS

The table below sets out a comparison of the main features of rights issues, open offers and placings:

	Rights issue	*Open offer*	*Placing*
1. Shareholders participate pro rata	Yes	Through assured entitlement	Usually not
2. Pricing (approximate discount to market price 'ex issue')	15–25%	10–20%	0–10%
3. Trading in nil paid entitlements	Yes	No	No
4. Underwriting	Yes	Yes	Usually not
5. Registration of prospectus	Yes	Yes	Depends on number of placees
6. Approximate time to complete	6 weeks	6 weeks	1–2 weeks
7. Widens shareholder base	Usually not	Usually not	Yes
8. Over- or under-subscription announcement	Yes	Yes	No

As existing shareholders do not usually participate in placings, the price of the placing should be as close to market as possible. Since existing shareholders do participate in rights issues and (usually) open offers, pricing is less sensitive; indeed, in the case of rights issues, a 'deep discount' (higher than the 20–30% range) may be adopted to avoid the need for underwriters (and the payment of underwriting fees). Normally, a 15–25% discount to the ex rights price is considered sufficient to encourage shareholders to take up their rights while still employing underwriters as a fall-back. This level of discount should also ensure that the nil paid rights will have a reasonable value, which promotes market-ability when trading commences. Since the main distinguishing feature of rights issues is this ability to trade in the nil paid rights, it makes little sense to price the issue so tightly that trading in the rights is inhibited.

In management's eyes, the small discount to market and the speed and certainty of completion makes the placing method highly attractive. Management may feel that in some sense they have done a 'better deal' for the company by issuing shares at a price close to market. On occasions, a large rights issue or open offer can depress the market price of the shares below the theoretical 'ex rights' or 'ex open offer' adjustment and towards the issue price itself, as the market contemplates the issue of a large number of shares at that price. In addition, the speed of completion and, in some cases, the lesser documentation involved in a placing means that the risk of a change in market conditions during the issue period is greatly reduced. In addition, the argument can be made that a placing gives management the ability to widen the shareholder base and attract institutions who might feel, particularly in a growing company, that the market is too narrow to build up the size of stake an institution would look for. Whether this is a benefit to existing shareholders or more a convenience to management is not entirely clear.

These same institutions are however among the firmest defenders of the rights principle in a more mature company. In taking this position, they may argue that they are championing the rights of all shareholders, small and large. However, large shareholders tend to be approached by the manager of the issue to act as sub-underwriters as well. Since they normally support a rights issue as a convenient way to re-invest cash flow, the underwriting is fully covered and can be considered either as an effective discount on the rights price or as a source of fee income.

The question of rights issue or open offer versus placing is one of the areas in which the perspectives of management and existing shareholders can differ sharply. In theory, their differing interests should be reconciled by appeal to what is to the wider benefit of the company. In practice, objectivity may be difficult to achieve when a professional management's understandable desire for a bigger and wider equity base is matched with shareholders' keen eye to their short-term financial advantage.

Part 4

Takeovers, mergers and disposals

Introduction

Part 4 of this book deals with takeovers, mergers and disposals. This Introduction is intended to explain some basic terms and concepts and to present an overview of the topics covered in the individual chapters.

Why takeovers are made (see ch 13 below)

The reasons why takeovers are made are examined under three headings. The first is commercial and deals with such aspects as increase in market share, growth, synergy, security of supply and diversification. Acquisition of a business in the same field (a 'horizontal' acquisition) will increase the combined group's market share. This type of acquisition is the most easily justified in terms of 'fit' but may fall foul of anti-monopoly legislation. Growth can be achieved economically and swiftly by acquisition but should not become an end in itself.

Synergy is the theory that two plus two can equal more than four. This proposition is a major argument that merger and acquisition activity benefits the economy as a whole. An acquisition primarily undertaken to secure supplies or sales is called 'vertical'. Particularly in a process industry, it is convenient to bring all the stages of operation under the control of one group but it can complicate business relationships.

Diversification, or spreading the risk, can be justified on a commonsense level – do not keep all your eggs in one basket. It is also the subject of increasingly sophisticated analysis. Acquisitions which fall into this category are called 'conglomerate' to distinguish them from horizontal or vertical integration.

The second heading is financial. An 'asset stripper' will concentrate on obtaining a discount to a company's net asset value, intending to recoup the purchase price from the sale of assets. Another financial objective may be to increase earnings per share following the acquisition. If an acquiror buys a business less highly rated on the stock exchange than their own by way of a share exchange, earnings per share of the enlarged group will rise. This strategy requires ever more and bigger acquisitions to sustain it. It also depends on the acquiror's price earnings ratio not being averaged down following the acquisitions. The opposite effect, when earnings per share declines as a result of a transaction, is called 'dilution'.

An acquiror may be able to reduce the gearing of the combined group by buying a cash rich company. A company with highly rated paper will attempt to buy assets for shares, increasing its asset backing per share and creating a platform for a further stage of growth.

Personal ambition is a major factor in making acquisitions. Personal commitment may be necessary to push a deal through at sticky moments. Some acquisitions are special situations, embarked on to obtain a management team, a stock exchange listing, access to tax losses or important operating licences.

Acquisition search: developing criteria, generating opportunities and preliminary screening (see ch 14 below)

The multiplicity of motives for acquisitions spills over into the planning process, complicating the development of criteria. Once the criteria have been set, the company needs to ensure that it makes effective use of all available market channels to generate opportunities. This process often throws up a bewildering range of half-formed ideas. Discipline is required in preliminary screening if analysts are not to be overwhelmed by the wealth of possibilities.

Criteria can be looked at under the same general headings as objectives, that is commercial, financial and special situations. In addition, size and the availability of finance will be critical. Commercial criteria include type of industry and the attitude of the management and workforce. Financial criteria can be set in beguilingly precise numbers but a degree of flexibility is essential. Whether paper is acceptable may be relevant. If an acquisition is for a specific purpose, the criteria more or less set themselves. An upper size limit should be set – few companies can take over companies much larger than themselves. Below a certain size on the other hand, an acquisition may just not be worth the effort. Size can be judged by reference to various factors, including price, turnover, capital which will be tied up and profitability. Finance will be more readily available for asset rich companies or those with a highly predictable cash flow.

Opportunities are generated internally and externally. Executives working in an industry will know more about it than outside professionals. Constructive use of this pool of knowledge should be encouraged. In addition, a company may establish its own merger and acquisition unit. External sources include advertising and the use of intermediaries. Merger brokers operate aggressively in the field. Experienced merchant bankers see a constant flow of opportunities across their desks. A merchant bank should be able to offer a package of finance to back its proposals. A close relationship with a merchant bank or other acquisition professionals has proved an ingredient in the growth of many business empires.

Preliminary screening boils down to a more rigorous and practical application of criteria to the range of opportunities which have been generated. A 'nose' for a realistic proposal can save significant waste of time. Screening should take into account the overall impact of an acquisition on the acquiror's business. The factors include increased official scrutiny which may result, the after-shock of a contested battle and the extent of the risk of the acquisition to the organisation as a whole. Unsatisfactory or downright bad acquisitions are an unsettlingly common experience. The best time to avoid them is at the screening stage when minds are open. A hard look at how effective a company's screening process is can pay large dividends.

Acquisition analysis: collecting and evaluating information (see ch 15 below)

A certain amount of information may be obtained from public sources on an anonymous basis. However, the information required by regulations to be available for public inspection is limited in scope and may be considerably out of date. The tightening of disclosure under listing requirements is helpful in researching public companies.

Except where a bid is expected to be contested, the target company itself will in due course be approached for information. This approach should be handled with kid gloves. Information requested should be kept to a reasonable minimum to avoid antagonising the vendors. This also prevents the acquiror's analysts being overwhelmed by figures. The information requested should be tailored to the key characteristics of the business being examined. An acquiror should be ready to accept a confidentiality agreement covering the information supplied. The really critical points are often quite small in number. A battery of questions directed at a particular aspect is likely to tip the acquiror's negotiating hand. Sensitive topics may be left to be covered by a warranty in the sale and purchase agreement. If they are made the subject of probing questions, the vendor may feel he is engaged more in an inquisition than an acquisition.

A sample questionnaire is included in ch 15. When requesting any of the items the acquiror should ask himself whether the information would make any difference to his decision to proceed or not.

If the information confirms that the acquisition is of interest in principle, the next step is to set a price range and decide on the type of consideration. Value in the context of an acquisition is not absolute and will be influenced by the acquiror's objectives. An asset stripper will need a significant discount to open market value on a willing buyer, willing seller basis in order to cater for a substantial programme of rapid sales. Vendors may be expected to sell at a cyclical peak in earnings so that an apparently reasonable price earnings ratio may prove illusory. On the other hand, a purchaser may increase the estimate of the target company's earnings to take into account savings from rationalisation after the merger.

In the case of conglomerates, it is likely that adding together valuations of each constituent business will produce a higher figure than one overall valuation based on net assets or earnings. This is legitimate provided that each business can stand on its own and could be sold as a separate unit.

The share price of a listed company is only an approximate guide to the price which may be needed for a successful acquisition. Market price relates to smallish transactions and so contains no premium for control. To overcome investor inertia, some premium, say at least 20%, must be offered unless the market price has some 'froth' in it. Shareholders may be reluctant to sell in any event at a price less than they originally paid for the shares. They may also be influenced by prices for other deals – 'market comparables' – and industry rules of thumb for the worth of businesses.

It is useful to set an upper price limit for an acquisition before negotiations begin. Although some flexibility is desirable to cater for fresh information becoming available as it often does during a bid, the dangers of being carried away 'in hot pursuit' are acute.

Acquisition analysis is usually based on long-term expected results. An acquisition which appears attractive on this basis may nevertheless not have an immediate beneficial effect on the published accounts of the acquiror. The market, on the other hand, tends to judge a management over the short term. If earnings per share are diluted following an acquisition, the market may not necessarily appreciate the longer-term benefits in view.

A package of different forms of payment, particularly the use of convertible securities, may help to alleviate the problem of dilution. An example of how this works in practice is given.

Other factors to be taken into consideration include goodwill, pre-acquisition profits and the effect of the acquisition on the balance sheet and gearing of the enlarged group. Borrowing restrictions and covenants based on other financial ratios will need checking.

Strategies for control: structure of offer and terms of payment (see ch 16 below)

The task of gaining control can be approached from various different angles. It may prove advantageous to purchase a major asset directly rather than the company which owns it. If a company is purchased, its worth, particularly in the case of a private company, may lie more in shareholder loans than in share capital. It is important to ensure that the entire shareholders' funds are purchased. Care is needed if shareholder loans have not borne interest and the price is calculated on earnings.

If a company has financial problems, effective control may be acquired by purchasing bank or other third party loans without the need to acquire shares. It may be possible to negotiate conversion rights to be attached to such loans. If the equity does subsequently prove of value, the acquiror's interests are protected. Control may also be obtained by subscribing new shares, thus strengthening the capital base of the company, rather than the purchase of existing shares. This route may avoid the need for a general offer in countries where an offer might otherwise be triggered under a takeover code.

If a purchaser decides to take the route of buying shares in a company, he should still consider whether he needs to buy the entire share capital. The advantage of having 100% control is principally that it eliminates any need to provide information to outside shareholders and protect their interests. If he controls 100%, the acquiror has unfettered access to the target company's assets and cash flow. On the other hand, the funds required are obviously decreased if less than 100% is purchased. A listing for the shares may be continued. The loyalty of management, employees and customers may be more easily retained. Partial control usually involves a holding of over 50% but in the case of a widely-held company a level as low as 20% may confer control. At the lower levels, an option to buy further shares becomes particularly valuable.

There are a number of ways of paying for control. Cash has the great merit of simplicity. It can be raised from existing surplus resources of the company supplemented by bank borrowings. Cash resources may be topped up by issues of securities particularly 'junk bonds'. Junk bonds have been popular in the case of leveraged buy-outs where a group of investors is put together for the purposes of acquiring a company. Where management is involved this type of operation is commonly called a management buy-out. Tax implications and presentational aspects may also affect the decision as to whether to fund a bid in cash. In some jurisdictions, legal problems may arise if it could be argued that a company is giving assistance in the purchase of its own shares.

Payment may be made on a deferred basis rather than for immediate settlement. A purchaser may need assistance in completing the transaction in the form of vendor finance. Deferred payment may also serve as a disguised reduction in price where the nominal amount paid is a sensitive issue. A deferred payment structure allows for a period of investigation before all payments are handed over. It also allows for 'earn-outs' – where the total amount payable is related to future performance. The idea of an earn-out, while attractive in principle, can be difficult to put into effect and the difficulties increase with the length of the earn-out period.

Securities of the acquiror may be offered as consideration. Ordinary shares of the acquiror are the most straightforward choice, but may have to be underwritten. Specific requirements of the acquiror or the vendor may result in a new class of shares being issued with special rights to meet the situation, for example, high dividend income or a dividend linked to the results of the business being acquired. Debt securities can also be useful where additional income is required. These are most appropriate where the acquisition is asset rich. The debt may be made convertible into ordinary shares. Warrants may be included in the package as a sweetener.

Making the offer (see ch 17 below)

The time when analysis stops and the initial approach is made is a critical phase. A clumsy approach may do irretrievable damage. Careful thought is needed to identify the right tactics. There may be some parties connected with the target company who are more sympathetic than others. An acquiror should be alert to a possible conflict of interest between shareholders who may simply be interested in the highest offer and management who are concerned for their jobs and power base. The use of an intermediary whose interest lies in reconciling the objectives of buyer and seller may be productive. With a public company, special efforts to maintain secrecy will be required. Pressure may mount from the authorities for an announcement before the parties are ready.

Negotiations depend on the skill of the participants to a large degree. Knowledge of the party on the opposite side of the table is fundamental. A front line negotiator, however experienced, must rely on a support team.

A recommendation of the terms of the offer by the target company's board is probably the single most critical factor for success. It can be regarded as having a value of its own. To obtain a recommendation it may be necessary to keep something in reserve so that the vendors feel they have won some concessions during the negotiations.

In the heat of negotiation, it is difficult to resist paying too much to clinch a deal. Limits set beforehand are useful safeguards. A seller on the other hand may play the reluctant bride and try to create a sense of rivalry even where no actual rivals exist. He may for tactical reasons appear willing to negotiate whether or not he is in fact prepared to do so. The acquiror must assess whether the negotiations are progressing or are simply a play for time.

In the case of a private company, there is little alternative to continuing the negotiations or abandoning the transaction. Where a public company is being considered, the option exists to appeal to shareholders over the heads of the existing directors and management. As in any frontal assault, this course of action requires a certain amount of courage. The main weapon is price. There will no doubt be a price which is attractive even to loyal shareholders. The timing should be designed to catch the target at a moment of weakness for itself and at a period when the bidder can make positive comments about his own business. Hopefully, potential rivals may be preoccupied with other projects.

Purchases in the market in advance of the bid and during it will help to create a springboard. Rapid purchase of an effective controlling stake is known as a 'dawn raid'. The acquiror must take care not to fall foul of local rules governing accumulation of such stakes and of bidding up the target company's share price against itself.

The offer document addressed to the target shareholders will be used as a platform for criticising the target company and emphasising the attractions of the offer and trumpeting the virtues of the offeror. The degree of paper or cash in the offer should be tailored to suit the preferences of the shareholders of the target company as far as they can be ascertained.

The art of self-defence (see ch 18 below)

There are three types of counter measure which may be taken against an unwanted bid. The first, good housekeeping, covers areas which a competent management would attend to in any case. Second, there are measures which have a commercial basis but whose primary purpose is to repel an unexpected bid. Third, there are short-term expedients adopted to counter a specific hostile bid after it has been announced.

Good housekeeping is a continuous process. It includes monitoring the company's share price and trying to keep it in line with the underlying value of the company. A share repurchase programme may be used to good effect. The single most effective deterrent against an unwanted bid is a share price which fairly reflects the profit potential and asset backing of the company. As the company's shareholders will be the ultimate arbiters in a takeover battle it is important for management to know who they are, communicate with them and monitor significant changes. All announcements should be reviewed carefully with a view to their public relations impact. The directors should avoid giving any 'hostages to fortune' in the statements they release. Management should from time to time put themselves in the shoes of an aggressor and consider what steps he might take to rationalise the company after an acquisition. Incumbent management should not wait to initiate appropriate action as they know the company's potential better than any outside party.

Measures adopted primarily to repel an expected bid take some time and preparation to put in place. Changes to the procedures for holding meetings or electing directors can make it more difficult for an aggressor to succeed in taking control. Obstacles can be built into the voting capital and financial structure.

Defensive shareholdings can be created by voting pacts, placing blocks in friendly hands or by cross-holdings. Valuable assets can be sold or placed out of the reach of an aggressor. Acquisitions can be made of businesses which are not attractive to a bidder or which make the group too large for him to swallow. The bidder can be bought off through greenmail, although this practice may whet another predator's appetite. A company can distribute cash or securities to its own shareholders via a recapitalisation, in effect a home-grown LBO. Alternatively, a threatened company may open negotiations with a more congenial partner.

After an offer is announced, it can be opposed in various ways. New information can be released to demonstrate for example that the existing management is doing a good job and that the price offered is too cheap. Such information frequently involves a profit and dividend forecast and a revaluation of assets. The terms of the bid can be attacked and so can the bidder. The bid can be criticised for the level and type of consideration. It can be claimed to be opportunist since this is likely in some sense to be true. The motives of the bidder can be impugned.

Various other spoiling tactics can be employed. They are available equally whether the bid is good or bad. The laws and market regulations concerning takeovers can be invoked, with claims of violations of procedures and inadequate disclosure. Anti-monopoly rules may be brought into play and time limits skilfully manipulated.

In the closing stages of a bid, perhaps the most critical factor is whether the market price is at a premium to the offer. A programme of share purchases by friends of the target company may be helpful, but must be carefully handled. Extensive advertising and public relations exercises may be mounted through the media. Stockbrokers and other professionals may be enlisted to lobby major shareholders. Appeals to shareholder and customer loyalty, and even patriotism, may be made. As a last resort, a management in distress may seek a 'white knight' to rescue it from the clutches of the hostile bidder.

Leveraged buy-outs (see ch 19 below)

LBOs are acquisitions funded largely by debt. Where they are management led, they are called MBOs. Although they existed previously, they grew rapidly and became considerably more sophisticated during the eighties. The reasons for their development include the reversal of the earlier conglomerate trend and the rise of the entrepreneur. The political climate, the availability of finance, the risk/reward equation and technical factors such as tax were also favourable to their growth.

A pre-requisite is a willing seller and a strong management team. The business must be capable of generating surplus cash from operations and other measures and should be stable and well-established. A key task for the management team is to put together a convincing business plan. Negotiation of the terms can be difficult with the team having to deal with their bosses, which may put them at a psychological disadvantage. However, they hold some cards, such as control of information flow and the 'nuclear option' of a walk-out.

A key area which distinguishes LBOs and MBOs from other acquisitions is the structure of the financing. This is like a pyramid, with a small (sometimes very small) amount of pure equity supported by quasi-equity, mezzanine finance and more conventional senior debt. A 'ratchet' may operate to increase management's percentage interest in the equity as specified targets are met. Junk bonds have played a large part in the financing which has become more conservative since the consolidation in this market. The working capital needs of the business after the LBO must not be lost sight of in the intricacies of the financing scheme.

After the LBO comes the hard work of managing the business under severe cash constraints. Areas of conflict can arise between management and financiers which often lead to a re-negotiation of the original financing package. Both management and the sophisticated investors who back LBOs are likely to keep their eyes firmly fixed on the exit which can come from a refinancing, a trade sale or a flotation. This last route is ironic considering that many MBOs result from listed companies 'going private'.

The popularity of LBOs has risen and fallen with almost equal speed. However, they are rooted in fundamentals of commercial life and human nature and are therefore likely to prove an enduring feature of the corporate finance scene.

Takeover Code and techniques of deal-making (see ch 20 below)

Takeover codes have been introduced in the UK and countries where securities regulations are based on UK practice. In the US, takeovers are primarily regulated by law. There is a lively debate between the flexibility of a voluntary code as opposed to the rigours of a legal system.

Under the voluntary Code, a Panel or Committee is established to make rulings while day-to-day administration is handled by an Executive. The Code is based on four general principles. The first – that all shareholders should be treated equally – is not regarded as self-evident in all markets. Its most important tenet is that all shareholders should receive a cash offer when control (variously defined) of a company changes. To bolster this rule, the concept of a group 'acting in concert' to control a company is important but can cause difficulties of interpretation. The second principle is that adequate information must be made available to shareholders to assess an offer. The Code sets out information to be included in documents and announcements published during an offer. Profit forecasts and asset valuations are a sensitive area. The third principle relates to a fair market in the shares of the participants and covers disclosure of dealings and their consequences. The final principle is that an offer should not be frustrated, so that shareholders have no chance to decide on its merits. The full body of rules of the Code are partly extensions of the general principles and partly deal with procedural aspects such as timetable and methods of acceptance. As further rulings are made, the Committee issues practice notes to keep the market informed.

An acquisition of a private company can only be carried through by negotiation with directors or major shareholders. The articles of association of private companies usually contain pre-emption rights and restrictions on the transfer of shares. Even a willing seller (and the intended purchaser) must take these into account if the transaction relates to less than 100% of the company.

The transaction will be documented by a sale and purchase agreement. This is made up of a number of fairly standard sections. One common area of difficulty is the extent of the warranties about the company being sold which a seller will be expected to give to the purchaser.

A business which has encountered financial difficulty may come under the control of a receiver or liquidator. In order to separate a continuing business from the problems of the past, a new subsidiary may be set up and the relevant assets 'hived down'. This will allow the purchaser to buy a business which starts with a clean sheet. It is unlikely that a receiver or liquidator will give warranties.

A much wider range of options is open when a public company is the target. An acquisition of a significant stake may be possible through a dawn raid. In the UK, rules have been introduced governing substantial acquisitions of shares (SARs), the effect of which is to slow down the pace of acquisition and force greater disclosure. A partial offer may be made for less than 100% of the share capital. A full bid may be made by way of a public offer, or, in some jurisdictions, a legal procedure called a scheme of arrangement. A scheme is an all or nothing procedure and has advantages in terms of saving transfer duty and speed in reaching 100% control, which make it a suitable method for privatising listed companies. It is more cumbersome overall and requires the recommendation of the target company. All the shares of the target company may be acquired under a public offer if acceptances are received from a minimum number of the shareholders to whom the offer is made.

Whether a partial offer, full offer or scheme of arrangement is employed, extensive documentation is circulated to shareholders on behalf of the acquiror. These documents cover areas laid down by regulation such as financial and legal information and disclosures of interest. Comments from the chairman of the offeror or offeree are also included and a letter from the merchant bank arguing the pros and cons of the offer. If shareholders' meetings are required, the notices will be attached to the letter.

Roles of professional advisers (see ch 21 below)

Mergers and acquisitions require a combination of skills to bring about a successful conclusion.

The prime movers are often merchant banks who have taken the lead in building up large departments of full-time professionals specialising in merger and acquisition work. They are actively involved in generating ideas and putting up proposals. They may assist with valuations and advise on the type of payment. They often play a role in the negotiating process. In markets where a takeover code operates, the merchant bank monitors compliance, submits draft documents to the secretariat and discusses contentious points with them.

The merchant bank normally has the role of co-ordinating the input of all parties involved in the production of the offer document to be sent to the target company's shareholders. The offeror looks to the merchant bank for assistance in putting together the financing of the offer, either directly by underwriting or loans or through its market skill in putting together a syndicate.

An accountant's report commissioned by the purchaser on the target company's business is often a basic building block. A request for an investigation may meet various degrees of resistance from the vendor. In compiling the report the accountants will highlight any items of potential under- or over-valuation and comment more generally on the adequacy of systems and the competence of management. They will be on the look-out for one-time adjustments to the accounts which could, for example, produce unrepresentative earnings used as a basis for pricing.

The accountants will be best placed to advise on the effect an acquisition may have on the acquiror's balance sheet and profit and loss account. Technical matters to be reviewed include the cost of acquisition in the acquiror's books, goodwill on consolidation and the extent of pre-acquisition profits.

In an acquisition of any complexity, legal advice will be required at an early stage. Procedural matters such as the conduct of meetings may be a critical element in deciding on tactics. Many lawyers are skilled negotiators and play a leading role in negotiations as well as providing advice behind the scenes. If a heads of agreement is used at a preliminary stage, drafting is almost inseparable from negotiating.

The sales and purchase agreement is a major responsibility of the lawyers involved. When a public offer document is prepared, the lawyers will have an overall brief to ensure rules and regulations are complied with and that proper disclosure is made. If the takeover is by way of a scheme of arrangement, the legal requirements will determine the procedure and timetable for the entire transaction.

A number of tactics, particularly in defence, are the province of the lawyers. Legal moves to repel or delay an unwelcome bidder are a major part of any well-organised defensive campaign. Offers and defences require a plethora of approvals by boards and individual directors which it would normally be the responsibility of the lawyers to organise correctly.

Tax advice is of critical importance. The correct structure for an acquisition can make the difference between a transaction which is highly rewarding and one which is marginal. Tax aspects include transfer duty when shares or assets are bought or sold, capital duty when securities are issued, tax on the income stream generated by the acquisition, tax on the eventual sale of the investment, the tax liabilities of the company being acquired and the tax position of the vendor shareholders. Tax advice may be provided by the accountants or lawyers working on the acquisition or may be given by tax specialists.

Where an acquisition involves listed companies, the involvement of a firm of stockbrokers is highly desirable. The skills and contacts of public relations consultants are likely to be required to ensure that their clients' arguments are getting enough air-time, to smarten up the offer documents and announcements and to lobby politicians and interest groups if necessary. From time to time professionals from other fields will be called upon for assistance. With large numbers of specialists involved, the role of co-ordination becomes as difficult as it is important.

Disposals (see ch 22 below)

It is logical for a management to spend as much energy and enterprise on identifying and preparing for disposals as it does on acquisitions. This rarely proves to be the case. Acquisitions are associated with growth and achievement. Disposals carry a connotation of decline and failure. Employees are worried about their own positions. A major task therefore is for management to encourage a positive attitude towards disposals. A management buy-out, where the attitude of at least a portion of management will be enthusiastic, is always worth consideration.

One of the prerequisites for a rational approach to disposals is a fair system of measuring performance. Management accounts may include allocations of costs and income which do not provide an appropriate basis for considering a disposal.

When a company has been identified for disposal, it should be groomed so as to appear in the best light possible to a purchaser. The purchaser will look at key factors and statistics. The seller can anticipate this analysis and prepare answers for the questions which may arise.

Succesful sales depend critically on timing. It may be advantageous to sell the company at a period when it appears to the purchaser that there is still something to go for. At this point in the cycle, finance may also be more readily available. Information must be provided to the purchaser but sometimes to supply everything asked for is counter-productive. Creating an auction-room atmosphere and encouraging a little rivalry can do wonders for the price achieved.

Intermediaries have an important role to play. They allow the principals to be flexible without fear of showing weakness. A skilful intermediary will make both parties feel he is on their side. A realistic vendor will realise that he may have to assist a purchaser with financing. A willingness to take some of the vendor's shares helps promote a feeling of partnership.

If a company is forced to make a disposal to raise money, one of the more promising assets of the group may have to be selected. Market perception of the vendor's financial position will be critical and skill is required in achieving the desired image. Other reasons for sales include defence against an unwanted takeover, a buy-out by a group organised by management and streamlining a company for flotation.

CHAPTER 13

Why takeovers are made

To gain an understanding of the processes involved in merger and acquisition activities, it is necessary to have some appreciation of the driving forces which lie behind them. Most of these forces are rational and it may well be that no acquisition of significant size, at least in a public company, is likely to proceed unless it is capable of rational justification. However, mergers and acquisitions form an area of business activity where the emotions and instincts of those closely involved play a major part. Why a particular deal is being progressed in a particular way becomes a complex matter. Anticipating the next move becomes as much a matter of psychology as of logic.

The reasons for making acquisitions are probably as numerous as people who make them. However, motives can be usefully grouped under three headings:

I   Commercial;
II   Financial;
III   Special situations.

Very often of course there will be elements of all three present in a particular acquisition.

I   COMMERCIAL

Many acquisitions are designed primarily to strengthen the commercial position of the company. This may be looked at from the following aspects:

(i)   Increase in market share/reduction of competition

An acquisition of a company in the same general line of business will increase the acquiror's market share in that sector. At the same time, the acquiror may strengthen its market position in another way by eliminating an active competitor. Acquisitions of this type (called horizontal) are the most easily justified by the acquiror in terms of 'fit'. A target company in the same line of business is likely to have a broadly similar structure and organisation. Its business should be fairly easy for the acquiror to understand and assimilate. Specific executives may be known to management. The industry grapevine will probably have alerted the acquiror to any significant problems that may exist and some which no doubt do not. After the acquisition, there may be obvious cost savings through reductions in the workforce, elimination of duplicated functions and economies of scale.

The opposite side of the coin is that mergers of this type are the most likely to attract official scrutiny. This is particularly so in jurisdictions where, and at periods when, anti-monopoly regulatory bodies are strong or fears of unemployment are high.

The very reasons which make this type of acquisition attractive, principally reduction in competition and the elimination of duplication leading to redundancies, are the factors which can most readily unite opposition groups.

(ii) Growth

Management has the responsibility for determining the future direction and policy of the business. The development of a new product range or entry into a new technology or geographical area can be achieved more quickly and perhaps more effectively by acquiring an existing business than by starting from scratch. In sectors which have a depressed stock market rating, it may also be possible to acquire assets and facilities through an acquisition at a lower price than the cost to build comparable 'green field' facilities. It must be borne in mind, however, that it is rare for the assets acquired to be precisely what the acquiror would have wished or in the condition it would desire.

Growth can become an end in itself, perhaps because it is taken as a proxy for dynamic management. In the short term, whether growth is simply growth in assets and sales or whether it is also growth in profitability and earnings per share can become obscured. Comparing the year-by-year performance of a fast-growing group on a consistent basis is a difficult task. Pressure is growing on companies to provide greater analysis of sources of profits in their accounts.

(iii) Synergy

It has been argued that in certain circumstances a complex business is worth more than the sum of its parts, in other words, two plus two can equal more than four. The thrust of this argument is that by putting organisations together the performance of the components can be enhanced and their potential increased by feeding off each other's strengths. Examples might be a company with a good product range combining with a company with strong marketing and distributing capability or a research-oriented company combining with a traditional manufacturer. Size alone can confer benefits, for example when negotiating with suppliers, customers and financiers.

In practice it has been difficult to demonstrate that these theoretical advantages have been realised. It is fairly easy to show that costs have been reduced following a horizontal merger. Benefits from synergy tend to be less tangible and more difficult to quantify particularly when accounting systems may not have been designed to capture the relevant information. Despite this, synergy remains one of the most important theoretical bases used to justify mergers and acquisitions because it opens up the prospect of benefits to the economy as a whole. The concept of synergy is therefore an important counter to arguments in favour of restraints on merger activity.

(iv) Security of supply and sales

Critical business relationships exist with suppliers and customers. In some industries, for example textiles and petroleum, the relationships are so close that it is difficult for the functions of supply, production and marketing to be conducted on a totally arm's length basis. There is therefore a tendency for these activities to be controlled inside one group. An industry where this type of merger has occurred is called 'vertically integrated'.

It should be said that what is presented as compelling business logic at one time seems later to owe much to herd instinct. An increased availability of a previously scarce raw material, for example crude oil, decreases the importance of a guaranteed source of supply. Although vertical integration brings more aspects of the business under top management's control, it also complicates the allocation of profits and costs. The performance of executives in charge of a particular division cannot be properly evaluated and monitored if key variables are out of their hands. Initiative may be stifled as freedom of action of the various parts of the organisation are constrained by the interests of others.

(v) Diversification

Management may seek to reduce risks by acquiring a portfolio of assets or companies rather than being dependent on one product or industry. To combine in one group businesses which are not equally affected by prevailing economic factors and cycles should produce a more consistent overall performance than to be heavily dependent on one business. Complex analysis may seek to demonstrate this statistically, backing up the commonsense belief in not keeping 'all your eggs in one basket'.

Groups consisting of businesses which do not have particularly close commercial relationships with each other are called conglomerates. It has proved difficult to demonstrate that conglomerates have achieved a superior performance through reduction of risk. Their rise seems to have been partly a product of 'merger mania' and of the philosophy that a good manager can manage anything. However, the practical difficulties of controlling very diverse groups may have cancelled out the theoretical benefits of diversification. Conglomerates built up of disparate parts have at a later stage of their development tended to rationalise their activities. Management pick out certain core businesses, spinning off or disposing of 'non-core' companies.

II FINANCIAL

It is rare that the commercial attractions of a potential acquisition will be so compelling that the acquiror decides to buy at any price. It may happen on occasion if a very big group wishes for example to gain access to a new technology, but normally there must be an attractive financial basis. Financial attractions may be considered under a number of headings:

(i) Bargains

Few people can resist a real or perceived bargain. This is as true of companies as anything else. When bargains occur in the corporate field, it is usually due to some element of weakness. The weakness may be in the company itself because of declining profitability or liquidity problems. The weakness may lie with a controlling shareholder under pressure to sell. In the case of a public company, the market rating may be poor for some reason not directly connected with the company, for example the sector being out of fashion with investors.

Potential acquirors may have identified a company as an opportunity and be patiently waiting for the right moment. Bargain prices are often dependent on opportunism. A company which is ready to strike holds a distinct advantage and many a 'cash mountain' is earmarked (at least in principle) for this purpose. A popular moment to bid for a public company is after disappointing results have just been announced and before a recovery can be forecast.

(ii) Discount to asset value

This is probably the most popular and most reliable financial basis for an acquisition. Aggressive individuals or organisations have been labelled 'asset strippers' because they make no disguise that this is their primary motivation. However, eminently respectable companies may also make asset backing the primary focus of their analysis.

Analysis will be concentrated on the balance sheet of the target company. Book values will not be accepted as accurate assessments of present market value but each item will be scrutinised for potential appreciation and for losses. Liabilities will be examined to see if adequate provision has been made and to what extent liabilities expressed as long term could fall due earlier. Contingent liabilities and any 'off-balance sheet' items will be assessed. Many sources of information will be tapped. Some figures may be rough estimates or even guesses, so a considerable margin for error must be allowed. Allowing room for negotiation, a situation may not be of real interest unless the estimate of revised net asset value is, in the case of a public company, at least 50% higher than the prevailing market price.

The type of company which tends to attract most attention is one with substantial fixed assets and yet a lacklustre profit and dividend record. Over a period of time the company may come to be valued principally in relation to its profits and dividends rather than its asset backing. This situation is likely to reflect uninspired management in general.

It sometimes happens that assets become more valuable if put to some alternative use in an area in which the current management may have no expertise. Management may be adequate as regards the traditional business but not alert to some change in the outside environment. A classic example is a business operating a department store on a site which becomes ripe for redevelopment. Acquirors with expertise in a relevant area may be able to derive more benefit from a particular asset than its existing controllers, however well they run their traditional business. Certain intangible factors such as tax losses may only be valuable in the hands of someone capable of ensuring profits are earned in the relevant entity.

(iii) Increase in earnings per share

(a) Technical position

A company may increase its earnings per share by issuing shares to acquire another company rated at a lower price earnings multiple. A simplified example would be as follows:

EXAMPLE

Assume: (a) An all-share offer by the acquiror for 100% of the shares of the target company.
(b) The terms are based on the market prices of the shares of the two companies.

Position before the acquisition:

	Acquiror		*Target*
Latest earnings	100		50
Number of shares in issue	1000		1000
Earnings per share	0.10		0.05
Multiple on which shares are rated	12 times		8 times
Share price	1.20		0.40
Market capitalisation	1200		400
Terms of offer (based on respective market prices)	1 new share	*for*	3 existing shares

Effect of the acquisition on the Acquiror:

	Note	*Post-acquisition*
Earnings	1	150
Number of shares in issue	2	1333
Earnings per share	3	0.1125
Multiple	4	12 times
Share price	5	1.35
Market capitalisation	6	1800

Notes: 1. Addition of latest earnings of 100 and 50.
2. Addition of shares in issue of 1000 and 333 issued under the terms of the 1 for 3 offer.
3. Enlarged earnings of 150 divided by enlarged share capital of 1333.
4. It is assumed that the enlarged group will continue to be rated at acquiror's multiple of 12 times.

5. Earnings per share of 0.1125 and multiple of 12 times.
6. Share price of $1.35 multiplied by enlarged share capital of 1333.

(b) Practical effects

The increase in earnings per share, from 0.10 to 0.1125, is a simple question of mathematics, following from the assumption that the terms of the share exchange are based on respective market prices. (This is in fact an over-simplification, as normally a premium over market would have to be paid for the target.) The increase in the market price of the acquiror after the offer from $1.20 to $1.35 depends on whether the combined group remains rated at the multiple of the acquiror prior to the offer, that is 12 times. If it does, or at least holds at above the weighted average multiple of the acquiror and the target (weighted by size of earnings), the market capitalisation of the combined group will be higher than that of the two companies separately.

An aggressive company may have gained for itself a high market rating on the expectation of rapid growth in profits. These expectations can be fulfilled, at least in the short term, by acquisitions on terms such as those illustrated in the example. Indeed, they may be self-fulfilling for the moment in that the ability to grow by acquisition (apparently proved) may be part of the reason for the premium rating. However, unless the acquisitions are very skilful ones, the rating of the acquiror will in due course suffer as the proportion of earnings contributed by lowly-rated companies increases. In addition, the size and number of acquisitions at low ratings needed to maintain this strategy over a period of time becomes ever larger. Consequently, the strategy carries the seeds of its own failure unless the acquiror and/or the companies acquired are also capable of achieving organic growth.

(c) Cash offer

In the case of a cash offer, a similar effect will be achieved if the return from the business acquired at the purchase price is higher than the funding cost. The funding cost in the short term (as it will affect the reported earnings) could be considered either to be the cost of debt incurred to finance the purchase or, if surplus cash is used, the interest foregone on the cash deposits. In the longer term, if acquisitions are funded purely by cash or borrowings, the increased gearing is likely to require further equity issues.

(iv) Gearing

An acquisition by means of a share exchange of a company which has low borrowings or surplus cash is likely to reduce the financial gearing of the enlarged group. In an extreme form, the acquiring company may issue shares to purchase an investment trust or other company with highly liquid assets. This type of transaction may be seen more as a disguised equity issue than a true acquisition.

An acquiror may take the opportunity to change the balance of its capital structure. The terms of an acquisition may include the issue of unsecured loan stock or convertible securities in addition to ordinary shares and cash. By juggling with the proportions of such elements in the total consideration, the acquiring group can increase or decrease the proportion of long-term debt in its balance sheet and adjust its overall gearing.

(v) Opportunity to issue highly rated paper

In the growth cycle of an aggressive listed company, there tends to come a period when it attempts to issue its shares (which are not likely to be fully backed by net assets at the issue price) to third parties in return for assets. The market rating of a share in the short term is likely to be set by expectations of profit growth. Maintaining rapid increases in profits requires an additional accumulation of assets to be amassed to form a basis for a second phase of growth. The management of a company may therefore take the opportunity to issue paper at a time when its market rating and share price are high but its net asset backing low. Whether this strategy succeeds in producing the profits necessary to sustain the share price will depend on the potential of the assets acquired and the acquiror's ability to manage as well as to 'wheel and deal'.

III   SPECIAL SITUATIONS

In addition to the commercial and financial aspects, specialised factors may be involved in the selection of an acquisition target. Empire building, to increase power or protect it, can be a powerful motive. Sometimes acquisitions are made to secure scarce resources, for example the services of a particularly talented manager or a licence which would be otherwise unobtainable.

(i) Ambition

Prestige and compensation in an organisation may depend more on size than results. Acquisitions are the quickest way of building up the size of the group.

An element of 'small town boy makes good' may come into play. An individual who has built up his company reaches a stage where he seeks to acquire more established and well-known organisations. Sometimes these are companies he has admired in the past or had to ask for help during his rise.

A successful acquisition often brings with it extensive publicity. Certain noted corporate raiders and their advisers have become national figures for a time. The exposure may mainly be a matter of ego. However, it can also be justified in terms of increased corporate and management visibility. This may lead to improved ratings in the stock market and a larger number of acquisition opportunities being presented by brokers.

A high degree of determination on the part of an individual or group is usually necessary to bring an acquisition to a successful conclusion, particularly if it is contested. During the course of an acquisition, occasions almost always arise where the parties concerned are ready to call it off. In these circumstances, the motivation and drive of a particular individual can be a critical factor.

(ii) Defence

It is commonly believed that the bigger the group is, the harder it is to swallow. Companies therefore sometimes attempt acquisitions in order to grow too big to be taken over by a feared rival. In addition, the more complex a group is, the greater is the likelihood that the bidder will be deterred or that regulatory authorities or other interested parties will find grounds to raise objections to a takeover. A company in a sensitive area, for example telecommunications or broadcasting, may be particularly favoured as an acquisition partly for this reason.

Companies espousing this philosophy should be wary of creating their own downfall. Ill-conceived acquisitions can lead to criticisms and disaffection from shareholders. Weakening the financial position of the group through expensive or inappropriate purchases ultimately plays into an acquiror's hands.

(iii) Management

Some acquisitions are made primarily to obtain the services of a manager or management team who have proved themselves competent at running a particular type of company or handling a particular type of crisis. Sometimes the specialised professional expertise or contacts of individuals are what is sought. An example would be the purchase of a stockbroker or advertising agency. In such cases, an important task for the purchaser is to create a climate where groups of people with a different approach to conducting business can learn to work together effectively. Otherwise, the purchaser may find that the most important assets of the company purchased walk out through the door.

(iv) Stock exchange listing

Control of companies may be sought which have little or no assets or business but which are listed on a stock exchange. Once control has been obtained, the acquiror will typically inject a business or assets into the company. Depending on the nature of the assets and the length of time they have been held or operated, a listing is obtained which might not have otherwise been possible. Such companies are commonly called 'shell companies' and are discussed in detail in ch 9 above.

(v) Tax losses

Companies which have been unsuccessful may have accumulated considerable losses for taxation purposes which may in certain circumstances be utilised by an acquiring group. Usually the company is valued on the basis of a discount to the amount of tax which will be saved. The feasibility of such an acquisition depends critically on the tax regulations in the country concerned and the current interpretation of them.

(vi) Licences

A licence, for example to conduct a banking business or operate a TV station, may be more easily obtained by acquiring a company which already holds such a licence than by a fresh application. Care must be taken to ensure that a change of control in the company acquired does not jeopardise the continuity or validity of the licence. If it is practical, this matter should be cleared in advance with the authority responsible for granting the licence or regulating companies which hold it. This may not always be possible for tactical reasons, in which case any agreement should be conditional on the appropriate clearance being obtained.

CONCLUSIONS

The main driving forces behind the launching of takeovers and acquisitions have been considered in this chapter. For the purpose of analysis, they have been looked at under three headings, commercial, financial and special situations. However, motives for takeovers tend to defy tidy categorisation. Most acquisitions can be justified from a number of points of view. If published explanations sometimes seem lame, there are likely to be other factors at work. It is important for those working in the acquisitions field, whatever their role, to keep in mind the whole range of possible motivations. This is an area where very little can safely be taken at face value.

CHAPTER 14

Acquisition search: developing criteria, generating opportunities and preliminary screening

The multiplicity of motives for takeovers discussed in the last chapter has the result that acquisition search is a complex process. To conduct an effective search it is necessary to develop relevant criteria. Criteria which have proved useful are discussed in 'I Developing and setting criteria' below. When the criteria have been established, procedures are needed for generating suitable proposals. Imaginative management can widen the range of opportunities which arise internally or are presented by the market. This aspect is considered in 'II Generating opportunities' below. A preliminary screening of potential targets is required to prevent analysts being overwhelmed by too many options. Screening candidates is partly a matter of rigorous application of the criteria and partly depends on an ability to see the main implications of an acquisition before detailed analysis commences. This topic is dealt with in 'III Preliminary screening' below.

I DEVELOPING AND SETTING CRITERIA

A clear statement of management's objectives in looking for acquisitions should suggest suitable criteria. The more precisely the objectives can be stated, the more definite will be the criteria for an appropriate acquisition.

In the previous chapter, the reasons why takeovers are made are discussed under three general headings:

  (i)   Commercial;
 (ii)   Financial;
(iii)   Special situations.

Criteria can be considered under these same headings. Other types of criteria apply whatever the motive for an acquisition. The main ones are:

 (iv)   Size;
  (v)   Financing.

(i) Commercial

If an acquisition is being considered principally for commercial reasons, typical criteria are likely to include the following:

(a) Type of industry/activity

Acquisitions intended to increase market share must be in areas of activity closely related to the acquiror's existing business. If the objective is growth in a general sense, companies engaged in different areas would be considered. Frequently, a company is prepared to consider a potentially more difficult acquisition in a business with which it is thoroughly familiar. If an acquisition in a new area, it must be capable of 'standing on its own feet'. A loss-making company or a company with management problems might not be considered whatever its other attractions.

If the acquiror is seeking benefits related to synergy, it will concentrate on the fit of business. A strong manufacturer may be looking for an organisation with a widespread marketing and distribution network. A company seeking to secure supply of a key component or additional sales outlets will focus specifically on these areas.

The last type of commercial motive discussed in the previous chapter was diversification. By definition, this will involve the acquiror actively seeking a business with significantly different characteristics from its own, perhaps in a totally unrelated industry. Although such an acquisition may reduce the overall risk profile of the group, the acquisition itself (of an unrelated company) falls into the most difficult category for the acquiror to analyse.

Criteria related to type of industry and activity may be defined in a positive or in a negative way. A company may take a positive decision to emphasise high technology or overseas markets. On the other hand, a company may decide it will in no circumstances consider an acquisition in say property or shipping. This type of rule should not be allowed to degenerate into dogma. A ruling which is soundly based when established should be reviewed periodically as business conditions change and the company itself evolves.

(b) Attitude of management and workforce

Acquisitions undertaken primarily for commercial reasons are vulnerable to the reactions of management and workforce. Unless a reasonable degree of co-operation can be established, many of the anticipated benefits may not be realised in practice.

Acquirors may decide that they will not consider an acquisition intended to realise commercial benefits unless management has been proved to be competent. They may also seek assurances that the majority of the senior executives are willing to stay. Incumbent management is likely to react initially with nervousness if not outright hostility.

The attitude of the workforce is perhaps less likely to be one of outright opposition as their position is less directly threatened by a takeover. However, if the acquiror has not previously had to deal with a unionised labour force, he may be unwilling to acquire a company whose workers are organised in this manner. Lack of experience in negotiating with unions may act as a deterrent. The acquiror may also be apprehensive about the spread of unions to his own organisation.

(ii) Financial

If an acquisition is intended principally to improve the financial position of the acquiror, strict financial criteria will be applied. Financial criteria are amongst the most difficult to establish in a way which does not prove to be counter-productive. If the returns required are set too high or applied too strictly, an ideal acquisition target may be defined which in reality is never encountered. In response, the acquiror's analysis may be adjusted towards the returns required and owe more to wishful thinking than objective reality.

A management which rigidly insists on buying companies at below market price may find that they investigate many transactions but complete none. If they do finally succeed in concluding a deal, the results may be disappointing. The emphasis on apparent cheapness can cause critical weaknesses to be overlooked.

Asset strippers aim to acquire companies at a discount to net assets. Allowing room for negotiation, a target may not be of real interest unless the discount is substantial, say one-third. Although it may seem that only a forced seller would accept such terms, there is scope for a good deal of disagreement in buyers' and sellers' estimates of what assets are actually worth.

If increase in earnings per share is paramount, it is unlikely that a company currently making losses will even be considered. However, a realistic acquiror should be prepared to give an acquisition say two years to recover to a position of reasonable profitability if its own financial position is strong enough. Unless some latitude is allowed, an acquiror will rule out the possibility of making a potentially attractive acquisition at the low point in a company's fortunes.

Some acquisitions are used to improve the gearing of the enlarged group. In this case a company which is already highly geared or one which is facing substantial capital commitments is unlikely to be considered.

If an acquiror's strategy is to issue highly-rated shares or other paper, the willingness of vendors to accept such paper may make an acquisition attractive which would not meet normal criteria. If a vendor has a pressing need for cash, this is likely to rule out the use of paper except in circumstances where a vendor placing can be arranged.

(iii) Special situations

In addition to financial and commercial aspects, other more specialised factors are often involved in acquisitions. This will make setting criteria a simpler process. For example, if a company is being acquired for its management, stock exchange listing, its tax losses or a licence it holds, then the criteria more or less set themselves. If an acquisition is being made as a defence against a takeover threat, it can be judged purely by its effectiveness in this respect. One important factor will be sheer availability at short notice.

In circumstances where motives include subjective elements such as empire building, criteria are unlikely to be set in an organised way. The motive may not be fully realised by the decision-makers themselves, far less openly acknowledged.

(iv) Size

There are likely to be fairly obvious limits to the size of a possible acquisition. Even in the case of a highly leveraged buy-out, there is little sense in the average company drawing up a complex scheme to take over a very much larger company.

It is also useful to set a cut-off point at the lower end of the scale. There is a large fixed element in the time and expense in evaluating an acquisition. The acquisition must be of a certain minimum size to justify the effort involved. A series of small acquisitions ties up management time without making a significant difference to the performance of the group.

Size may be defined in different ways. A trading company may have an impressive turnover figure without a large asset base. A company with a big balance sheet may not command a high purchase price for the equity if it is in financial difficulties or heavily geared.

An acquiror may wish to consider maximum and minimum size criteria under various headings:

(a) Purchase price

What is the most a company is prepared to pay or can afford to pay? This figure may depend on the possibility of using paper as part of the consideration.

(b) Turnover or value added

These may be the most useful indicators of how substantial a business is being considered. Care is required as some companies may have a high turnover with little value added. Others may have a smaller turnover but with value added representing a significant proportion.

(c) Assets, liabilities and capital requirements

The most immediate impact of an acquisition is frequently an increase in the balance sheet footings. Key ratios may come under pressure. An acquisition must be judged not only in terms of its initial effect (including the price paid) but taking into account any additional capital which may be required. Weakness in capital structure or heavy capital commitments may have been the reason the company was vulnerable to a takeover in the first place.

(d) Market share

There is a school of thought which believes that controlling a substantial proportion of a particular market is the best guide to whether a company can survive and prosper in the long term. A company with a toehold in its market may fail if a period of intense competition is encountered even if the company is large in absolute terms. An appropriate minimum criterion for percentage market share will depend on the industry structure.

(e) Profitability

Most companies making acquisitions establish a minimum rate of return which the target should be capable of generating. The minimum hurdle rate of return may be reduced if the acquisition is in a familiar business or increased if it operates in high risk areas of the world. Some discretion must be exercised as to the year in which this target return is intended to be achieved.

(f) Number of employees, diversity of markets served and spread of business

A further way of measuring size is by reference to the numbers of people employed and the numbers of markets served or products produced. This may be taken as a proxy for the complexity of the business as a whole. The more complex an acquisition, the more likely it is that something will go wrong.

(v) Financing

It is of little use planning to buy a business the aspiring acquiror cannot finance. Managers who have been successful in building up businesses by acquisition try to finance each proposal to a large extent on a project basis, minimising the call on the financial resources of the holding company and avoiding giving its guarantee. How easily an acquisition can be financed depends partly on the characteristics of the target company and partly on the requirements of the vendors.

A company with valuable fixed assets or a predictable surplus cash flow will be more easily borrowed against. Businesses which have a high proportion of goodwill in the price paid and are subject to abrupt market changes or cycles will not commonly be considered by financiers to provide good collateral. The acquiror is likely to have to fund such acquisitions substantially out of its own cash flow.

A desire not to miss any possible opportunity can lead to a reluctance to define criteria too closely. This is particularly the case when acquisitions are being sought for financial or opportunistic reasons. Precise definitions may be seen more as closing down attractive options than a useful sharpening of focus.

In the case of acquisitions undertaken primarily for commercial reasons, it is productive to avoid the 'we-are-interested-in-everything' approach, which can amount to a failure to set a policy at all. Too much reliance may be placed on advisers or brokers presenting suitable proposals. No outside party can tell a management what type of acquisition they should seek. Management must itself define its own objectives and set criteria which are consistent with them.

II GENERATING OPPORTUNITIES

Once a management has set its criteria for making acquisitions, it must develop procedures for generating suitable proposals. The criteria selected can then be applied to narrow down the range of opportunities the market presents. One important principle is to identify opportunities before they have become stale. Experience suggests that attractive acquisitions are progressed quickly. Those that have been in the market for some months are rarely worth the trouble of analysis.

It may be useful to divide sources for acquisition opportunities into two categories, those which are generated internally, that is by the staff of the company through their private contacts or through their executive function in the company, and those which are generated by or through external professionals in the merger and acquisition field.

(i) Internal sources

(a) From non-specialists

The senior staff of a competently run business know more about that area of business and the major participants in it than an external professional. Consequently, the best ideas for acquisitions within a company's existing sphere of business will often come from the staff themselves. Management should try to provide some forum or channel of communication so that ideas can be put forward and discussed, with some credit and involvement in analysis going to the originator. As executives may be more conscious of brand names and marketing networks than the ownership of corporations, assistance in providing information on the corporate structure of the industry may stimulate the flow of ideas.

(b) Merger and acquisition unit

In addition to opportunities identified through involvement in a particular business field, the company may also establish a specialist merger and acquisition unit. One of the functions of this unit will be to search publicly available information to find targets which fit the criteria which have been laid down. Except in a very major conglomerate, such units are unlikely to be entirely independent or engaged solely in merger and acquisition work. They may be located for example in the treasurer's or controller's departments or within a corporate planning function. Such arrangements promote economical use of manpower. However, the approach of the staff will be coloured by the environment in which they find themselves. They will be more effective if they act in an independent entrepreneurial way to locate the widest range of opportunities.

(ii) External sources

(a) Advertisements

Companies rely on external sources to supply or prompt many of their acquisition ideas. One obvious source of possibilities is simply to advertise for them. In practice, unless the type of acquisition is a standard one, sellers will be reluctant to reply to such an open approach. It seems that a modification of Groucho Marx's law applies, that you would not wish to buy a company whose owners answer your advertisement.

(b) Intermediaries

The role of the intermediary is well established in the merger and acquisition field. Intermediaries may be experienced businessmen and negotiators. Often they are senior accountants or lawyers with expert knowledge of certain industries. Others are pure merger brokers whose modus operandi is to match buyer and seller without necessarily knowing much about either.

Investment and merchant banks have access to a continuous stream of proposals through their professional and client contacts. Often, they can offer a package of services, including provision or introduction of suitable financing and the placing of securities in support of an acquisition.

Many significant business empires have been built up through a close association with one or more merchant banks. The development of a personal relationship is fundamental. As a merchant bank becomes familiar with the philosophy of an acquiror, it can increasingly anticipate his reaction. If the group becomes a significant client, the merchant bank will take the initiative in presenting proposals in order to keep the client relationship active. A merchant bank is not as transaction orientated as a merger broker but will still seek to get a transaction moving as quickly as possible. A client who is known to react swiftly and is prepared to pursue opportunities in spite of the inevitable uncertainties will soon gain a favoured position. However, the client must recognise that the intermediary may receive little or no fee unless the acquisition is completed and is therefore strongly motivated to encourage the client to press ahead.

(c) Financial pressures – an ill wind

Receivers and liquidators are a productive source of potential acquisitions. Unlike many sellers, they do not have any emotional attachment to the businesses or assets it is their responsibility to realise. They are frequently under time pressure, particularly if customer and supplier relationships are fundamental to the value of a business as a going concern. Not only are they firm sellers but they may be willing to accept a discount on the open market value in return for speed, certainty and simplicity of the transaction.

Relationships with outside professionals are usually conducted at a senior level. A company may also promote contact between its analysts and the junior staff of merchant banks to create an additional channel of information. Merchant bank executives are usually allocated on a client basis and competition to present good proposals to clients is fierce. Which client sees which opportunity first may be a matter effectively settled at a fairly junior level, allowing the more senior executives to remain above the fray.

III   PRELIMINARY SCREENING

Once the criteria have been developed and opportunities generated, the preliminary screening process, which may partly be carried out by computer, comes down to a rigorous application of the criteria. In seeking suitable acquisitions, it is possible to go down a large number of blind alleys. Promising proposals can fall down at the eleventh hour leaving nothing but a good deal of wasted time and the frustration of having the prize snatched away. Experience can assist the company's staff in developing a sense of what type of proposal is realistic. From the outset, they should adopt a questioning attitude as to whether a proposal has the ingredients necessary for a successful outcome. If a proposal does not make good commercial or financial sense to all the participants, it is likely to be only a matter of time before it founders.

A number of subjective factors play a role in the preliminary screening process.

(i) Relationships

There may be unanticipated commercial consequences arising from an acquisition, particularly in an industry where vertical integration is involved. An arm's length commercial relationship between supplier and customer frequently proves easier to handle than the relationship between parent and subsidiary. Rival suppliers may feel that a competitor who becomes a member of the group will always receive favoured treatment.

If an acquisition takes a group into an area in which its own customers are active, the business put at risk may cancel out the expected benefits of the acquisition. Existing participants in the industry may feel that their supplier is trespassing on their own preserve. The resultant loss of business may make the uncertain benefits of entering a new field too costly.

(ii) Management

An acquisition may be intended to secure the expertise and business generating abilities of its management. However, loss of independence and changes in working environment may result in disenchantment with a large group. In a service business, for example advertising or insurance brokerage, the members of the firm acquired may be very capable of leaving to set up on their own. Although it may be possible to impose certain restrictions on them for a period of time by means of service contracts or other agreements, this can result in the almost equally unsatisfactory position of a senior management with no real commitment to their job.

(iii) Matters of judgment

The intangible aspects of taking a company into an area in which it has no previous experience should be examined at an early stage. Acquisitions of companies in sensitive areas such as broadcasting and gambling can lead to official scrutiny of a group which may not have had to deal with regulatory authorities in this manner. Companies engaged in material litigation can absorb significant amounts of senior management time. Entry into overseas markets by way of takeovers of domestic companies may spark off a xenophobic reaction.

Management should assess whether an acquisition can be concluded on an agreed basis or whether it will be contested to the bitter end. A contested takeover can provoke a counter-attack on the acquiror's financial position, management performance and business ethics. This can in turn unsettle the acquiror's bankers and shareholders. Unless an acquiror has the stomach for this kind of infighting, contested takeovers are best avoided.

Another test to apply at the screening stage is the extent of the down-side risk of any acquisition. Management should ask themselves what is the worst that could happen in a 'disaster' scenario. Owing to a great reluctance to cut losses on high profile acquisitions, a management may be drawn into supporting a difficult situation far longer than it should. In extreme circumstances, an acquisition may threaten the survival of the whole group. This type of target clearly needs a different type of evaluation from the more run-of-the-mill project.

CONCLUSIONS

Setting criteria, generating opportunities and carrying out preliminary screening overlap to a considerable extent. They are themselves closely linked with and derived from the reasons for making acquisitions in the first place. It is possible to approach this aspect of mergers and acquisitions by attempting to set such precise criteria that they virtually pick out acquisition targets and dictate whether they should be pursued to the next stage. However, this approach, while logical, may produce too rigid a system which results in a failure to identify and take advantage of attractive acquisitions. The approach suggested in this chapter has been to set criteria based on the objectives of the takeover programme. The generating of opportunities is left as a separate exercise. In this way, a wide range of choice is initially presented. A preliminary screening process is then required to apply a more rigorous application of the criteria. The analysis should be extended to take into account matters of judgment as discussed above.

This procedure is far from perfect. A significant gap can develop between the specified criteria and the actual desired characteristics of an acquisition. The planners and analysts may put up a series of proposals only to find that management reaction to them is largely unpredictable.

It seems a common experience that many poor quality acquisitions are made. Mistakes which arise early in the process when minds are in theory still open should be the easiest to avoid. Some warning signs that an acquisition programme is on the wrong track from the outset are:

(i)   reluctance to spell out criteria clearly;
(ii) reluctance to screen out targets which are glamorous but dangerous;

    (iii)   a preponderance of ego or 'gut feel' over analysis;

    (iv)   poor use of intermediaries and misunderstanding of their motivation.

Once the initial go-ahead is given, the thrill of the chase can make it progressively more difficult to pull back.

CHAPTER 15

Acquisition analysis: collecting and evaluating information

Once a target company has been identified, the next step is the collection of information so that a more detailed financial analysis of the company may be carried out. This analysis forms the basis of the assessment of valuation and what price should be paid and whether it should be paid in cash or shares or some more complex package. The effect on earnings per share and gearing are highly relevant to this decision.

A cynical acquiror will always assume that there is some good reason why a company is for sale. A major objective of the analysis will be to identify any weakness which has led to a company becoming 'in play'.

A poor acquisition can have consequences which are not limited to the initial price paid. There is a strong resistance to admitting that an acquisition has been a mistake and instead a tendency to 'throw good money after bad' by trying to improve a hopeless situation. The health of the whole group may be affected, even companies with no direct relationship to the struggling acquisition, by the drain on financial resources and management time. The best chance of avoiding a damaging acquisition is through the initial analysis.

I COLLECTING INFORMATION

Analysis can only be as sound as the information on which it is based. Information on acquisition targets may be derived from public sources or by an approach to the target itself.

(i) Publicly available information

(a) Statutory requirements

Under the provisions of company law in most countries, a company is obliged to file certain information for public inspection. The information normally includes details of the authorised and issued share capital, the list of registered shareholders and the current directors. Certain information on profits and balance sheet may also be provided, although in the case of private companies this information may be limited.

Information held on file for public inspection tends to be up-dated annually. A fairly generous time limit is allowed for the provision of the required information. It frequently happens that the latest publicly available information is considerably out of date, especially as authorities do not always have the time to chase up prompt filing by the very large number of companies which have been established.

(b) Press and trade comment

Some comment and analysis may be obtained from press cuttings if the company is one which has attracted public attention. Credit analysis companies and similar organisations are another potential source. In addition to searching publicly available information, such organisations may have carried out interviews with selected suppliers, customers and creditors of the group. Trade and marketing associations may be able to supply literature on products and other commercial aspects of the company.

(c) Stock exchange related sources

Companies which have a public listing must produce annual accounts and publish results periodically, usually twice a year and sometimes quarterly, within a certain time limit from the end of the relevant period. In addition, the provisions of the listing agreement entered into with the stock exchange will usually require the company to publish details of transactions of a material size (measured against say its net assets and profits) or transactions with its directors or substantial shareholders and more generally to disclose promptly all price-sensitive information. They may provide additional information to stock-brokers as the basis of reports which are circulated semi-privately. If the company has been engaged in raising capital in the public markets or taking over another company, relevant documents will have been issued containing more detail than appears in the accounts.

(d) Registers

In many jurisdictions, transactions involving land are taxed and must be registered in such a way that the details are made public. Similarly, a public register of charged assets may be kept to enable creditors to assess the financial risk they run in dealing with the company. From these two registers, key information on the fixed assets of the company and the extent to which they have been charged to support borrowings may be obtained.

The acquiror may be relying on public sources because he does not wish to alert the target to his intentions. Drawing on the various sources described above does carry some risk of a leak occurring. Although public sources can be consulted anonymously, an alert observer may notice that a particular file is frequently out for use. A company whose management is nervous of a threat may quickly realise that questions are being asked in trade associations. The acquiror may be able to shield his own identity by having his enquiries carried out by a third party. However, the more extensive the enquiries become, the more difficult it will be to prevent rumours starting that someone is 'sniffing around'.

(ii) Asking the target company itself

Except in the case of a bid which is expected to be opposed, after an acquiror has done what homework he can based on public sources, the next step would be to approach the target company to open negotiations. If the initial approach meets with some response, it will be followed by a request for information.

(a) Establishing that the approach is 'bona fide'

The moment at which many negotiations founder is when a company which may be attracted by a proposal first realises the extent to which it will have to bare its soul. It is therefore important that the request be handled tactfully and that the acquiror convinces the target that the acquiror is a bona fide purchaser and not just on a fishing expedition. Assurances that funds are available helps credibility and initial requests should be restricted to relevant information which can reasonably be made available. This also helps prevent an acquiror from being overwhelmed by a mass of information. The danger of not seeing 'the wood for the trees' is a real one when substantial analysis has to be carried out from scratch, often under time pressure.

The key characteristics of a business can often be identified beforehand. The information requested should be designed to highlight these characteristics. An acquiror should ask the question 'what am I buying?' and tailor the information requested to allow him to answer that question. Sometimes the really significant points in a particular transaction may be quite limited.

When an important aspect has been isolated, questions must be phrased in a careful way. Intensive questions on a specific point may tip a negotiating hand, emphasising to the other side points the acquiror considers of significant value. Questions on major assets or profit trends will come as no surprise, but if the acquiror is interested in something more unusual, a battery of questions is bound to alert even an unwary target company to a factor they may have overlooked.

Some requests may cover areas such as the directors' own personal dealings or highly sensitive commercial aspects. In these cases, checks may only be needed of a negative kind, to establish that nothing untoward has happened. If this information proves hard to obtain, it may be possible to 'skin the cat' in other ways, for example by including warranties on the relevant points in the sale and purchase contract.

(b) Confidentiality agreement

It is likely that the target will specify that any information it agrees to supply will be covered by a confidentiality agreement to be signed by the purchaser. This may be a simple or complex document depending on the taste of the target's lawyers. The main elements are that the purchaser recognises it is receiving sensitive information, undertakes to safeguard it and disclose it only as necessary for analysis of the acquisition, to return it without keeping copies if the transaction does not proceed and not to use the information for any other purpose.

A list of the items which might be included in a request for information is shown below. It should be borne in mind that not all items will be essential in every case and that in specialised companies, a different emphasis may be needed. The acquiror should ask himself 'if I knew this piece of information, would it make any difference to my decision?'

QUESTIONNAIRE

(a) Statutory/legal

1 Memorandum and articles of association.
2 Authorised and issued share capital, including details of voting and dividend rights and of shares issued or bought back within the last year.
3 Details of capital convertible into shares and of any warrants or options outstanding and terms of any loan stock trust deeds.
4 Chart of group corporate structure, giving names and main activities of subsidiaries, place of incorporation and noting any minority interests.
5 Details of any litigation or material claims (actual, pending or threatened) and of material contracts.
6 Minutes of recent board and shareholder meetings.

(b) Financial

7 Latest audited accounts for the company, group, individual subsidiaries and, where appropriate, associates for as many past years as is useful.
8 Copy of the consolidation schedule used in drawing up the consolidated accounts.
9 Profit and cash flow budgets or forecasts for the current and, if available, subsequent years and projected balance sheet.
10 Statement of borrowings and cash position and capital commitments, guarantees, leases and other financial commitments. Amounts of any significant facilities undrawn and impact of any significant loan covenants. Details of any significant foreign exchange exposure.
11 Monthly management accounts for the current year.
12 List of properties and other major fixed assets with current valuations, any charges secured against the assets and, if relevant, a schedule of tenancies and insurance coverage.
13 Details of any tax losses and of assets with book value higher than their tax written down value.
14 Details of any intangible assets such as licences, brand names, trademarks or patents.
15 Details of pension or provident fund scheme. Is it fully funded? Is it over-funded? Details of any long service payments due in case of redundancies.
16 Details of any investments, with their market value, if listed.
17 Details of any contingent liabilities, obligations on behalf of joint ventures or associates or similar 'off-balance sheet' items.

(c) Market statistics (if listed)

18   Summary of monthly or weekly share price movements, price earnings ratio, dividend yield and net asset backing over say the past 12 months. Has the share under- or over-performed the market?
19   Analysis of level of turnover in shares and buying cost to major shareholders.
20   Details of major shareholders and spread of shareholdings.

(d) Directors, management and employees

21   Names of directors, their business background, their involvement in the group and their shareholdings.
22   Details of contracts of service.
23   Organisation chart.
24   Numbers of employees, where located, typical training or qualifications and union involvement, if any.

(e) Commercial

25   Description of business, technology, products and services. Details of any long-term supply or purchase contracts.
26   Sales/marketing organisation and procedures, trade or conference memberships, import or export quotas, licences, franchises and distribution agreements or agencies.
27   Geographical spread of production and sales.
28   Level of research and development expenditure, new products, competitive position, payment reputation.
29   Details of any organisation, affiliated or not, on which the company's business critically depends. Top ten customers and the percentage of sales they account for.
30   Details of any joint venture or similar arrangements.

It should be emphasised that to slap down a standardised list of questions is one of the surest ways to kill an acquisition proposal. A selective approach will elicit a more positive response from the vendor and start the acquiror's analysis off on the right track.

II   EVALUATING INFORMATION

Assuming a decision is made to proceed if terms can be agreed, the evaluation phase falls into two parts. The first is setting a price based on an objective valuation of the target company, adjusted for analysis of the particular circumstances and also horse trading as to what is needed to do the deal. The second is assessing the impact of the acquisition on the published profit and loss account and balance sheet of the acquiror and adjusting the components of the offer accordingly.

(i) Quality of information

As information is received, a view should be formed about its quality and reliability. How much is audited, how much based on management estimates. Have budgets been met in the past? Can any loopholes be covered by warranties? In the context of an acquisition, there is a trade-off between immediacy of information and accuracy which should be taken into account.

(ii) Setting the price

The major methods of valuation have been discussed in Part 1 of this book, and in broad terms, can be applied to the valuation of a company in the context of an acquisition. However, particular aspects and valuation techniques assume different degrees of importance and relevance.

Major aspects to be considered are as follows:

(a) Net asset value

The approach to assessing a company's net asset value should be adapted to the strategy of a bidder after the acquisition is completed. If an essential part of his strategy is to realise significant sums in cash over a short period, it is necessary to be sure that assets earmarked for disposal are valued on a quick sale basis. The market may be aware that asset sales are likely after the acquisition. This will affect the vendor's bargaining position and the price realised.

Different views may be taken of a stake in an associate company. A purchaser who is in a position to control the company (perhaps because of an existing stake) may attribute a higher value than would a passive investor.

(b) Multiple of earnings

The quality of earnings of an acquisition target should be scrutinised by reference to the factors discussed in Part 1. The acquiror may be able to identify areas of cost savings should the acquisition be completed. Some upward revision in earnings estimates may therefore be legitimate as part of analysing the consequences of the acquisition.

The purchaser of a company which is available for sale should be wary that the company may have reached a cyclical peak in earnings. Many purchasers assume that the price earnings multiple on which an acquisition is valued will decline as future growth comes through. However, in cyclical industries the price earnings multiple at the purchase price may well increase as earnings dip with the next cycle. Similarly, if an acquiror is striking at an opportunist time of depressed earnings, it must obviously not be too surprised if its own analysis shows the purchase to be on a rather high immediate multiple.

(c) Cash flow basis

In evaluating cash flow, it may be that cash generated by the acquisition will include other elements besides operating cash flow, such as sales of fixed assets.

A company which has been run by an inactive management is likely to have some fat in working capital. For example, stocks and debtors may have been kept at higher levels than necessary. If such funds can be released, they can be regarded as a legitimate part of the cash generated from the acquisition.

Calculating the return on the purchase of a company by discounting an expected stream of cash flows can involve the assumption that cash generated is reinvested at the same rate of return. This may not be the case if the acquisition target is a business where the proceeds are unlikely to be reinvested, for example a mine or a quarry which is being worked out or a 'cash cow', ie a business which generates cash and does not require significant funds to be reinvested. It may be necessary to modify normal internal rate of return methods, so that funds reinvested are assumed only to earn the average return on capital of the acquiring group. This may well be lower than the return expected on the acquisition, especially if the acquisition is attractive principally for financial reasons.

(d) Composite

In conglomerate groups, it is likely that a valuation which looks at each part of the business separately may be higher than a valuation simply based on group earnings or consolidated net assets. Some parts of the group may generate substantial profits but have a low book value. Some assets with a high book value may for the moment be generating little or no income. A simple valuation of the consolidated group may gloss over this aspect.

If this basis of acquisition is to be accepted, the seller must be prepared to adopt an approach equivalent to a controlled liquidation or at least a partial break-up of the group. If the purchaser is not willing to accept this, he may be better advised to let the existing management handle the asset sales and buy only the parts of the business which interest him.

(e) Share price

If a company is quoted, the most natural starting point is the market price. However, it must be accepted by a purchaser that the share price is set by dealings in a small number of shares and may have little relevance, depending on the circumstances, to the price which is necessary to achieve control of the whole company.

The simple force of inertia will require the offeror to pay a premium over the market price. If a shareholder can buy and sell in the market at a certain price there is no need for him to take the trouble to consider the terms of an offer. A premium over market is therefore necessary simply to get shareholders' attention. The level of premium will vary with circumstances, but, as a rule of thumb, might be considered to be in the region of 20% to 40%.

Attention must also be paid to the target company's price history. While negotiations are in progress or investigations are being made, leaks or rumours may occur which are likely to cause a rise in the share price. This 'froth' may result in a price which settles at a small discount to the market's guess of where a bidder might eventually pitch his offer. In these circumstances, the purchaser may assess the price which may have to be paid on the basis of the share price prevailing before the rumours started. If the rumours prove false, the price is likely to fall back to the previous level.

It may also be useful to look at the price history over a number of years, particularly the peaks and the levels of turnover in the shares at those peaks. The offer price may look attractive compared with current values. Shareholders have a habit of remembering the price they originally paid. If that price was higher than the offer, they may be reluctant to take what they would still consider to be a loss. The share price lows may be useful for calculations to show the attractions of the offer. On the negative side, they may indicate substantial possible tax liabilities for shareholders deemed to have made a disposal under the offer.

(f) Comparables

Both acquiror and target are likely to be sensitive to the price at which any similar recent transactions have been completed. This information may be difficult to obtain precisely but it is worthwhile spending some effort on research. It is helpful to both buyer and seller to know that a certain offer is 'in the ball-park'.

(g) Rules of thumb

Many businesses have rules of thumb as to how they value assets. Hotels, for example, may be valued at a benchmark rate per room, although the hotels themselves may vary greatly in location, quality and clientele. It may be thought that such estimates are so simplistic as to be almost useless. However, their sheer simplicity has a powerful appeal and they may provide at least a rough cross-check. This check is worthwhile if only because others in the industry and analysts without access to more sophisticated information may do the same exercise, in which case reaction to the deal may be significantly affected by these yardsticks, however crude.

(h) General

The general techniques of company valuation apply to valuing an acquisition but with a sharpened focus. An assessment should also be made on a strictly practical basis of the price it is thought necessary to secure control of the company. If this price is significantly above an objective valuation, strong warning signs should be registered against proceeding.

Especially in a situation which is likely to be contested, it is useful to set an upper limit before negotiations begin and while cold logic and rationality still prevail. In the heat of a contested battle when victory becomes more important than price, it is easy to lose sight of the objective value. A maximum price formula established in advance is the best safeguard against living to regret an expensive acquisition. It is legitimate to allow some flexibility, as during a contested takeover, the target company will frequently release new and more favourable financial information, on which the acquiror may be able to justify a higher valuation.

(ii) Effect on acquiror's published earnings and balance sheet

The purpose of the valuation phase of the exercise is to arrive at a soundly based price range and an assessment of what price it may be necessary to pay to succeed, which may be above or below valuation. However, even a soundly based acquisition can have unexpected effects on the acquiror's next published accounts, since the valuation placed on an acquisition is in effect a summary of results covering a large number of periods. Typically, the acquisition may look expensive in the early years and more reasonable later on when problems have been solved and improvements to performance have come through. However, shareholders tend to judge management over the short term and an unfavourable impression made when the transaction is first announced can be very difficult to remove. A company which ignores this factor may itself become a takeover target.

(a) Effect on earnings per share

In devising the terms of an offer a major objective is that the earnings per share of the acquiror should increase (or at least not decrease) following the acquisition. The opposite effect where earnings per share are decreased is called 'dilution'.

In the case of an acquisition for cash, the immediate cost may be simply the interest foregone on short-term deposits or investments in which surplus liquidity has been deployed. If the acquisition is funded by borrowing, the interest cost on the debt incurred will be easily calculated.

Where an acquisition is small or expected to grow quickly, it may be possible to offer the target company's shareholders new shares in the acquiror without significant dilution to the acquiror's shareholders. Often, however, this is a luxury which the acquiror cannot afford, since a premium over market price will have to be offered to the target company's shareholders whereas the acquiror's shares will be issued at market price. The position will be worsened if the market price of the acquiror comes under pressure following the announcement of an offer.

To soften the impact of an acquisition the acquiror may offer a more complex package than shares alone. Particularly in countries where taxation is assessed on a group basis, offering cash or loan stock as a proportion of the consideration is likely to improve the acquiror's earnings per share after the acquisition. This is because the earnings yield on the acquisition (the earnings divided by the purchase price) is likely to be higher than the after tax cost of debt.

Convertible loan stock may be a useful ingredient. The coupon payable on convertible loan stock will be lower than on a straight loan stock owing to the value of the conversion rights, whereas the conversion price may be set at a premium to the current market price of the shares. The immediate impact on earnings is therefore beneficial and by the time conversion takes place, combined earnings may have increased to maintain earnings per share. Regulations may require earnings per share to be shown both on a pre- and post-conversion basis in the accounts. With a judicious mixture of types of consideration and a reasonable conversion premium, the effect on earnings per share can still be favourable even on a post-conversion basis.

(b) Example of tailoring the terms of an offer to avoid dilution

An example of how this type of package works is set out below. The example is an extension of the example shown in ch 13 above which illustrated that earnings per share will increase by using highly rated paper to acquire businesses with a lower rating. The example below demonstrates that even if (as often happens in a bid) it is necessary to pay a premium over market price so that the acquisition is not necessarily made on an advantageous price earnings ratio, nevertheless by introducing other elements into the terms an increase in earnings per share can be achieved.

EXAMPLE

Assume: (a) An offer by the acquiror for 100% of the shares of the target company, partly in shares, partly in loan stock.
(b) The terms are based on a total value for the target company of 500.
(c) The acquiror's shares are issued at market value.
(d) The convertible loan stock is convertible at a 10% premium to current market value of the acquiror's shares.

	Acquiror	*Target*
Latest pre-tax profits	133	67
Tax at 25%	(33)	(17)
Latest earnings	100	50
Number of shares in issue	1000	1000
Earnings per share	0.10	0.05
Multiple on which shares are rated	10 times	10 times (at offer price)
Market capitalisation	1000	500
Offer terms		
40% in shares		200
40% in 7% Convertible Loan Stock (CLS)		200
20% in 10% Unsecured Loan Stock/cash (ULS)		100
		500

	Pre-conversion	*Post-conversion*
Effect on earnings per share		
Pre-tax profits of target	67	67
Less: interest on CLS	(14)	—
interest on ULS	(10)	(10)
	43	57
Less: tax at 25%	(11)	(14)
Earnings from target	32	43
Earnings of acquiror	100	100
Total	132	143

Shares of acquiror in issue	1000	1000
Shares issued for acquisition	200	200
Shares issued on conversion to CLS	—	180
Total	1200	1380
Net earnings per share	0.110	0.104

In the above example, the cost of debt at 10% is in nominal terms the same as the assumed earnings yield on the acquiror's shares which is also 10%. However, because interest payments are allowable for tax, an improvement in earnings per share from 0.10 to 0.11 is achieved. An equally important factor is the assumption that the coupon on convertible loan stock will be 7%, significantly lower than on the straight loan stock. After conversion, an improvement in earnings per share is still registered. This is partly because of the tax relief on the interest payment on the straight loan stock and partly because it is assumed that the conversion price for the convertible loan stock can be set at a premium to the current market price of the shares. This results in the issue of fewer shares than if shares have been issued at the outset.

(c) Goodwill

When an acquisition of a company is completed and it becomes a subsidiary, the accounting treatment involves allocating the purchase price amongst the underlying net assets, both tangible and intangible, of the company on the basis of fair value to the acquiror. The values of the assets of the company acquired are adjusted accordingly in its own books or on consolidation. The value of brand names or licences can be reflected as intangible assets, separate from goodwill. If the purchase price exceeds the fair value of the assets, goodwill (or premium) will arise on the acquisition.

Goodwill arising on acquisition can be written-off immediately against reserves. This however affects the balance sheet through a corresponding reduction in the net assets of the enlarged group. The idea of 'clearing the decks' at the outset may attract the acquiror but it may be a luxury for a group without a strong balance sheet.

An alternative treatment in the accounts of the acquiror is to amortise goodwill on a systematic basis over its useful economic life or over a fixed period (say 40 years). In this case, there will be an impact on the reported profits of the acquiror over the relevant period (there is no effect on cash flow). The permanent retention of goodwill, which can in theory be argued for on the grounds that the value of goodwill does not decline in a successful company, is not now normally regarded as acceptable by auditors.

In view of the above accounting treatments, an acquiror who pays over 'fair value' of the tangible and intangible assets acquired (which is likely if an acquisition is valued on an earnings basis) has in effect a choice between taking an immediate 'hit' on the balance sheet or taking a series of smaller hits on the profit and loss account over a period of time. This would appear to discriminate against acquisitions of companies with low asset bases but high earnings, although such companies will typically have significant intangible assets which form the basis of their profitability and can be valued or revalued at the time of acquisition.

(d) Gearing

If a company is bought for cash, the existing equity base of the acquiror must be large enough to support the business acquired as well as its own. In effect, the shareholders' funds of the target company have been repaid in cash, increasing the gearing of the enlarged group.

To the extent that the acquired company has existing borrowings or immediate capital requirements, the gearing of the enlarged group will be further increased, possibly to dangerous levels. The acquiror must confirm that the terms of its own loan capital permit the acquisition on the basis proposed. Covenants to maintain a specified level of net current assets or debt to equity ratio may come under pressure. In addition, the transfer of control of a company can sometimes trigger repayment of its debts. Against this, the company acquired may have surplus liquid assets or assets which can be sold to counter the apparent increase in gearing.

In the case of a share exchange, gearing will not automatically be increased. Whether the gearing of the combined group will be higher or lower will depend on whether the company being acquired has financed a higher or lower proportion of its assets with borrowings than the acquiror.

The type of assets of the company being acquired must also be considered. A service company with little asset base may not add significantly to the new group's borrowing power. However, an asset rich acquisition may enable new funds to be raised even if the assets themselves are not immediately saleable.

It is sometimes possible to arrange for an issue of new share capital to existing or new shareholders in anticipation of an acquisition or immediately following one. At the time of an acquisition, considerable documentation will be available about the company. It may provide a suitable opportunity to arrange for further equity to be raised as a separate exercise and leave the offer in cash. This allows the overall capital structure of the enlarged group to be strengthened without making the terms of the offer itself more complex.

CHAPTER 16

Strategies for control: structure of offer and terms of payment

In most acquisitions, there will be scope for some flexibility in three critical areas which are discussed in this chapter.

(I) What is the most appropriate method of control of a particular target? It may not always be necessary to purchase the company to achieve the objective.

(II) What level of control is desired? Sometimes it will be essential to obtain 100% control; at other times it may be the last thing an acquiror wants.

(III) What options are open in paying for control? Payment can, for example, be in cash or securities and may be made on an immediate or deferred basis.

I METHODS OF GAINING CONTROL

The task of gaining control can be approached from various different angles depending on the reasons for the acquisition, the resources of the acquiror and other more technical factors.

(i) Assets or company?

If the reason for making an acquisition is primarily to control a major asset and not the business, it may be feasible to purchase that asset rather than the company which owns it. The factors to consider include the following:

(a) Simplicity

The complications of acquiring an asset are less than those of acquiring a company. If a company is acquired, it is necessary to investigate all its assets and liabilities, including contracts it may have entered into and other actual or contingent obligations. On the other hand, it is usually possible to buy an asset such as a property or a ship by itself, without any entanglements.

(b) Finance

Banks may be prepared to finance a higher percentage of the purchase price where they can take a direct charge over the asset than if their security is at one stage removed, through shares in a company. Interest costs may be lower, reflecting the bank's perception of lesser risk. Security documents are likely to be shorter and in a more standard form, decreasing legal fees and management time required.

(c) Taxation

Taxation implications may exert a deciding influence on the matter.

In some countries, tax on the transfer of an asset is greater than tax on the transfer of shares and payable by the purchaser. In a transaction involving shares, buyer and seller usually split the duty payments equally.

The vendor's profits or income tax liability may be increased if the asset is sold rather than the company. If assets are owned through a chain of off-shore holding companies established for tax reasons, the vendor will usually prefer to sell this structure rather than the asset itself. However, if the purchaser agrees, he inherits this structure, which may not necessarily suit him, and must be aware that the cost of the asset in the company's books for tax purposes may be much lower (for example, because values have risen with inflation) than the value which is reflected in the price paid for shares. A provision for contingent tax should be included in the calculations of the value of the company.

An asset purchase will not be possible where the attractiveness of an acquisition depends on the business connections of the company such as its suppliers, customers and other commercial relationships.

(ii) Shares and shareholder loans

(a) Shareholder loans normal with private companies

A private company may well be established with a small share capital and subsequently funded by loans from shareholders or other related parties. This method has the advantage of minimising any capital duty on the issue of new shares. It is also more flexible as the advance can be repaid without any question of reduction of capital or the need to have sufficient distributable reserves to declare dividends.

(b) Care required if valuation based on earnings

If a company is capitalised in this way, it is important to ensure that the entire shareholders' funds are purchased and not simply the share capital. Calculations of value must be carried out on a consistent basis. Very often it is convenient not to charge interest on shareholder loans. This means that if the company is valued on an earnings basis, the valuation will correspond to the entire shareholders' funds, whether they are made up of share capital or loans or both. No question of repayment of loans to shareholders in addition to the purchase price can arise. On the other hand, if the loans have been treated on an arm's length basis and interest charged, then an earnings-based valuation will relate simply to the worth of the issued share capital. The repayment of any shareholder loans and the interest rate they are to bear are matters to be considered separately.

(c) Transfer tax

In some countries, there may be no or a lower rate of transfer tax on the assignment of loans. There may therefore be considerable tax savings available by purchasing shareholder loans in such a way that the value attributed to the share capital of the company being acquired is reduced.

(d) Shareholder loans/deposits

Particular care must be taken when a bank or financial company is being acquired. Part of the funding arrangements and deposit base may be tied to, or depend on, the outgoing management and shareholders. If, as is usual, a premium is being paid over net asset value partly to reflect the value of the deposit base, it must be clear what deposits are likely to be withdrawn following the change of control. This is not only a question of value but of liquidity. The worst possible start to the acquisition of a financial institution is to suffer a loss of confidence and a run on deposits after a change of control.

(iii) Obtaining control via loans

It will sometimes be the case that a company's shareholders' funds have become largely irrelevant. Where a company has encountered financial difficulty, the lenders to the company may have the effective control due to the erosion of the company's equity base. Depending on the terms of the loans, it may be possible to acquire control by buying the benefit of the loan rather than by buying the shares. For example, the terms of the loan may give the lender the right to take security over assets through a floating charge and to put in a receiver/manager to run the business. This would allow the prospective purchaser to control the company's affairs while an investigation is carried out as to whether deeper involvement is wise. This can substantially reduce the risks involved in a purchase where quick action may be required to prevent liquidation of the company.

The terms of the loan may, by agreement of the board and the shareholders of the company, be amended to include the right of conversion into equity. Alternatively, the prospective purchaser may be granted options to subscribe new equity in due course, thus enabling the acquiror to control the share capital if the equity proves to have a value. In the meantime by purchasing the benefit of a loan or advancing further loans, the acquiror can signal to the market that he is a creditor not a shareholder and is not committed to stand behind the obligations of the company. On occasions, a purchaser who becomes a major shareholder of a company is seen as having taken moral responsibility for the company overall. This can lead either to embarrassment if the company is subsequently allowed to fail or to financial loss if the purchaser feels obliged to support it.

(iv) Obtaining control by injecting new capital rather than purchase

(a) New capital needed more than new shareholder

If control of a company is available for purchase because of a shortage of capital, it is sensible to consider obtaining that control by an injection of new capital rather than a purchase of existing shares or loans. The company being acquired will no doubt require financial support in any case. It is more attractive for the purchaser to kill two birds with one stone by subscribing for sufficient new shares to obtain majority control while at the same time providing cash to the company. If shares are bought from existing shareholders, cash goes out of the system. The financial position of the company is not improved unless there is an agreement for the shareholders receiving the cash to support the company in some way.

(b) Advantages under Takeover Code

If no existing shares are purchased, the new controlling shareholder may be able to obtain a waiver from making a general offer to all shareholders to purchase their shares. This would normally be required when control passes under the terms of the Takeover Code, in countries where a code operates.

(c) Attitude of existing shareholders

This procedure requires that existing shareholders are willing to retain their shares while being diluted by the new party. This may not be palatable but may be preferable to an outright sale at the nadir of the company's fortunes. However, the willingness of the existing shareholders to accept this structure may be a warning to the purchaser that the company's position is critical.

(v) Management control

Sometimes control can be obtained at management level in a way which achieves the 'acquiror's' purpose without any acquisition being made. A majority on the board of directors may be secured through a proxy fight without significant purchases of shares. The mere threat of a takeover bid or proxy fight may persuade the board of a company to accommodate the wishes of a third party.

This method is only really effective if control is desired to achieve a specific objective rather than for the overall financial benefits of owning the majority of the shares in a company. For example, a property developer eyeing a company with a large land bank may be perfectly content to secure a joint venture agreement over the development of that land. To acquire the company and assume responsibility for its business and employees is an unnecessary complication. The whole benefits of control to the developer can be achieved through one agreement.

II LEVEL OF CONTROL DESIRED

If an acquiror has decided to purchase a company rather than its assets, he should then consider whether he wishes or needs to control all the share capital of a company. On some occasions, a lesser amount will be sufficient.

(i) 100% control

(a) Flexibility

The major advantage of owning the entire share capital of a company is flexibility in what can be done after the acquisition has been completed. Assets can be transferred or sold without having to consider the interests of minority shareholders. Funds can be channelled more easily to wherever they are needed. Future projects, business and costs can be allocated without the need to be fair to outside equity partners. Banks who have given financial support to fund an acquisition may place proportionately greater security value on the entire share capital of a company than on any lesser percentage.

(b) Public company requirements

If the company being acquired is a public company, the retention of minority shareholders may prove particularly burdensome. The share price and level of turnover (sometimes embarrassingly low) will continue to be published. Some transactions will require the approval of shareholders in general meeting. The report and accounts and other documents have to be published and sent to shareholders. The annual general meeting has to be held in public, allowing questions to be raised by outside parties. Material transactions with the controlling shareholder may be criticised by minorities. The controlling shareholders themselves will be unable to vote on such transactions. If the minorities are hostile or become very small, the outcome of such meetings may be difficult to forecast.

As a consequence, it frequently happens that controlling shareholders eventually decide to buy out small minorities. This is done principally to reduce the level of disclosure required, to minimise administration costs and to consolidate the management of the company fully with its parent.

(ii) Partial control

There are a number of reasons why an acquiror may not wish to purchase 100% of the share capital of the target company.

(a) Cost

One obvious advantage of a partial purchase is that the total consideration to be paid is correspondingly lower. In some cases, it may simply not be possible for an acquiror to fund a purchase of 100%.

(b) Commitment of management and other parties

Even if finance is not a constraint, it may be desirable to leave key parties such as the management team with a share in the business in order to provide them with a reason for staying on and an incentive in running the business. A purchaser may be particularly concerned at the prospect of losing senior executives soon after a takeover when its own capacity to replace them is likely to be low. The retention of a shareholder in outside hands also helps to preserve the image of independence. This may be desirable in the case of a group with a long tradition and a loyal customer base.

(c) Gaining or retaining a listing

If the target company is publicly quoted, its listing may have been one attraction in making the acquisition. To retain the listing, it will be necessary to demonstrate that there remains a sufficient spread of shareholdings in public hands to ensure an adequate degree of marketability. In this case, it is advantageous if certain shareholders agree from the outset not to accept an offer or not to accept it for the entirety of their holdings.

The new controlling shareholder of a listed company may wish to retain the listing for essentially the same reasons as persuade shareholders to take a company public in the first place. The most relevant reasons in the context of an acquisition are to be able to use paper for future acquisitions through the newly acquired vehicle and to raise loans against the security of the shares. Unlisted shares are unlikely to be as acceptable to vendors of companies as consideration or to banks as security.

(d) Percentage required

Partial control usually relates to holdings of over 50% of the share capital. The outcome of voting at general meetings is not in doubt on matters which require a simple majority. In the case of a company with a wide spread of passive shareholders, effective control may be gained at a much lower shareholding level than 50%, provided that the new shareholder is able to obtain board representation and the appointment of key executives. This is reflected in the takeover codes of countries where such codes operate. The level of shareholding at which a general offer for a public company is required varies considerably but can be as low as 20%.

(e) Options

Partial control may be backed up by an option to purchase further shares (possibly all the remaining shares) at some later date. The attraction to a purchaser is that further time is allowed for investigation and increased familiarity with the company before a commitment to go the whole hog is made. An option can also serve as a method of deferred purchase while eliminating the possibility that the vendors will sell their remaining shares to a third party.

In such cases, the option price may be subject to increase (or decrease) depending on the performance of the company in the intervening period. This may be seen as an attractive feature to both acquiror and vendor at the time of the transaction. The acquiror may consider that the sellers are not washing their hands of the company and have an incentive to achieve profit growth. On the other hand, the vendors may feel that they do not entirely forego the future potential by agreeing to sell now.

III PAYING FOR CONTROL

There are a number of different ways in which an acquiror can consider financing its acquisition. Sometimes this will require negotiation with the vendors; at others, negotiations will be with third party financiers so that the vendors receive the same type of consideration irrespective of how the acquisition is financed.

(i) Cash

Cash has the great merit of being simple, understandable and hard to argue with. The attractions of cash are likely to be most apparent to the seller but some noted takeover exponents consider that cash payment imposes a useful discipline on the buyer also. A number of factors need consideration.

(a) How can cash be raised?

If an acquiror has sufficient liquid assets, it may simply pay for an acquisition out of its own funds. This allows it to act immediately and without reference to third parties. For an acquisition of a significant size, an acquiror is likely to wish at least to supplement its own resources by external funding, either at the time of the acquisition or after it has been completed.

The most common source of finance is bank lending. Credit lines may have already been negotiated, although they may not necessarily be available or suitable as acquisition finance. As a major acquisition is outside the ordinary course of business, the company should brief its bankers beforehand or, if confidentiality forbids this, at the earliest stage possible. Most acquisitions need longer-term finance than the company's normal requirements. The acquiror may wish to negotiate with its bankers for extended maturities.

If the finance is required, the question of security for the borrowings will arise. In some countries, legal problems can occur if a company being acquired could be considered to be giving assistance in the purchase of its own shares. This is a point on which detailed legal advice is required. Unless the acquiror is very lightly geared or the acquisition is a small one, repayments of bank borrowings to fund a cash bid are very likely to come, at least in part, from the cash flow (including asset disposals) of the company being acquired. Even under the strictest interpretation of the legislation, it seems that the company acquired could pay very substantial dividends to its new parent to service loans, provided it has sufficient distributable reserves.

Funds can also be raised for acquisitions by the issue of securities to institutions and other third parties. The issue of high yielding bonds ('junk bonds') became an important source of financing acquisitions, particularly in the US, in the mid- to late-eighties. Such bonds attracted investors as they typically generated (at least initially) high fees and yields.

The payment of the high coupons and the repayment of the principal depended significantly on strong trading, low real interest rates and on funds being released from disposals of the assets of the company being acquired. If the disposal programme did not proceed to schedule, economic conditions worsened or if the acquiror misjudged the value of the assets in the first place, the worth of 'junk bonds' were brought into question. They represent the replacement of a significant part of the acquisition's equity by debt obligations of the acquiror company. This implies that it is possible to run the enlarged group with a significantly lower level of equity than was the case previously. This strategy does not leave much margin for error.

(b) LBOs and MBOs

In a leveraged buy-out, a group of parties come together to acquire a company funded principally with loans intended to be repaid out of asset disposals. Where management is involved this type of operation is called a 'management buy-out'.

Many leveraged buy-out operations begin to look like a controlled liquidation, at least of a part of the business. Indeed, the main logic underlying such transactions is that there exists a profitable core of businesses to which a group can be stripped down, freeing up significant, perhaps not fully productive assets, for disposals.

LBOs and MBOs have become a significant element in corporate finance work and are discussed in detail in ch 19.

(c) Taxation

Acceptance of cash by the vendors can give rise to tax liabilities. They will be considered to have disposed of their shares and any capital gain will be realised at that point. This may simply be the penalty of having made a successful investment. However, there may be some advantage in offering vendors the alternative of taking shares or other paper. In this way, they may be able to 'roll-over' their investment so that no taxable gain will arise until they dispose of the securities they receive in exchange for their original holding.

(d) Cosmetic advantages of a paper alternative

The fact that cash is simple also means that there is no disguising that a sale is actually being made. It is not possible to suggest to vendors that they retain any kind of stake in the future of the business. If some alternative, even partial, can be offered in paper in addition to the cash, this not only gives the vendors another option but may also make them feel they are not being forced to part with their investment in the company altogether. They become to some extent partners in the new enlarged business.

(ii) Deferred terms

As part of the negotiations between buyer and seller, it may be argued that all or part of payment for an acquisition should be on a deferred basis instead of for immediate settlement. One reason may be because the acquiror cannot afford to put up 100% of the purchase price initially but there are a number of other circumstances in which deferred terms may be appropriate.

(a) As vendor finance

Deferred payment may be considered to be mainly to the advantage of the purchaser. It may be offered by the vendors if they realise that to demand cash is likely to restrict the chances of a sale. In some cases, the assets being purchased may not be acceptable as security for conventional bank borrowing. Vendor finance not only makes the transaction possible but gives the purchaser an indication of the vendors' confidence in the quality of the assets and the price being paid. For the vendors, provided security is retained over the asset, the worst outcome would be to take back the asset and retain the deposit. Sometimes, title to the asset will not pass until the vendor finance is repaid.

Vendor finance is most suitable where a relatively straightforward asset such as a property is being sold. In the case of a business, the damage done by the changes of control can make this structure undesirable.

(b) As part of negotiation on price

Payment by instalments can be a useful negotiating device where a seller insists on the amount he must receive and the purchaser's best offer falls short. A compromise can be achieved through a series of deferred payments. These may add up to the nominal sum the vendor has in mind but have a discounted present value (allowing for interest) equal to the price the purchaser is prepared to pay. While this may seem purely cosmetic, it is surprising how frequently a vendor is concerned to claim he has achieved a particular figure, perhaps to avoid a book loss.

(c) To provide for a period of investigation

The purchaser will investigate an acquisition at the time of the transaction to find out what problems may exist. Without being in full control of the business, a purchaser cannot be entirely confident he has identified all the potential pitfalls. Difficulties may not become apparent for some period of time. If the whole purchase price is paid on completion, the purchaser may have to sue the vendor to recover any damages due. If, on the other hand, the purchaser retains some portion of the purchase price, he has the option to refuse to pay the balance if he feels the terms of the sale and purchase agreement have been broken. The vendor must then prove that the purchaser is withholding money unfairly. No question arises as to whether the vendor can actually repay the sum in dispute. If the vendor's business proves to have some financial weaknesses, it is likely that the purchase price, once paid over, will prove difficult to recover.

(d) To allow for a performance related price

The price for an acquisition may vary depending on future performance. It is sometimes useful to have a performance related element in the consideration so as to give management an incentive and to allow vendors to share in future growth. In such cases, payment has to be by instalments as the amounts due cannot be known at the outset. This structure is known as an 'earn-out'.

An earn-out may be appropriate where the business being acquired is valued by reference to earnings and the underlying net asset value is comparatively low. A purchaser may be willing to make a down payment equivalent to net asset value, with the balance contingent on earnings achieved over say the next three years. The vendor receives the net asset value at once and the goodwill element in the price will be realised if the profitability which the vendor has no doubt stressed in negotiations actually comes through. By adopting this formula, a cautious purchaser and a seller insisting on full value may be able to reach an agreement which would otherwise elude them.

Difficulties can arise with this structure. The new controlling shareholder may wish to change the accounting policies of the company or take a more conservative view on items, such as stocks and debtors, where an element of judgment is involved. This will affect the reported profits in a way which may not reflect the performance of the business. In addition, disputes may arise over policies which are good for the long-term development of the business but may depress short-term profits. The new controlling shareholder may wish to incur expenses to promote growth for the future. The vendors will wish to maximise profits in the period during which the variable consideration is calculated.

The difficulties experienced tend to increase the longer the earn-out period. After three years the changes which are likely to take place in the business make sensible calculation difficult. Re-negotiation or termination may be necessary if the purchaser decides he must integrate the business closely with his own.

(iii) Exchange of securities

An alternative to payment in cash immediately or on a deferred basis is to offer an exchange of securities. This is only likely to be a practical possibility where the securities being offered are, or will be, listed on a recognised stock exchange and so have a reasonable degree of marketability. The securities offered may be equity, debt or instruments combining both these elements.

An offer which includes an element other than cash can present problems of understanding for the shareholders to whom it is offered. The more elements there are in such an offer, the greater the likely problems become. It is a useful rule not to include more types of security than is really necessary and to ensure that the securities which are offered are as familiar as possible.

(a) Ordinary shares

The most obvious choice is ordinary shares of the acquiror which rank in all respects equally to shares which are already in issue. The acquiror must weigh up the percentage in the equity of the enlarged group which is being allocated to the shareholders of the company being acquired. The acquiror must expect that shareholders of a target company may not necessarily see the merits of the acquiror's paper as clearly as the acquiror itself.

The provision of a cash alternative by underwriting or some other method will establish the worth of the securities being offered. Firm arrangements are desirable to deal with a large number of shares being issued to investors who may not be long-term holders. In the absence of such proposals, the announcement of the bid may trigger a period of price weakness in the acquiror's shares. This can play havoc with calculations of the worth of the bid based on market prices before the announcement.

(b) Shares with different rights

Despite additional complications, it may be advantageous to offer shares with different rights from the existing ordinary shares. If the target company pays a high dividend, it may be necessary to offer shares carrying preferred dividend rights in order to be able to offer an attractive increase in income to the target's shareholders. An alternative might be for the acquiring company to raise its own dividends to match that of the target. However, this requires the higher dividend to be paid on all the issued shares of the acquiror, which may not be practicable.

As well as shares with improved rights, shares with restricted rights may be utilised in acquisitions. Shares which do not, for the moment, carry any rights to dividends may be acceptable to vendors as consideration for an asset which does not currently generate income. An example is a property for development where the development period might typically be two to three years. In this case, shares could be issued which carry no rights to dividend during the development period, after which they would rank equally with the other shares. Until they do, they are unlikely to be freely tradable in the market.

Shares can also be issued with rights linked to the particular business being acquired. This is a useful device where the acquiring company is very large with a different major activity to that of the target company. The target company shareholders may feel little interest in being shareholders of a company so dissimilar to their original investment. To counter this, the dividend of the new shares may be linked to the performance of the business being acquired and not to the group as a whole. Accounting problems may arise but an acquiror may feel this is acceptable where in any case it is intended that the acquisition should be run independently.

(c) Debt

Shareholders of the target company may also be offered debt obligations of the acquiring company. They may see an advantage in ranking ahead of shareholders in a company with which they are not familiar. The coupon on debt should provide a higher current income than dividends on an equivalent value of ordinary shares which should attract investors valuing high yields. The acquiror on the other hand can offer a higher value without surrendering equity in the enlarged group. Where the company being acquired is asset rich, inclusion of some debt may seem appropriate to both sides. The vendors feel due consideration is being given to the assets contributed by their company, while the purchasers' equity is not diluted. The debt issued is prudently backed by assets and may be serviced by income from or disposals of such assets.

The inclusion of debt increases the debt/equity ratio of the enlarged group in the same way as a cash payment. However, depending on the repayment schedule of the debt, the impact on cash flow will be significantly reduced.

Debt may be issued on terms which enable it to be converted into ordinary shares. This allows the issuer and the holder to hedge their bets. If the underlying equity does not perform well, the debt will still hold its value to a considerable extent. If the company does well, holders of the convertible will benefit from conversion. The dilution effect to the issuing company's shareholders will be delayed until increased earnings can compensate for the larger number of shares in issue. As an alternative to conversion rights, warrants to subscribe for the acquiror's company's securities (usually ordinary shares) may be included in the package.

CHAPTER 17

Making the offer

An acquiror should try to tailor his method of approach to the particular circumstances of the case, as discussed in 'I Initial approach' below. Negotiating is an art in itself, but some basic points are covered in 'II Negotiations' below. 'III Launching a contested bid' below deals with tactics if no progress is made. Even the most delicate approach and skilful negotiating technique sometimes come up against a brick wall, in which case it is time to call up the bulldozer.

I INITIAL APPROACH

Where a company is owned and managed by different sets of people, a choice must be made as to which to contact first and what line to take. Sometimes the use of an intermediary can allow for more flexibility than a principal-to-principal approach. If the target company is listed, there will be constraints imposed by the need to keep negotiations confidential.

(i) Shareholders vs management

In companies with a wide spread of shareholdings and a professional management team, the executive control of the company is in the hands of management, divorced from the ownership of the company which lies with the shareholders. It is management's responsibility to run the business in the interests of the shareholders and in normal circumstances there is little reason to expect them to do otherwise. However, the interests of the two groups may diverge sharply in the case of an actual or threatened takeover bid.

Management may be concerned principally with retaining their power, prestige and livelihood, particularly if they are not well protected by service contracts. Shareholders, on the other hand, are understandably attracted by the chance of realising an immediate and substantial gain in the value of their investment. Particularly in the case of a cash offer, they may not feel greatly concerned about how the company is run afterwards or who is running it.

This divergence of interest may have two undesirable consequences. If an incumbent management is convinced that they have no future after an acquisition, they may well try to discourage proposals being put forward or disguise the fact that they have been. If they are forced to recognise the existence of an offer, their first reaction may be to criticise its terms whatever the financial advantages to shareholders. Emotive language may be used against the offeror who will be labelled a 'corporate raider' or 'asset stripper'. This may of course be true or partly true but misses the point. Shareholders wish to be told whether the long-term prospects of yet-to-be achieved profits justify rejecting the bird in the hand. Arguments put forward by managements as regards the need for stability to ensure the long run success of the company can sound very high minded but may be spiced with a dash of self-interest.

On occasions, managements have been prepared to pay 'greenmail' to an aggressive acquiror of shares who is bought out using the company's resources. This rewards the opportunistic buyer at the expense of the existing shareholders. It tends to leave the company with a weakened capital structure while denying the body of shareholders an equal offer for their shares. Once one raider has been bought off, another may pounce.

A similar danger for existing shareholders is a management which is wooed by an acquiror. Management may be flattered by comments on their abilities and the importance of their remaining in office after the acquisition. If they become convinced that a takeover would enhance their own position, they can make ideal advocates of the proposals to shareholders. It is not uncommon to find proposals from acquaintances or associates of existing management being recommended to shareholders as being in their interests only to be topped by a less welcome party whose appetite has been aroused by the prospects of a bargain. In this situation, the tactical advantage lies heavily with the less welcome party. The board of the target company has not only lost credibility by its premature recommendation of a low offer but has also deprived itself of a major defensive ploy, the argument that the price offered is too low.

(ii) Use of intermediaries

A mutual acquaintance, merger broker or other agent may be of assistance in making the first approach. A seller may indicate a willingness to deal to a third party without being thought to display weakness. In a direct contact, the potential seller might well be more cautious. The role of a 'marriage broker' to break the ice is as useful in this context as in a number of others.

A third party using 'shuttle diplomacy' between principals has more chance of narrowing the gap between two sets of proposals without being hung up on a particular structure or price. A skilful intermediary will seek to make both parties feel he is on their side. As someone who is committed to neither and paid only if a deal is consummated, his interest lies in seeking ways to reconcile the objectives of buyer and seller.

If emotions run high, a direct meeting between acquiror and the target company's management or shareholders may be bad tempered. A clash of personalities can hinder the conclusion of a proposal which might otherwise have a good chance of success.

(iii) Publicly listed companies

If the target company is publicly listed, special considerations apply. A leak of the possibility of an offer being made or that negotiations are in progress may cause a rise in the share price. This works against the interest of the offeror by making his proposals look less attractive when compared with the market price ruling immediately before a public announcement. A sharp price rise may also embarrass a management which is seeking to be helpful.

Precautions aimed at keeping discussions confidential by restricting knowledge of them to the minimum number of people are essential. Holding talks on neutral ground is worthwhile if proposals reach an advanced stage. On the other hand, a management which wishes to frustrate an offer may resort to a deliberate leak.

The stock exchanges and other regulatory authorities are alert to unusual levels of trading of companies' shares and will monitor the position as a matter of course. Sometimes pressure will mount for an announcement which the parties regard as premature. Ritual denials can look very foolish in light of the unveiling of a detailed transaction, sometimes hours later.

If the proposals are not likely to be welcome to the target company, the acquiror may decide to maintain secrecy in order to achieve a surprise attack. If it is decided that negotiations in advance will be fruitless, the acquiror will wish to give the target the minimum time possible to marshall its defence and present its case. Announcements immediately prior to major holidays such as Christmas and New Year are not unknown. A public company offer usually has to be open for a minimum period (say three weeks) but holidays are not excluded.

II NEGOTIATIONS

Merger and acquisition negotiations tend to be particularly prone to breakdowns and other disruptions. It is hard to remain detached and objective while selling a business which has taken years to build up and which may be closely identified with one individual. Equally, the process of buying a company can be wrapped up with ambition and prestige of the individuals involved. Takeover battles make good reading and, if one becomes public, the added glare of publicity can magnify the problems. The following paragraphs suggest some guidelines through this potential minefield.

(i) Knowledge of the other party

During investigation of a target, some information should have been obtained concerning its directors and shareholders. As the first approach would normally be to the chairman of the target company, a knowledge of this person's character and personality may be particularly valuable. The initial contact with the chairman is probably the moment of greater danger as, if this goes badly, all subsequent negotiations may be irretrievably soured.

It may sometimes be possible to use a divide and rule tactic, splitting the directors into two camps. Experience suggests that an unsolicited approach to buy a company is one of the few things which will unite directors who may have been quarrelling bitterly over other matters.

If it seems likely that an appeal will be made to the general body of shareholders over the heads of directors, the personalities of the major shareholders (or, if institutions, their representatives) will be relevant. Do they regard themselves as 'loyalists' or will they treat a bid in an objective way? Has the company done anything in the recent past, such as missed a profit forecast, which would have unsettled them?

(ii) Assembling a team

A team approach to negotiations can be very productive. It is not easy for one person to grasp all aspects of a transaction and impossible for him or her to analyse thoroughly all the various alternatives which may be open. A properly briefed team of advisers is necessary to keep a negotiator effective 'in the front line'. The composition of such a team will depend on the business of the target company but will normally include a firm of accountants and lawyers as well as a merchant banking adviser and, if the company is listed, a stockbroker.

Presentation of the arguments and analysis carried out by the team may be put forward more effectively by a single person. Some effort may be expended by the negotiator to conceal the depth of analysis and planning which lie behind an approach. The negotiator may be significantly assisted by a go-between whose role is to find solutions to the problems rather than to negotiate the toughest possible deal for one side or the other. Negotiations which result in a deal which is too tough on one side frequently collapse at a later stage.

(iii) Timing

The outcome of many negotiations is dependent upon timing. The state of mind of the vendor may critically affect his attitude to a sale. At times of difficulty, either for the economy as a whole or for a particular company, a realistic attitude towards doing a deal is likely to prevail on the part of the vendor. This however is precisely the time when a purchaser will need most courage to push forward.

Confidence born of a thorough analysis of the target is important. A well thought-through programme to assimilate the acquisition into the acquiror's group can pay great dividends at this stage. If the purchaser delays until the market recovers, he is likely to find that the seller has changed his mind or at least increased his expectations of price.

(iv) Win a recommendation

Recommendation of an offer by a target public company's board is probably the most important factor in success. Recommended offers fail principally if they are topped by a third party, in which case the initial suitor can at least retire with a dealing profit if he has built up a share stake as a platform for a bid.

Obtaining a recommendation tends to deter third parties from entering the fray. Buyers who might have been interested may be reluctant to disturb an agreed deal. They fear rebuff and are conscious of the premium price they would have to offer. There may also be the risk of legal sanctions if they can be considered to have persuaded a seller to break a contract.

If a recommendation is not achieved and the bid vigorously opposed, it can often be repulsed. Even if it succeeds, a substantially increased offer may well be required, resulting in a pyrrhic victory which the purchaser lives to regret. On other occasions, the ultimately successful party enters later in the day and the bidder who has made the running finds that the prize is elusive.

A recommendation is so important that it can be regarded as a factor separate from the financial and business position of the target company. It has a value which may be estimated as equivalent to the cost of fees, expenses and management time of a contested bid, plus the intangible damage to business morale and image which may be caused by failure.

(v) Keeping something in reserve

Company chairmen spend a significant proportion of their working lives in negotiations of one sort or another. They like to believe that they are successful negotiators. Unless the target company is so vulnerable that it has to accept anything it can get, a purchaser should keep something in reserve in the initial approach which can be conceded at a later stage. The chairman or his advisers can feel that extracting this concession is their contribution to the deal.

Care must be taken that, in allowing some scope for improvement in an offer, the initial level is not pitched so low that it cannot be considered a serious offer. If it can be dismissed as a sighting shot, the purchaser may find he has to begin all over again from a higher base, without extracting any worthwhile response from the target. The alternative is to let the bid drop at a level which is far below what the offeror was in fact prepared to pay, which is even more unsatisfactory.

(vi) Setting limits

It is important for an offeror to consider his upper price limit before serious negotiations begin. Once personalities are engaged, it is all too easy to be carried away in 'hot pursuit' of an acquisition. Success becomes an end in itself, a matter of corporate and personal pride which can overwhelm other factors and lead to poor judgment.

It is legitimate to review prices set in advance if more information becomes available. This is in fact likely to happen during negotiations or as part of defence documents issued by a target company. However, strict control must be exercised to ensure that the information provided does indeed justify revision of the limits set in the cooler atmosphere before a bid began. Prices paid in contested bids tend to demand unrealistic rates of growth or very high increases in asset values to be justified.

III   LAUNCHING A CONTESTED BID

It is necessary for the potential acquiror to monitor the progress of negotiations carefully. It is worth expending a good deal of time and effort to obtain a board recommendation for an offer. On the other hand, it will be to the advantage of a board, even one which is determined to resist, to engage in negotiations if only to gain time to marshall their defences. An acquiror must be alert for a phase of negotiations which represent a target simply playing for time and which are highly unlikely to lead to any fruitful conclusion. At this stage, the acquiror will have to decide whether to let the transaction die or to make an offer without the blessing of the target company's board.

(i) Private companies

In the case of a private company, the room for manoeuvre is limited. The acquiror is normally faced with a vendor who controls the share capital and management of the company and is therefore not susceptible to pressures in this area. In addition, the standard articles of association for a private company contain a pre-emption clause, providing for shares being disposed of by one shareholder to be offered to other existing shareholders before they can be purchased by a third party. This presents a further hindrance to a forceful approach.

An acquiror may nevertheless be able to gain some advantage by establishing a timetable and pressing ahead with the events required before a deal can be completed. This assists in building up momentum and making a transaction seem more definite in the eyes of the principals. Setting of deadlines (as long as they are not unreasonable) for completion of various stages contributes to a sense of steady progress. The acquiror must be able to move decisively at each stage, including being prepared to incur professional expenses and line up the necessary finance even when it is by no means certain that it will be required.

(ii) Public companies

In the case of public companies, the option is open to appeal to the body of shareholders over the heads of the directors. Even if it has not been possible to achieve a recommended offer in the initial negotiations, it is sometimes possible to gain a recommendation after an offer is announced but before offer documents are sent to shareholders. To achieve this, something may be left in reserve when the initial offer is announced so that the negotiations can be seen to have extracted an increased price or other concessions in return for the recommendation.

(a) Price – a premium is needed

If a recommendation cannot be secured, the offeror has relatively little room for manoeuvre and must rely on fairly blunt instruments. The major factor becomes simply the price he is prepared to pay. The opening price offered must be at a significant premium to the market price before the bid in order to grab the attention of shareholders. Although no hard and fast rules can be set, a premium of around 20% over market seems a common starting point.

In considering the premium, an analysis of the recent price history and levels of turnover must be taken into account. In many instances, the share price will tend to increase in the period prior to the announcement of a bid owing to market speculation and information leaks. The price is said in these circumstances to be 'frothy'. It would be reasonable for the acquiror to base his calculations on the price level which prevailed in the period before any rumours surfaced.

If a bid is timed after a steep decline in share price, many existing shareholders are likely to have acquired shares at prices significantly higher than the current market price. Although the acquiror may be able to make some mileage out of the premium at which the bid is pitched, he must nevertheless realise that shareholders may be reluctant to sell at prices which will result in a loss to themselves, in spite of the healthy premium over the prevailing market price. It may be found that there was particularly heavy turnover at certain prices, in which these prices will be particularly sensitive to the shareholders who bought at that time.

If it can be said that the offer price is at a premium to the all-time high of the target company's share price, this is likely to be a powerful argument. All shareholders will make some profit. If the all-time high was reached some years ago, it will be relevant to look at the highs over the last two or three years to see if a more limited statement relating to those years only is possible.

(b) Timing

The timing of the bid may be partially determined by the progress and speed of the negotiations which precede it. Sometimes an acquiror will spring a surprise attack and time the announcement at a period of maximum difficulty for the target to mount an effective reply and organise its defence. A holiday season may be chosen or the attack launched just after an announcement of poor prospects or other problems by the target, particularly if this news comes at the time of the annual report. In these circumstances, it will be very difficult for the target to publish an optimistic forecast. As there will be a relatively long period before the next year end, prudence will demand a considerable safety margin should be built into any forecast. If the chairman is already committed to some rather gloomy remarks about the future, he cannot turn round and forecast a sudden improvement without putting his own credibility in doubt.

Similar arguments apply if an acquiror can identify rivals for the target company. In that case, it will be advantageous to select a period when the potential competitor has other priorities or problems.

If the terms of the offer include an element of equity-linked paper, the acquiror should prepare the ground by choosing a time when it knows it can forecast good results and positive developments in its own business. This will be useful not only for supporting its own share price but in order to make favourable comparisons with the business and results of the target. The acquiror should pay attention to the rating of its shares in the period leading up to the offer. The higher the price of the shares and the greater the support of the shareholders, the more attractive the terms of the bid will appear to be for the acquiror. The share price is more likely to bounce back from the marking down which is often the initial market reaction to the announcement of a significant bid.

(c) Platform for the bid

A common procedure is to accumulate a block of shares in the target company to serve as a platform for the bid. There are a number of advantages to this. It may serve to lower the overall cost of the bid as shares are bought at market price rather than at the premium level at which the bid will be pitched. It also helps to give credibility and momentum to the offer if a significant number of shares are already 'in the bag'. In addition, it allows a dual strategy on the part of the acquiror as regards rival offers. The knowledge that the initial offeror has a significant stake may in itself deter possible rivals. However, if a rival does emerge and is ultimately successful at a higher price than the initial bid, the initiator has the consolation of a dealing profit to offset expenses and show some reward for his efforts.

(d) 'Dawn raid'

If substantial blocks of shares can be identified beforehand, it may be possible to deliver a virtual knock-out blow by purchasing in the market or from selected major holders. Rapid purchase of an effective controlling stake is known as a 'dawn raid'. Some markets have introduced checks on the vigour with which dawn raids can be mounted. These restrictions are designed to allow a target company breathing space to put forward its defence and provide up-dated information to shareholders so that they can make an informed decision on whether to sell their shares. Such regulations may prevent an acquiror from carrying off the prize in one fell swoop via a dawn raid, but the arguments in favour of building up a stake in advance of an announcement remain powerful. Typical restrictions imposed by dawn raid rules are discussed in ch 20 below.

(e) Drawbacks to market purchases

Purchases in the market or from major holders must be handled carefully if they are not to backfire. Market purchases may have the effect of supporting the share price of the target company or even of pushing it up. This may result in the acquisition actually becoming more expensive for the acquiror. If he is not able to buy many shares, the saving on those shares will be relatively small, whereas the offer for the remainder may have to be pitched higher in order to appear attractive compared to the price before the announcement of the offer. The higher offer will apply to many more shares than have been acquired at the cheaper price in the market. Takeover codes (where they apply) commonly provide that all shareholders should be offered a price equivalent to the highest price paid for shares during the offer period. Consequently, purchases at a price higher than the offer value will require the entire offer to be revised, even for shareholders who have already accepted at the lower levels.

The ability to purchase substantial blocks of shares in the market after an offer has been announced may be a warning sign that some shareholders feel the offer may not be successful. If they also feel the share price will fall if the offer lapses, their best policy will be to sell in the market while the bid is still on the table. A purchaser buying such shares risks being caught with a substantial (and expensive) minority holding if his offer fails.

(f) Offer document

The wording of contested bids is fairly strong by the standards of professional documentation. This is one of the few occasions when the normally restrained language may go out of the window and the professionals involved have the opportunity to let their hair down. The main points covered will be:

Criticism of record.   The offer document sent out on behalf of the offeror will normally criticise the record of the incumbent management of the group under attack in terms of its financial record and business abilities. Published documents such as annual reports and circulars to shareholders will be carefully studied and any broken promises, over-optimistic comments or missed forecasts contained in them will be gleefully seized upon. The verbal warfare by circular may be backed by prominent advertisements in the press and sallies by supportive stockbrokers, journalists and public relations consultants.

Increases in capital value and income.   A more staid part of the document will cover the financial arguments for accepting the offer. The aim in this section is to show that the shareholder enjoys a significant appreciation in the capital value of his investment under the terms of the offer. It will also try to show that his income (before and after tax) increases, or is at least maintained.

Attributable assets and earnings.   As an acquiror's shares will often be more highly rated than the target company's, it will not necessarily follow that, in a share exchange, an increase in capital value will be backed up by an increase in attributable assets and earnings. The acquiror should be aware of the likely defence in this area and do what it can to minimise the opportunity for a counter-attack. It may be limited by the wish not to dilute the attributable assets or earnings of its own shareholders, which would inevitably be the case if it was offering the target company increases in attributable assets and earnings.

The best that can probably be achieved in this area is that any dilution in the earnings and assets attributable to the selling shareholders will not be sufficient to outweigh the benefit to them of the increase in capital value. The target company's management cannot go too far on this point without leaving themselves open in turn to attack. Why are their shares apparently so lowly-rated despite the asset backing and earnings record?

Drawing the defence.   Vigorous assaults may at the least persuade the target company to release more detailed and probably more favourable information about themselves. This will enable the acquiror to analyse the position in greater depth to satisfy itself that its own proposals are sound. To the extent that the information is favourable, the acquiror will have the ammunition to persuade its own shareholders and financiers that a higher offer is prudent and not just the blind pursuit of success.

Limits of criticism.   Care should be taken that criticism of the target company and its management does not become a double-edged sword. If the criticism is of the company, the question may arise as to why the acquisition is so desirable in the first place. If the criticism is of the management, after the offer closes, assuming the acquiror does not intend to replace executives wholesale, the wounds of battle may make relations very bitter. A defensive and resentful management can cause a malaise in the period after an acquisition which jeopardises the value of the business being acquired. The South may rise again.

(g) Components of the offer

The offeror should attempt to tailor the components of its offer to suit the shareholders. The main elements are:

Shares or other securities. If shareholders are likely to have significant capital gains tax problems, they may prefer to receive securities in exchange for their existing holdings rather than cash. If they receive cash, there is no doubt that they have disposed of their shares and the gain would be crystallised. If they receive securities, it is normally possible to 'roll-over' the gain until the securities received in exchange are disposed of. Shareholders may prefer to feel that they still retain an interest in the business after they sell their shareholding. If they receive shares (or other equity-linked securities) in a group which includes the company in which they are currently shareholders, they will still participate in its future success. If they have no option but to receive cash, the deal may take on a rather different complexion and possibly require a higher price for success.

Cash. On the other hand, shareholders may believe that if they are going to sell out they should receive cash, which gives them maximum flexibility for reinvestment. Why should they become shareholders in a group which they had not independently selected as a desirable investment? There may be a feeling that it is rather a cheek to offer paper instead of cash and that this is not a proper form of payment. The more complicated the securities involved in the offer become, the more likely this argument is to be heard, until the purchaser is accused of paying for the acquisition with 'funny money'.

Underwriting and its benefits. The most versatile arrangement is to offer shareholders a choice between taking securities or an equivalent amount of cash. This can be achieved either by the company providing the cash alternative itself or by arranging for the securities which will be issued to be underwritten. In such circumstances, it is not unusual for the cash offer to be set somewhat below the nominal value of the paper offer. Care must be taken to ensure that the gap does not become too large as this gives the target company an opening to attack the credibility and value of the paper being offered.

If the company is providing the cash alternative itself, it may (subject to availability of funding) set the level of the cash alternative as it desires. However, if underwriting is being employed, the level of the cash alternative will be determined by the discount demanded by the underwriters. This discount will become an even more sensitive negotiating point than usual.

CONCLUSIONS

The scope for subtlety on the part of the acquiror lies mainly in the opening moves, in the way the target company is first approached and negotiations are conducted. The prime objective of the approach and negotiations is to secure an agreed or recommended deal. If this cannot be achieved, an aggressor must rely on decisiveness, determination and a sheer ability to pay. But in inter-corporate warfare, for most moves there exists a series of counter-moves and the emphasis shifts to the resourcefulness of the intended victim and the art of self-defence.

CHAPTER 18

The art of self-defence

It has been said that the price of liberty is eternal vigilance and nowhere is this more true in the case of a public company whose shares are widely spread. Companies with no dominant shareholder group are always potentially vulnerable to an unwanted takeover bid. The announcement of a takeover bid can strike such a company's management rather like a heart attack. After it has occurred, there are only a limited number of steps which can be taken and time is running out. In addition, there may be legal or other regulatory or practical restraints on management's freedom of action once a formal offer has been announced. A management which wishes to prolong its life should adopt preventative measures in advance and review them on a regular basis.

The measures described in this chapter are divided into three categories. The first section deals with areas which can be considered good housekeeping, in other words, matters which a competent management would deal with as sound business practice rather than because it was nervous about a possible unwanted bid. The second section covers measures which, while having a commercial basis, would be primarily undertaken to deter or repel an expected bid. The third section deals with the tactical steps which may be taken to defeat an unwanted bid after it has been announced.

I GOOD HOUSEKEEPING

Good housekeeping measures relate primarily to an awareness of and sensitivity to the market. This includes shareholders, potential aggresors and the investment community in general.

(i) Share price – keep it up

The surest defence against an unwanted takeover bid is not to receive one. The single most effective deterrent is a share price which fairly reflects the profit potential and asset backing of the company. The most vulnerable companies are those with depressed share prices standing at a substantial discount to net asset value.

Some managements claim indifference to the ups and downs of the share price. In their eyes, their job is to concentrate on the company's fundamental commercial and financial health, ignoring the whims and fads of the stock market. This approach, although understandable, invites opportunist attacks from a more market-aware operator.

In the long run, a company's share price is likely to reflect the fundamental factors affecting itself and its industry. But there will be periods when this is not the case, and it is these periods an aggressor will watch for.

It is of course true that maintenance of a healthy share price is not wholly within management's control but neither is management helpless. Steps which are likely to assist the share price include:

(a) Repurchase of the company's own shares

Repurchase of shares is permitted in many jurisdictions. With shareholders' consent, directors may obtain a mandate to repurchase up to say 10% of the issued share capital at their discretion. When seeking shareholders' consent, directors must explain how repurchases can be prudently financed and whether there will be any adverse impact on the company. The effect on gearing can be dramatic, as share repurchases simultaneously reduce net assets and increase borrowings (or reduce cash).

If shareholders' consent is given to a repurchase programme, there will normally be restrictions on how many shares can be repurchased and at what price. This is to avoid the company becoming the dominant force in the market for its own shares. Immediate disclosure is required of the number of shares repurchased and the price. Alternatively, the company may purchase its shares through a tender offer, open to all shareholders for a stated period and at a stated price.

Depending on the jurisdiction, shares repurchased are either cancelled, and the share certificates destroyed, or held in treasury and so available for reissue. Warrants and convertible loan stock may be repurchased as well as shares and in certain circumstances these securities may also be called by the company.

Where such repurchase is not permitted, management may encourage major potential buyers sympathetic to them to enter the market in times of price weakness. Such a process tends to prevent a poor technical position developing in the market and helps to keep the price firm. It also serves to demonstrate management's views of the minimum value of the company.

(b) Cultivate a good market image

Responsibility for shareholder, market and press relations should be recognised as a significant function. The responsiblity should be one which is specifically allocated, whether it is carried out by company executives, external consultants or a combination of the two.

It is good sense for management to promote cordial relations with the major shareholders who can be identified. This may be done by telephone calls, by lunch meetings or other forms of entertaining and by off-the-record briefings on management's plans. In giving such contacts substance, care must be taken not to disclose to certain favoured shareholders specific price-sensitive information concerning the company which is not available to the market generally.

Management should also consider the merits of granting interviews and making background information available to research analysts employed by stockbrokers, fund managers and other professionals. A favourable broker's circular can assist the market rating of the shares and help in building up an institutional shareholder base.

Management should try to keep abreast of the preferences of the stock market which change from time to time. In differing phases, a market may emphasise low gearing, export sales, currency exposure or some other factor. Some markets show a distinct liking for bonus issues of shares or stock splits which keep a share price within a certain range.

A further step is to ensure that positive news or developments about the company receive favourable coverage in the media on a regular basis. There is a school of thought which favours this activity being handled by the company's own staff, particularly the chief executive or other senior director, if they have any talent for public relations. There is a natural tendency for the media to be flattered by being granted access of this kind, as there is to regard a public relations consultant as either a buffer or a channel for 'misinformation'. However, an individual may be a very capable executive but have little ability for communication outside the company, in which case the task is probably better handled by a professional firm.

(c) Keep in mind the benefits of a steady profit and dividend record

Major transactions should be reviewed at the time they are undertaken to assess their immediate impact on the profit and loss account and balance sheet. Cosmetic considerations should not be given decisive weight when considering major corporate decisions. Nevertheless, it would be naive to assume that shareholders' opinions will not be influenced by short-term results. As a highly successful investor remarked, in the long run, we are all dead. One of the skills shareholders demand from management is an ability to produce reasonable results in the short term while at the same time building for the future.

Financial years which are likely to show outstanding results offer a chance to review and provide against doubtful or uncertain items to establish a strong base for less good years. The dividend paid should be adequately covered by recurring income. The market may not applaud a large dividend increase for one year if the increased dividend cannot be maintained for the next.

(d) Updating information

If fixed assets form a significant proportion of a company's balance sheet, consideration should be given to periodic revaluations of assets, say once every three years. The annual report may also disclose other types of information not necessarily required but useful for shareholders to base an analysis of the company's worth.

Some managements are reluctant to supply data on the basis that they may be giving ammunition to a bidder. However, a determined bidder may find out anyway; providing information to the market at large may well be the safer course if it results in the share price reflecting the underlying value more closely.

(ii) Shareholders – who are they?

If a takeover is announced for a widely-held company, the attitude of shareholders is likely to be decisive. It is therefore good sense for management to identify the company's shareholders and monitor changes.

Some managements seem ignorant or careless of the shareholder base of the company they manage and, equally important, how it is changing. Directors may be only familiar with a few long-standing shareholders, often friends and acquaintances, a smattering of institutions and the little old lady who asks a question each year at the annual general meeting. This probably presents a thoroughly misleading picture of shareholders in general and what their attitudes are likely to be in the circumstances of a takeover bid. Management's awareness can be improved in a number of ways:

(a) Monitoring the registers

A sensible precaution is for the company secretary's department to compile on a regular basis (perhaps monthly or weekly in times of high stock market activity) a report on the numbers and composition of shareholders and the transfers recorded in the period. Holders of, say, more than $\frac{1}{2}$% of the company's voting capital or of securities convertible into that amount of voting capital should be listed individually. Any changes in their shareholding and any new shareholders reaching this level should be highlighted.

Significant holders of preference share capital or debentures may also be relevant. Holders of such securities can normally block proposals which affect their rights. Preference shareholders may have considerable voting power on other matters if, for example, the payment of the preference dividend is in arrears.

Most public companies hire a specialist outside firm to maintain the register of their shareholders. Such a firm will normally computerise the register, in which case various analyses of the shareholders and the changes should be readily available.

(b) Nominees

Shares may not necessarily be under the control or ownership of the registered holder. The use of nominees to act as the registered owner of shares makes it more difficult to interpret shareholding lists. Nominee companies are not always sinister, often being used more as a convenience than as a cloak. Many nominees can be safely identified with a certain institution or group, either by a similar name (rather obvious acronyms are favoured), the same address or other clear connections, leaving a balance of potentially threatening holdings. In some countries, regulations permit a company to require nominees to reveal identity of the beneficial owner of the shares. However, there may be some time lag before this information is forthcoming.

(c) Monitoring market activity

As a potential aggressor may not register shares promptly, the report on registered holdings should be supplemented by regular conversations with the company's brokers regarding concentrated buying from unusual sources. The level of turnover in the company's shares on the stock market and the price fluctuations should also be monitored to highlight any disturbing trends.

(d) Disclosure levels

In some countries, the accumulation under the control of one party of a certain level of shareholding (however registered or held) requires public disclosure or notification to the company concerned. In the UK, for example, an important check is at 3% of the voting capital, a level which many signal potential trouble but hardly confers control.

(iii) Public announcements

(a) Avoid a 'timetable-driven' announcement

A watchful management will pay particular attention to content and presentation of all public announcements. Announcements of corporate results are often dictated by accounting or auditing timetables, with little opportunity allowed for an overall review of presentation and impact. Under the pressure of time to get an announcement out, implications which later seem quite obvious can be overlooked. Omissions can make management seem incompetent or insensitive to shareholder concerns.

(b) Expectations

In the case of an announcement of results, the market is likely to have formed expectations in advance which the company's brokers or other market contacts can be asked to relay to management. If the actual figures are significantly different from the market's expectations, an explanation should be prepared in advance. Explanations made later, perhaps under public pressure, rarely succeed in being wholly convincing.

Inconsistent comments, changes of policy, missed forecasts and other unpleasant surprises are useful sources of ammunition for potential bidders. All statements should be reviewed to identify what 'hostages to fortune' are being given. Comment or loose wording which runs the risk of coming back to haunt management in the future might be best omitted in the first place.

(c) Delay means bad news

It is useful to bear in mind that the market tends to assume that delayed announcements of results mean bad news. If the news is bad, a delay in timing is not going to help.

(iv) Putting yourself in the aggressor's shoes

A useful exercise for management is periodically to view their own company in the way an aggressive bidder might. The exercise should include a valuation of all major group assets both on an existing use and on a best alternative use basis. Businesses with a below-average return on capital should be considered for management buy-out or other means of disposal at an acceptable price. Other possibilities include spinning off a part of the business whose worth may not be obvious to the market.

Incumbent management is in a position to know the company's potential better than any outside party and is able to apply the same analysis and techniques as a raider would. Inertia, sentiment or commitment to people or past decisions can make this a difficult or painful process. However, the options identified may strengthen the financial position of the company as well as anticipate and therefore neutralise a bidder's strategy.

A mechanism to identify such opportunities should be established so that they can be considered for implementation before management's hand is forced. Such moves may be rejected as undesirable for the moment for many valid reasons but contingency plans should at least be prepared which can be activated at short notice.

Management may have fears that rationalisation along these lines will present the company to a bidder 'on a plate'. Experience suggests that taking the necessary steps to improve the performance of a business is much less likely to attract a hostile bid than neglecting them.

II   MEASURES TAKEN PRIMARILY TO REPEL AN EXPECTED BID

The measures discussed in this section are those for which some preparation is normally required (although some may, in emergency, be attempted after a bid has been announced) but which a management would probably not undertake except in anticipation of some hostile move. They therefore fall into a kind of twilight zone where the immediate benefit to shareholders may be questioned. On the other hand, a management may argue that it is part of their duty to protect the company in a wider sense and that they are therefore justified in taking measures which have the effect of safeguarding their position so that they may carry out their responsibilities without extreme short-term pressure.

The actions are divided into five categories:

  (i) Changing the rules.
 (ii) Building obstacles into the financial or commercial structure.
(iii) Creating defensive shareholdings.
(iv) Making critical disposals or acquisitions.
 (v) Pre-empting the bidder.

The specific actions which fall into these five categories will change as laws, market sentiment or public opinion about their legitimacy change. However, the principles of how to repel a bid remain the same although they may appear in different guises at different times.

(i) Changing the rules

Procedures for managing a company's affairs are set out in the articles of association or bye-laws. The rules of the game may be changed by management initiative (sometimes without reference to shareholders) in a number of ways:

(a) Place of incorporation of company

The directors may take steps to move the place of incorporation of the holding company to a jurisdiction which has more favourable rules from the point of view of incumbent directors. This process normally involves the merger of the existing holding company with a new company incorporated for the purpose.

(b) Directors

Rules concerning the nomination and election of directors not currently on the board may be tightened. For example, a lengthy period of notice and disclosure of candidates' personal, financial and business interests may be required. Election of directors may also be 'staggered' calling for, for example, one-third of the directors to be elected every three years, a move which may prevent a new controlling shareholder from obtaining a majority on the board for two years.

Existing directors may be given long-term service contracts. This does not prevent them being fired, but may make it a very expensive process to do so. Such arrangements are sometimes referred to as 'golden parachutes' but can backfire by making directors appear more concerned for their own welfare than the shareholders' interests. Amounts paid to retiring directors are usually disclosed. They can receive wide publicity and prove deeply embarrassing to individuals.

(c) Proceedings at meetings

Rules may be introduced banning special meetings except with the consent of the board or requiring extended notice for resolutions to be put to meetings of the company without management's blessing. Higher majorities may be required for certain critical motions, such as those approving mergers or a repurchase of shares from a holder who has recently assembled a significant stake.

(d) Voting rights ('A' and 'B' shares)

Under the articles or bye-laws of a company, classes of shares may be issued with different voting rights. A class of preferred shares, for example, may carry a multiple of the votes applicable to ordinary shares. Ordinary shares may be issued with different par values and dividend rights but the same number of votes. Some stock exchanges refuse listings for shares if different voting rights of this type are being introduced for the first time. Companies with such a voting structure already in place are normally permitted to maintain it.

Opinions vary as to whether control can reasonably be divorced from financial returns. A founding shareholder may place great weight on retaining control, or at least a significant voting interest, which can conflict with the need of a growing company to increase its equity base. If investors can be found who are sympathetic to the view that the founder's control is key to the company's growth, why not permit them to invest on a financial basis without equal voting rights? The contrary view holds that the existence of a two-tier structure is fundamentally unsound and in due course likely to lead to abuses of control, by which time it is too late to remedy the situation satisfactorily. This view holds that the voting rights are an integral part of the value of the share.

(ii) Structural obstacles

Obstacles may be erected through the financial structure of the company or its commercial arrangements.

(a) Authorised share capital

Sufficient authorised but unissued share capital should be maintained to give management the flexibility, without further reference to shareholders, to issue new shares. This gives scope for issues of new shares to supportive parties and to dilute a threatening shareholding. There will normally be a limit—say 20% of issued share capital—on the number of shares which can be issued without the sanction of a meeting of shareholders, even if sufficient authorised share capital is available, and all such issues must be justified commercially.

New classes of shares with particular rights to be designated by management may be authorised, the basis for the 'poison pill' defence. In this manoeuvre, the defending company may declare a special dividend or bonus issue of a new class of share capital or of rights to subscribe for such capital. In some cases, the rights are only exercisable after a third party acquires more than a certain percentage of the outstanding share capital. The holders of the new shares may be entitled to receive payments or purchase shares in a new merged entity after a bid in such a way that the bid would be rendered prohibitively expensive for a bidder.

(b) Loans and loan stocks

The terms of listed convertible or unsecured loan stocks may include a provision that the stock becomes immediately convertible or repayable at par in the event of a change of control of the issuing company.

The origin of this type of provision was as a legitimate protection for the providers of long-term loan capital. It allows them to obtain repayment if the borrower's management changes in such a way that the loan stockholders' confidence is lost. However, the provision has sometimes been built in by the issuer itself in order to increase the cash requirements of the bidder. The terms of some syndicated bank loans also contain a provision that the loan may be callable in the event of a change of control of the borrower. In many instances, a default or early repayment of one loan may through cross-default clauses trigger wholesale repayments of a company's borrowings.

(c) Commercial arrangements

Companies may have valuable agency or licence agreements which are liable to be terminated in the event of a change of control. As in the case of bank loans, this practice has a legitimate commercial basis in that a licensor or other principal wants to know the party with whom he is dealing. However, it can also be used by a company entering into such agreements to erect further obstacles to a takeover.

(iii) Creating defensive shareholdings

As ultimately it is the votes that count, measures to form solid voting support are very effective.

(a) Voting pacts

Voting trusts or other voting agreements or arrangements between shareholders may be established. Sometimes family members, for example, or groups of associates, may agree that their shares should be held by a single company which votes for them as a block. This prevents an outsider from picking off individual members of the group or driving a wedge between groups who may not always see eye to eye.

(b) Allied shareholdings

An allied shareholding may be created by placing a block of shares in hands considered to support existing management. This might be done for cash or by the purchase of assets from a group or individual with long-standing connections with the company. The consideration would be satisfied by way of an issue of new shares. However, the asset or business acquired may not be ideal in commercial terms. There is also the danger of a change in attitude of the holder or an approach by an aggressor with an offer which cannot be refused.

(c) Cross-shareholdings

Cross-shareholdings, where two (or more) companies take substantial shareholdings in each other, have been commonly used to protect control. The position may be created originally by an exchange of shares, purchases in the market or other types of transaction. In a case where a third person has a substantial shareholding in one of the companies concerned, control of a large pool of assets may be secured for a relatively small investment.

Cracks in this structure may appear if any of the companies develop financial weaknesses. The interlocking nature of the shareholdings considerably hampers the making of issues of voting capital to third parties to raise further equity. The companies may therefore be locked into a vicious circle where new capital becomes increasingly difficult to obtain.

(iv) Disposals and acquisitions

(a) Disposals

It is part of sound management policy to review and, if appropriate, dispose of under-performing businesses. However, businesses or assets which cannot be sold easily or at an acceptable price but which may have great potential value to shareholders may require a different approach. They may, for example, be spun off through a distribution of shares to the existing shareholders of the company. In this way, shareholders have distinct shareholdings in two separate entities. This may serve to sharpen investor focus on both companies by unbundling a package of interests, in which case, the combined share prices of the two holdings should be higher than the share price of the group before the spin-off.

The value of certain assets, such as oil or forestry reserves, may be made more directly accessible to shareholders by putting them in trusts and distributing units in the trust to shareholders. In this way, the shareholder can participate in the benefits of the income generated by the asset without the intervening layer of the corporate structure.

If there is one particular asset (sometimes referred to as a 'crown jewel') which is thought to be of particular interest to a potential bidder, it may be put outside the control of the company by one of the above methods or other arrangements whereby the management of that particular asset passes to other hands. In this way, the attractions of the company to a bidder are reduced.

(b) Acquisitions

A programme of acquisitions if properly planned will promote the growth of a company and improve the market rating of its shares. However, as sheer size is felt by many managements to be a barrier to a hostile bid, acquisitions may be made partly with a view to rendering the enlarged group too large for a predator to swallow. If such an acquisition is made for cash, it will also increase the level of gearing of the enlarged group which may be a further deterrent to an aggressor. Acquisition of a business in a specialised or sensitive area which involves government or other regulatory approvals can be an effective ploy of this type.

(v) Pre-empting the bidder

(a) Greenmail

Management may be inclined, where the law permits, to use the company's own resources to buy off a shareholder who has built up a potentially threatening stake. In cases where the price paid to such an aggressor is above the prevailing market price, this practice has been dubbed 'greenmail' and comes uncomfortably close to a management using shareholders' money to protect their own interests. It seems particularly blatant where a third party may have had as its principal objective to be bought off at a dealing profit rather than to seek control of the company or to take a long-term investment. A number of companies in the US have introduced measures preventing the payment of greenmail, on the assumption that this will dissuade an aggressor motivated by short-term profit. As a defence, it has had the drawback of displaying weakness, so that a management which pays greenmail once is likely to find itself faced with a similar demand soon afterwards.

(b) Defensive merger

On a 'better the devil you know' principle, some managements form under-standings with a similarly-sized group to whom they can turn in the event a less agreeable suitor seems likely to press his case. This appears to be the driving force behind some mergers which lack any obvious commercial logic.

(c) Recapitalisation

A company can carry out what is in effect an LBO or a partial LBO (see ch 19) on itself. This is commonly referred to as a recapitalisation exercise or 'recap'. Such a move is usually prompted by a takeover threat from an outside party for whom the main attraction is the cash resources or strong balance sheet of the target company, combined with a depressed share price.

One method is to pay a large cash dividend which not only exhausts available cash resources but requires heavy borrowing to complete the funding. This can be done rapidly if the company in question has sufficient reserves to declare a dividend of the size required. The dividend itself can be paid partly in cash and partly in loan stock (or preference shares) of the company if it is not practicable to obtain bank financing for an all-cash dividend. The objective is to get available resources into existing shareholders' hands and create additional gearing in the company's balance sheet to ward off the predator.

If the payment of a large dividend is not practicable, a more elaborate reconstruction exercise can be attempted. A new company is established whose shareholders are substantially the same as those of the original company. The new company then acquires the original company with cash raised by an LBO-type financing structure. Shareholders thus receive a substantial amount of cash plus equity in the LBO vehicle, sometimes referred to as 'stub' equity, as the value of the 'ticket' is in the loans. The effect is to secure for the existing shareholders the profit that the LBO financiers would have made.

III TACTICS AFTER THE ANNOUNCEMENT OF A HOSTILE BID

The third category of measures are those mainly applicable only after the announcement of a hostile bid, in other words, short-term tactical moves designed to combat a specific threat. After its announcement, an offer can be opposed in three broad ways:

  (i) Releasing positive new information.
 (ii) Attacking the terms of the bid and the bidder.
(iii) Taking actions designed to block or frustrate the bid.

(i) Releasing positive new information

A skilful bidder is likely to time his move at a time when it is difficult for the target to release encouraging news, for example just after an announcement of poor results has been made or following warning remarks on prospects by management. The main areas on which the shareholders and investors generally will expect to hear the company's views are:

(a) Profit and dividend forecast

If increased profits and dividends can be forecast this serves not only to make the offer price look less attractive but also underlines the good performance of current management. Such forecasts must be reported on by the company's auditors and financial advisers. A past record of good growth and achieved targets assists in establishing the credibility of a forecast in circumstances where the directors would like to show an encouraging increase in profits.

(b) Revaluation of assets

If significant assets have been carried on the company's books at cost for a number of years, a revaluation may disclose a substantial surplus over book values which would tend to make the offer price appear less generous. Some allowance should be made for any tax which might be incurred on the disposal of assets at the valuation price.

(c) Other positive developments

A company may have projects on hand which can be announced at an important moment to bolster shareholder confidence in the future of the company. Such announcements might include promising new products and orders, contracts which are being signed or negotiated, hiring of new management and other similar items.

A target company must be aware that release of positive new information may be a double-edged sword in circumstances where the aggressor has considerable financial strength. The first offer may be a 'sighting shot' to force disclosure of information on the basis of which an increased offer can be justified. A management should therefore carefully consider how much new information it needs to release in order to repulse a particular offer. There may be arguments in favour of releasing information step by step saving the best until fairly late in the process so that it is difficult for a bidder to react with substantial changes to the terms of their offer.

(ii) Attacking the terms of the bid and the bidder

Attack is often the best form of defence. It is a rare bid and bidder that have no Achilles heel. Possible vulnerable points include:

(a) Value and type of consideration

An obvious tactic is to argue that the offer is not high enough, specifically that it does not adequately reflect the profits, dividends, assets and prospects of the company. Shareholders may be subject to taxation through a forced disposal of their shares, which will reduce the face value of the offer. An analysis of past share price performance may show that the offer price is below the market price at some period.

If the bid is not all in cash, the value of the securities being offered in exchange may be attacked. The bidder's shares may be vulnerable to the same type of criticisms as can be advanced against a target company.

If other more complicated types of security are being offered such as convertible or unsecured loan stock, the consideration may be attacked as 'funny money'. In a closely-matched contest, shareholders may through familiarity prefer to keep shares deliberately purchased rather than to accept shares in another company offered in exchange.

If a bid is in paper, the contribution of the two companies to the earnings and assets of the enlarged group may show that the shareholders of the target company are being 'short-changed' as regards earnings or asset backing. Indeed, unless the bid is over-generous to the target, some disadvantage to the target company shareholders is inevitable and can be highlighted. Typically, the bidder will be seeking to use paper with a high market price to acquire earnings or assets at a discount.

(b) Commercial and timing arguments

Often a bid can be attacked as being opportunist, taking advantage of some period of weakness in the target which may be temporary. Indeed, the bidder is unlikely to be motivated by pure altruism. The commercial and industrial logic of the transaction may be questioned, although strictly speaking this may be of little relevance to a shareholder offered cash or a considerable proportion of cash in exchange for his shares.

The argument may be put forward that if the company is as bad as the bidder makes out then why does he want it at all. Alternatively if a company is good, why should the bidder reap the benefits and not the existing shareholders? Sometimes the tables can be turned and pressure brought to bear on the shareholders of the bidding company to prevent that company making a high bid. If a bid is so attractive, in some sense it must penalise the bidder's existing shareholders.

An offer for the bidding company by the target has the potential to reduce the market to total confusion. This is the so-called 'Pac Man' defence.

(c) Motives of bidder

Contested takeovers may rapidly become personalised, the more so the longer the bid continues. It tends to be seen as a duel between the two chairmen or other prominent executives of the companies. Public exchanges between the two sides can degenerate into mere abuse and personal attacks. A common tactic is to question the motives of the controlling shareholder or chief executive of a bidder, suggesting that the bid is made for reasons of ego or empire building and that such a person is unfit to manage the target company.

(iii) Throwing blocks

The third category involves not chiefly a debate on the pluses and minuses of the bid but spoiling tactics which can be applied almost equally well whether the bid is essentially good or bad.

(a) Legal/regulatory

In the US, a major part of the defence to a hostile bid is a resort to the courts for injunctions to delay or block the takeover, including attacks on both the bidder and his associates and financial advisers and backers for misleading or inadequate disclosure and violations of procedure. Takeovers may also be subject to government or other regulatory approvals particularly as regards anti-monopoly rules so that lobbying for such approval to be withheld is a possible tactic.

Whether a bid is vulnerable to such obstacles will depend primarily on size, sensitivity of the industry and the political clout of the bidder and the target. It may also depend on the political climate of the time. Most countries, for example, have restrictions on foreign control of local companies. How these restrictions are interpreted and enforced may vary with the attitude of the government of the day towards foreign investors. Equally, the strength of a domestic lobby at a particular time, for example the trade unions, may make the employment consequences of a particular bid a more sensitive factor than it otherwise would be.

(b) Market purchases

In the closing stages of a bid, perhaps the most critical factor will be whether the market price is at a premium to the value of the offer. A programme of share purchases in the market by associates of the target company will help to achieve this. In some countries, it is necessary to be able to demonstrate that the company has not provided any financial support for share purchases, including giving 'stop-loss' guarantees.

(c) Publicity and appeals to other factors

Management will send circulars and other material to shareholders containing information helpful to their case. Newspaper advertisements may also be taken out. The help of related parties such as stockbrokers may also be enlisted to prepare and send positive circulars to major clients who are shareholders or potential shareholders of the company.

Management can often appeal to a sense of loyalty in its shareholders particularly if the business has a long history and tradition. Companies with well-known products or brand names may be able to rouse the support of customers and suppliers. Employees who may be anxious about the effect of a change of control on their jobs can also be recruited.

(d) White knight

If management feels that the other moves open to it are unlikely to prevent the success of a hostile bid it may seek another suitor, commonly referred to as a 'white knight'. By gathering a consortium of institutional backers, management can become its own white knight through a management buy-out.

With the encouragement and support of existing management, a white knight knows that there is a high chance of success. In addition, an appropriate white knight will often have some interest in preventing the rival merger which may lead, for example, to a powerful competitive group being formed. These factors appear sufficient to guarantee no shortage of eager white knights, despite the fact that their late entry into the fray involves the payment of a price which they sometimes live to regret.

Blocking tactics may prove highly effective and are attractive in the heat of the battle. However, it may be questioned whether some moves, particularly legal and other technical steps which may be taken to block an otherwise attractive offer, are genuinely in the interests of the shareholders or whether their main effect is to preserve the power of an entrenched management.

CHAPTER 19

Leveraged buy-outs

Many acquisitions are financed by loans and to that extent qualify to be called leveraged buy-outs (LBO). However, during the eighties, a particular type of transaction developed not only financed by borrowing but where the acquiring vehicle is set up specifically for the purpose of the acquisition and has little equity capital and no other business. From isolated, one-off cases, LBOs became more standardised until they generated their own specialist industry.

Where an LBO is led by existing managers of the company, it is referred to as a management buy-out (MBO). Less frequently, a management team not involved in the business will raise finance to make an acquisition or will be backed or recruited by a team of financiers to do so. This is referred to as a management buy-in.

The reasons for the development of LBOs as a technique are discussed in Section I below. The general stages and procedures for a typical LBO are described in the following sections. The steps needed to achieve a successful LBO are covered in Section II. The structure of the financing, which has become a key element in implementing an LBO, is set out in Section III. The subsequent management, refinancing and 'exit' for the investors is described in Section IV. LBOs have been among the most controversial transactions in the corporate finance field in recent years. Despite their rapid rise and the subsequent decline in activity, they are likely to be an enduring feature of the corporate finance scene. A brief assessment is set out at the end of the chapter.

This chapter is largely written from the perspective of the buy-out team and its advisers. The point of view of the vendor is covered in ch 22 – Disposals. Many features of LBOs are common to other acquisitions and if dealt with in other chapters are not repeated here. This chapter concentrates on aspects, such as financing, which change critically in the context of an LBO.

I REASONS FOR DEVELOPMENT

The LBO has its origins partly as a reaction to previous trends, such as the conglomerate, and partly because it was an idea whose time had come.

(i) Reaction to the conglomerate trend

The rationale for the conglomerate merger is discussed in ch 13 above, particularly the view that a strong centralised management can create value in applying its skills to a disparate group and reduce risk through diversification. Such merger activity saw the grouping together of businesses which did not always prove well suited to each other.

The stock market sometimes values the whole at less than the sum of its parts, a phenomenon most easily observed in the case of a company holding a portfolio of securities or properties. This discount creates pressure to sell, especially if the parent company comes under attack from corporate raiders. Other reasons for sale are financial difficulties where acquisitions had been funded with bank debt or disillusionment if the business fails to perform up to expectations. Groups identify 'core' assets or businesses, areas of critical mass which make the greatest financial contribution to the group or where the group is or could become a market leader. Businesses not falling into such areas are designated 'non-core' and, by implication, become candidates for sale.

The philosophy of the conglomerate is to decentralise and allow maximum freedom to local management, so that they can be held accountable to head office for performance. When conglomerates divest, it is therefore natural for them to consider backing local management to make the purchase. In addition, local management already know the business so the need to give sensitive information to outsiders is eliminated. The risk of leaks of the possible sale, taken as a sign of weakness, can be more tightly controlled.

(ii) Emergence of the 'entrepreneur'

Head offices might be prepared to consider local management as purchasers, but would management rise to the challenge? That they often did so was partly due to a shift in the market's perception of the 'entrepreneur'.

At times, the word 'entrepreneur' has been a term of abuse or so obscure that the main difficulty was how to spell it. However, in the eighties, the role of entrepreneur rose in prestige due to political trends favouring this approach to business. To be an entrepreneur became politically correct. The desire of managers to become owners was kindled and the prevailing political philosophies made it easier for banks and other financiers to lend their support.

(iii) Availability of finance

Assuming a willing seller and willing buyer, it had previously been largely impracticable for a group of managers with expertise but little capital to finance a buy-out of a substantial business. However, private investors, venture capitalists, investment banks and specialist funds or partnerships rapidly responded to the attractive deal flow which started to cross their desks. Meanwhile, bankers hit by losses from third world lending viewed LBOs as welcome relief. They appeared to be less risky domestic projects related to established businesses which had a proven track record and management.

(iv) Rewards

(a) Managers

Early LBOs could make the management group substantial fortunes based on small initial investments. A small investment in absolute terms can be burdensome for a given individual and it was in many instances the financiers who actually insisted on the management group having a significant equity stake, even if they did not have large resources. Consequently, the 'pure' equity component was often very small – say less than US$1 million spread among a number of individuals, some of whom became multi-millionaires within a 2–3 year period. This prospect attracted more and more management teams to put together their own proposals.

(b) Advisers

Management teams whose fortunes were being made were not inclined to object too strongly to high 'success' fees for advisers if the 'no-go' costs were limited. For the advisers themselves, MBOs became a veritable Aladdin's cave. There were fees for putting together the initial structure, carrying out due diligence, doing documentation and arranging bridge finance and syndication. There might be opportunities to co-invest through shares, warrants or options. The new company was likely to have to undertake disposals, creating further business opportunities. At the 'exit' phase, there would be capital restructuring, refinancing and the management of the flotation or sale to handle. Legal advisers, reporting accountants, valuers and other professionals all could draw from the same apparently inexhaustible well.

(c) Financiers

Returns for equity investors in excess of 50% per annum in the early years were touted. For lenders too the returns were initially above market with attractive spreads being supplemented by front-end fees and sometimes a sweetener in the form of conversion rights, warrants or options.

(v) Technical factors

(a) Taxation

It is probably no coincidence that LBOs are most popular where interest charges are allowable against tax in a flexible manner and corporate tax rates are fairly high. This substantially reduces the after-tax cost of using debt to acquire companies making taxable profits. In the US and the UK, it is usually possible to structure the financing of the transaction so that interest charges incurred by the acquiring company are allowable against the operating profits of the underlying subsidiaries. In parts of Europe this is more difficult and in many areas of the Far East it is not possible. Tax considerations can make highly leveraged deals look more attractive when cash flows are given greater emphasis in the analysis than the effect on the acquiring company's balance sheet.

(b) Security over acquired company's assets

LBOs are simpler to finance if a structure can be created where the loans to the acquiring company can be secured against the assets of the underlying subsidiaries. If this is not so, the lenders to the LBO can be stranded at the holding company level while the creditors of the operating companies have a preferred position. It is possible to merge the acquiring vehicle and the company acquired but this can be a cumbersome process and leaves the lenders exposed if problems arise before the merger is completed.

II   STEPS TO ACHIEVE A SUCCESSFUL LBO

(i) Is it 'on'?

Given the general climate may be favourable for a buy-out, each deal also requires a specific trigger. The main factor is an indication that the controlling shareholder may be prepared to sell or at least to open negotiations.

A promising situation is one where there is scope for differing approaches to valuation of the business. The controlling shareholder will tend to value the business based on the existing performance and methods of management. An LBO team may be able to develop a different approach leading to a different valuation. In this scenario, there is room to reach a price with which both seller and buyer can be well satisfied.

(ii) The management team

The management group may start with one individual and grow to say five executives. It is rare for one individual to have all the qualities required. Financiers feel uncomfortable if there is no back-up and generally regard the calibre of the team as a single most important factor in a successful outcome. A balance of business flair and financial discipline is desirable and checks will be made on character and integrity. An ability to work closely together is essential to survive the inevitable tensions of high pressure and prolonged negotiations.

Management must not only have a solid track record but be motivated to take responsibility for an independent business. Motivation comes primarily from the equity interest they acquire under the structure of the LBO but they must also be committed to making the transition from managers to owners, accepting the risk and the loss of big-company 'perks' for a period. The team must also be tough enough to take the decisions needed. One of the main justifications for an LBO is that local management, once properly motivated, can fulfil the functions performed by head office without a similar overhead. This principle will be put to the acid test.

The particular management talents required in an LBO may not be the strong points of the executive who initiates the LBO or who contributes the most funds. The degree and management responsibility of individuals should be dictated by needed skills and ability, not necessarily size of shareholding in the management group.

(iii) The business and the business plan

(a) The business

Not every business is suitable for an LBO. A proven track record of profitability is preferred, but there are likely to be some weaknesses, without which the deal would probably not be available in the first place. However, a business which does not exhibit most of the following characteristics is unlikely to be a candidate:

Established market position: An LBO must have a core business capable of being run on a stand-alone basis. Companies with established product lines and high, defensible market shares, perhaps reinforced by brand names, in fields with mature technologies are favoured.

Positive cash flows: The financing of LBOs leaves little in reserve for unpredicted cash calls. Basic operating cash flow should be positive or capable of rapidly becoming positive. Savings in operating costs will be identified on the assumption that the LBO team will manage their operation in a leaner way once it is really 'their' money at stake.

Not capital intensive: There is little scope for ambitious capital expenditure budgets in the early years of an LBO. Decreases in working capital and disposals of non-core or unproductive assets may be needed to supplement operating cash flow.

Gearing: The balance sheet of the target company must be strong enough to support the additional borrowings inherent in an LBO financing structure. Highly geared companies make poor candidates.

Non-cyclical: A business which is in a cyclical industry, is highly seasonable in sales or subject to sudden fluctuations in financing needs may not be suitable. Stability and predictability are valuable characteristics when the margin for error is low.

(b) The business plan

The preparation of the business plan is one of the key components of the LBO. It serves as a valuable aid in crystallising the team's ideas and forces them to consider the various influences on their business in a systematic way. Their assumptions can then be tested by their advisers and financiers and the plan modified to meet the points raised. It is likely to emerge more conservative but with inconsistencies ironed out and obvious weaknesses addressed.

The plan may describe the history and development of the business and summarise its products and production process, plants, technology, component suppliers, competitors, customers, marketing and distribution capability and other main relevant features. Past results will be analysed and future forecasts derived from them with differences (usually improvements) in sales levels and margins explained. The balance sheet will be set out with comments on the realisable value of assets and the status of liabilities. A cash flow forecast will be built up from operating cash flows plus cash derived from anticipated balance sheet changes. This will be the basis of justifying the price to be paid and demonstrating how the finance raised for the purchase can be serviced.

The LBO team knows their business best and should produce the initial version of the plan. They may welcome assistance from professional accountants and bankers and, in any event, the financiers are likely in due course to require a formal accountant's review.

Such business plans often show sharp changes from past performance and may stretch further into the future than a professional review would normally cover. For this reason and also to give the LBO team a feel for a range of outcomes, a sensitivity analysis will be performed to identify what factors have most impact on cash flow and what happens if changes or delays occur. The team can then concentrate on the likelihood of this happening and devise counter measures for the most critical scenarios. It is also helpful for financiers to confront such possibilities in advance so that the terms of the financing, particularly the covenants attached to the loans, can accommodate them.

A sensitivity study of this kind will be computerised for practical reasons. However, such computer applications often work by calculating many variables as a function of one. Sales is usually the chief determining factor. Consequently, errors in the sales forecast compromise the value of the sensitivity analysis especially in the later years of the forecast, where differences are magnified by assumptions such as a constant growth rate.

(c) Negotiations

The first test of the calibre of the management team is negotiating the terms of the buy-out itself. Too low a price may be dismissed as a 'try-on' with no result except ill-feeling. Too high a price may stifle the project at birth. Although management may draw on assistance from their professional advisers, and some financiers insist on being involved, the main responsibility will fall on the team.

It is a task at which they may be at some psychological disadvantage. They have been accustomed to a reporting role, acting under the supervision of executives with whom they must now negotiate as equals. They may fear at least a forfeiture of trust and at worst a threat to their jobs if they encounter an adverse reaction. One difficult card they may play is to suggest they may themselves walk out if their approach is rejected. There may be a fine line between tough but ultimately successful negotiations and being taken at their word.

Although management's position is unenviable in some respects, in other ways they hold the upper hand. They have intimate knowledge of the strengths and weaknesses of the business they manage. They control the flow of information to group head office which relies on them for reports on the business's competitive position and for estimates of future performance. It may be expected that once a buy-out team has formed an intention to proceed, they are unlikely to paint a particularly rosy view of the immediate prospects.

III   STRUCTURE OF FINANCING

Financing LBOs is a specialist activity, handled by buy-out or venture capital organisations or specialised departments or divisions of large financial institutions. The availability of finance tends to be cyclical and influenced by recent experience and the political atmosphere.

The structure of an LBO financing resembles a pyramid where a small amount of 'pure' equity is supported by a larger amount of 'quasi' equity resting in turn on a layer of mezzanine debt and a base of senior debt.

(i) Pure equity

The amount of pure equity may be insignificant in the context of the overall financing. Its small size is a function of the desirability of allowing the management team to hold considerable voting power and ensuring that they have a significant financial stake in the ultimate success of the business.

(ii) Quasi-equity and management 'ratchet'

(a) Redeemable preference shares

Since the amount of 'pure equity' is insufficient to support the level of borrowings required, 'quasi-equity' must be contributed from sources other than the management team, typically by a venture capital fund or similar entity. One suitable form is redeemable preference shares which can be converted into ordinary shares. The situation calls for a flexible form of equity, which can be redeemed if performance permits but can be converted if cash flow becomes tight. From the financiers' point of view, the desirable features of quasi-equity are that it should yield income when there may be no dividends on the ordinary shares, that it should represent a reasonable level of potential equity interest (say up to 50%) if things go wrong and that it should have a built-in incentive for the management team to serve investors' interests.

(b) The ratchet

This last feature may operate through a 'ratchet'. The principle is that the management team may start with a fairly low percentage equity (say 5–10%) but if they meet certain targets, their percentage interest increases to up to, say, 25–30% or higher. One way such an increase can be effected is by a redemption of the convertible preference shares held by the investors. For example, as certain target cash flows are achieved or if a certain target valuation is met on flotation or sale to a third party within a given period, part of the investors' equity will be redeemed at par (or perhaps with a small premium) resulting in an increase in the percentage held by management.

(c) Level of gearing

The level of gearing which is acceptable in an LBO has varied from market to market and also depends on the morale of the banks and other providers of loan finance. LBOs are by nature highly geared transactions, with overall gearing ranging from about ten times at the upper limit to one or two times at the lower end of the scale.

(iii) Mezzanine debt

(a) Characteristics

The next level of financing after the preferred shares is referred to as mezzanine finance. Mezzanine debt carries above-market interest (say 3% higher) and might be fixed rate. On the other hand, it is likely to be unsecured with no right to capital repayment for several years (perhaps until after the remaining debt is repaid). It may carry only limited rights to initiate legal action against the issuer. In return, it may be issued with warrants or with conversion rights as a sweetener. Where cash flow is tight in the early periods, zero coupon or payment-in-kind bonds may be used. Interest payments may increase over time to give the management team an incentive to complete disposals (and so repay the debt) at an early stage.

(b) Junk bonds

In the US, as LBOs began to require an extra tier of funding, issues of so-called 'junk bonds' became popular. Such bonds were originally issued by companies whose securities could not qualify as 'investment grade' (ie the highest four categories as measured by the principal rating agencies in the US). Many companies which were in a general sense highly creditworthy failed this test and the junk bond market, after its pioneering years, developed rapidly, in part due to aggressive marketing techniques. Increasing numbers of participants were drawn into this area. Junk bonds, based as they were on a view of the business and cash flow of the company as well as its assets, became a natural channel for financing LBOs. Mezzanine finance was made available by companies and financial institutions which were not venture capitalists or commercial banks. The process became incestuous, in that companies might invest the proceeds of one junk bond issue into similar issues by other companies.

In periods when the junk bond market is dormant, mezzanine finance may be supplied by the vendor in the form of a note taken back.

(iv) Senior debt and working capital

This grade of debt is of a more conventional kind, secured by mortgages on property and a charge over the other assets of the company. It will have a fixed amortisation schedule with covenants imposing strict sanctions on the company if repayments are not made when due. As it is designed to attract banks, it may well have a floating interest rate which is more suited to bank funding.

While the specialised demands of the LBO financing receive great attention, it is crucial to ensure that sufficient borrowing capacity is reserved to finance the working capital needs of the business. Negotiations will be needed with bankers for existing bank lines to be maintained and for any additional short-term facilities needed to support the business plan.

In a complex deal, the lines between the different kinds of finance can become blurred. Some investors participate at more than one level, seeking a 'blended' return. Indeed, it appears that institutions which have participated only in senior debt have fared poorly. When things go right, they receive a higher than usual spread; however, it takes a large number of good loans of this type to compensate for one deal which turns sour. When LBOs go wrong, even an apparently well secured loan may need a substantial provision. On the other hand, equity stakes in the same deals involve in practice relatively little additional exposure but offer a handsome up-side when things go well. Consequently, institutions participating only in senior debt appear to limit their up-side without significantly reducing their risk.

IV   AFTER THE LBO – MANAGEMENT, REFINANCING AND EXIT

As explained above, a major step in the LBO is the preparation of the business plan. As the plan is constantly reworked during the negotiating phase, it may come to have an air of unreality. However, once the deal is done, the business plan is the blueprint for action.

(i) Management

(a) Emphasis on cash flow

Owing to the high level of gearing, cash flow is of utmost importance – far greater than reported profits. Particularly in an LBO of a previously listed company, management may feel liberated from the 'tyranny' (as they see it) of quarterly or half-yearly published results and a daily moving share price. However, they now have another master, which is cash. To manage cash flow tightly, typical steps would include:

– sale of surplus property and other assets
– sale and leaseback of property required in the business
– minimising capital expenditures as well as operating expenses
– squeezing working capital requirements by managing stocks and debtors more efficiently and controlling credit
– selling businesses which command a high price earnings multiple while retaining cash cows.

(b) Areas of conflict between management and financiers

It is doubtful whether all such measures are likely to be in the long-term interests of the company. There can be no objections to 'running a tight ship' and many divisions of big companies no doubt have some fat to be trimmed. The circumstances of an LBO require that the closest attention should be paid to cash flow on a monthly, weekly or even daily basis. On the other hand, repayment schedules may limit needed capital investment and dictate sales of assets which could be of long-term value to the business. Expenditure on research and development and marketing may be restricted.

Management and financiers have a common goal only to a degree. Management, once confident of the survival of the business and a reasonable gain to themselves, may have goals in terms of expansion and innovation which are not easy to reconcile with financiers' desire to recover their capital and invest in another project. This conflict may be resolved by a comprehensive refinancing on more conventional terms or an 'exit' for the financiers by a sale of the business or a flotation of the shares.

(ii) Refinancing and exit

(a) Loans

The loans used to finance LBOs are supported by as much conventional security as can be obtained in the particular case. However, typically some part of the lending will be based on projections of cash flow not backed by tangible assets. Consequently, an array of covenants will be required by the lenders relating to coverage of interest and repayments by cash flow based on the business plan. If these covenants are triggered, the position will have to be reviewed with the banks.

If things go seriously wrong, a restructuring of debt may be required. In this instance, the equity share for management may be decreased and some mezzanine debt converted into equity. Some debt/equity swap of senior debt may also be required. Management's share will be further diluted and their control threatened.

If things go right, and particularly if substantial disposals are made to supplement other sources of cash flow, a refinancing by more conventional terms may be on the cards. This will allow management to run the business by more usual yardsticks by replacing mezzanine debt with loans from banks.

(b) Sale of shares/flotation

Both management and financiers want to know where the exit is likely to be before they enter into an LBO. For many companies, including those which have been public and gone private through an LBO, the preferred route is a flotation. This will allow the senior and most expensive debt to be repaid, so that the results can be presented on the basis that the relevant interest expense had not been incurred in the first place. Providers of mezzanine finance and equity capital see their investment restructured and are likely to cash out in whole or in part. Management cannot expect to sell a significant portion of their shares at this stage as it would damage confidence in the flotation. However, they gain liquidity for their investment and the ability to realise a profit in due course.

Other exits include a trade sale or a gradual degearing from cash flow. On occasions, a trade purchaser will pay a premium for control not available from a flotation.

CONCLUSIONS

LBOs in one form or another have been known for a long time. However, during the eighties, their number and size increased dramatically and, more controversially, they became the vehicle for ambitious groups to launch assaults on much larger companies. Alarms began to ring in the boardrooms of even the best-known companies, leading to political pressures being brought to bear.

At about the same time, the whole system began to fall victim of its own success. The original deals tended to be natural LBO candidates and priced conservatively, with adequate safety margins for lenders and attractive returns for equity investors. As the success of these deals attracted further participants and capital, prices were bid up and situations not necessarily suitable for LBOs were structured in this way. Aggressive or hostile deals became common. This resulted in transactions which could only succeed if everything went right; they were not sufficiently robust to withstand normal economic and stock market cycles, let alone the pervasive force of 'Murphy's law'.

The risks that lead financiers were prepared to run to secure mandates also increased. Instead of spreading risk through syndications at the outset, the 'bought' deal became common and syndication was an after-thought; instead of using their skill and contacts to recruit investors and funds, financiers took the equity on their own books and used the well-worn term 'merchant banking' to describe what was essentially commitment of their own equity; instead of securing long-term funding from other institutions, 'bridge finance' was offered with only a rough idea of where the other side of the bridge was.

Some buy-outs have made rapid fortunes for the management group launching them and lucrative fees for the merchant banks and advisers who assisted. It is tempting to conclude that such profits must have been made at the expense of someone, presumably the original seller who sold too low. However, market mechanisms have corrected this imbalance, with the prospect of excess profits driving up the prices at which buy-out deals could be concluded and increasing the number of players.

An LBO will tend to run into difficulty if it is in competition with other types of purchase. A trade purchaser may see value in synergy and economies of scale which an LBO by definition cannot offer. A cash-rich purchaser may have a low opportunity cost of capital and be prepared to accept a lesser rate of return than LBO backers would contemplate. On occasions, a listed buyer deploying highly rated paper may stand at a similar advantage.

Despite the roller coaster ride which LBOs have given investors and financiers, they are unlikely to disappear. Their rise was based on enduring features of commercial life and human nature. Organisations will for various reasons continue to under-perform over lengthy periods. Not all of these will be suitable for an LBO but in certain instances a frustrated management and ambitious investors will be able to see what is wrong and launch an attempt to put it right.

CHAPTER 20

Takeover Code and techniques of deal-making

Takeover Codes (referred to in this chapter as 'the Code') have been introduced in the UK and in countries where securities regulations are based on UK practice. In the US, the problems of the 1929 crash had led to a legal approach being adopted through the establishment of the Securities & Exchange Commission in the mid-1930s. However, it was not until 1968 that the first Code appeared in London following the tactics adopted in a series of contested takeovers which showed that the previous guidelines (the so-called 'Queensbury Rules') were inadequate. Subsequently, the Code has been updated periodically and amended to counter questionable tactics as they emerge. The authority of the Code has become established and no takeover of a public company in jurisdictions where the Code applies can be undertaken without close attention to its principles and rules, which are set out and discussed in Section I of this chapter.

The formal procedures and techniques used to implement mergers and acquisitions call for different skills and personalities than the cut and thrust of negotiations, attack and defence. The detailed steps involved are complex and vary with the provisions of the relevant company law, tax regulations and even fashions in professionals' views of how aspects of a transaction should be tackled. Certain basic principles, however, remain constant and are capable of useful application in a wide range of circumstances. These principles are the subject of Sections II and III of this chapter.

In the case of private companies, it is likely that there will be restrictions on the sale and transfer of shares which will have to be taken into account. As it is only possible to proceed by negotiation, the formal sale and purchase agreement assumes a central position in the transaction.

In public company acquisitions, a wider range of procedures is possible. There is more flexibility in the level of control and the methods by which control is achieved. It will also be important to know how shareholders who do not agree to the proposals can be dealt with. The contents of circulars and any other communications to shareholders of public companies are subject to strict control.

I TAKEOVER CODE

A voluntary code on takeovers and mergers is in effect in the UK and in countries such as Australia, Hong Kong and Singapore where regulation of takeovers has been traditionally based on UK practice. In the US, takeovers are primarily regulated by law.

(i) Voluntary code vs legal system

The proponents of a voluntary code stress the speed and flexibility with which it can operate. Speed is an important virtue in the context of a takeover, particularly a contested one, where fortunes may ebb and flow at a pace which can outrun legal process. The Code is interpreted by a Panel or Committee made up in large part by practitioners in the takeover field. Not all concepts and rules need to be precisely defined as considerable reliance is placed on the 'spirit' of the Code. This discourages participants from exploiting technicalities and loopholes in the rules which might be regarded as a legitimate tactic where regulation is by law alone.

In addition to the Panel or Committee, there is a full-time secretariat ('the Executive') and provision for appeals against Panel rulings. Their response time is rapid, often by telephone and informal influence can be brought to bear by the authorities to good effect. Practice notes supplementing the rules will be published regularly to provide up-to-date information about significant decisions made by the committee or the secretariat, and these notes are a particularly useful guide to current points of concern.

The Executive relies heavily on the co-operation of the participants in the market, who may be future or ex-colleagues. Particularly when things go wrong, such arrangements may appear to be cosy and to carry an inherent conflict of interest. Questions are raised as to whether self-regulation can really have teeth. An unscrupulous operator who is prepared to bend the rules breaks no law simply by refusing to comply. The practice of 'cold-shouldering' – denying an offender access to financial markets – depends on a tight knit financial community for its effectiveness. Where breaches are discovered, often as a result of a scandal, criticism is heard that a more vigorous system may have succeeded in bringing them to light at an earlier stage.

(ii) General principles and rules

Voluntary codes are based on a core of general principles. Some specific rules are largely extensions of these principles. Other rules govern particular aspects of procedures, for example, timetable. The general principles can be summarised under four headings, as follows:

(a) All shareholders should be treated equally

This principle might seem far from self-evident. In some markets, it is freely acknowledged that a block of shares which confers control should be valued more highly than a small holding. However, a central tenet of the Code is a mandatory offer rule. This rule states that if an aggressor acquires control of a company, it must extend an offer to all shareholders, in cash or with a cash alternative, at the highest price it has paid for shares in the target company for a specific period (say 6 months) before the obligation is triggered. Moreover, in recognition of the fact that a shareholder can wield great influence over a company without having a majority of the shares, the definition of control ('the trigger point') has been set variously at 15–35% of the voting rights. The requirement for a mandatory offer can be waived by the Executive if approved by shareholders at a general meeting usually in circumstances where the incoming shareholder obtains control through the issue of new shares (for cash or injection of assets) and has not purchased existing shares. Such procedure is known as a 'whitewash'.

To prevent associates accumulating a controlling interest in different hands, the Code includes the concept of 'acting in concert' to obtain control of a company. Members of a 'concert party' are treated as one entity for the purpose of the mandatory bid rule. To some extent, whether two parties are acting in concert in a particular situation is a matter of judgment and some of the trickiest decisions the Executive is called upon to take relate to this concept.

The mandatory offer rule also extends to cover the position where an aggressor's holding lies between the trigger point and statutory control (ie over 50%). Under a so-called 'creeper' clause, the aggressor may add only a certain percentage (between 2% and 5%) to his holding in any period of 12 calendar months. If he exceeds this limit, a full bid is triggered.

Also derived from this principle is a rule stating that if an offeror acquires more than a certain percentage of the voting rights (say 15%) over a set period (say 12 months) before the bid is announced, then if a bid is made, it must be in cash or accompanied by a cash alternative. The Code also stipulates that it is not possible to offer special terms to a particular shareholder which cannot be, or are not, extended to all shareholders.

There are also rules to protect the rights of those who are not yet shareholders, but have rights to become so, ie warrantholders and holders of convertible securities and options issued by the target company. The Code states that a 'comparable' or 'appropriate' offer or proposal should be made to them. This is normally interpreted as meaning that they should be offered the 'trace through' price, that is the amount receivable had the security in question been converted into shares, less the amount required to exercise the conversion or subscription rights. This ignores the time value and other elements in the valuation of such securities, as discussed in ch 1. A clause is now sometimes inserted in warrant particulars the effect of which is to reduce the subscription price if a bid is made. In this case, the trace-through formula will result in a higher offer for the warrants.

(b) Disclosure of adequate information to shareholders

Shareholders should be put in a position where they can make a timely and informed decision on the merits of an offer. There are sections of the Code setting out what information must be provided as a minimum.

Up-to-date financial information must be set out by the offeree. This covers not only past results but a statement on prospects. Most target companies will want to make a profit and dividend forecast if at all possible. The Code stipulates reports to be made on such forecasts by the auditors and financial advisers of the target company. Where a significant proportion of the assets consist of property, an independent professional valuation is recommended. Disclosure is also made of directors' and advisers' shareholdings and dealings in the offeror and offeree companies so that shareholders can assess the influences on their recommendation.

The position of the offeror is somewhat different. If the offer is in cash, it may be thought that little information is needed by the offeree's shareholders except the conditions and terms of payment, a guarantee that the cash is available and a statement about how the offeror would run the company if it obtains control. This statement includes their intentions as regards employees, any major asset sales and continuation of the offeree's business. The UK Code, however, requires past financial information on the offeror to be included in the offer document even if the offer is in cash.

If the offer is in paper, shareholders of the offeror will need the same information as they have received about their own company in order to assess the merit of exchanging familiar shares for unfamiliar.

To ensure that directors have guidance from professionals in preparing and presenting this information, and on the terms of the Code itself, there is a requirement for the appointment of competent independent advisers to the offeree. A merchant bank usually performs this role. In general terms, the information provided to shareholders during a takeover is required to be prepared and verified to the same standard as for a prospectus.

(c) Fair market

The major requirement for ensuring a fair market is full and timely disclosure of dealings and arrangements relating to dealings. The holdings of the various parties are disclosed at the outset and subsequent dealings are reported on a daily basis.

The details of dealings are relevant to the Code in various ways. If the offeror buys shares in the market at higher than the offer price, he must increase his offer to that price and give all acceptors the benefit of it. The provision of 'stop-loss' or other guarantees may result in one party being deemed to be acting in concert with another. This may have consequences for the terms of the offer and who has the obligation to make it.

Guidelines are laid down for the initial and subsequent public announcements. Arrangements may be made for suspending market dealings in the shares briefly when critical new information is released. Any conditions to which the offer is subject must be announced from the outset and must be stated in such a way that there is an objective test of whether they have been satisfied or not. The directors of an offeror or offeree company have a responsibility to act solely in their capacity as directors, without regard to their own position.

(d) No frustration of an offer

The board of a company in receipt of an 'unwelcome and unacceptable' offer may react with outrage and consider that a 'no holds barred' defence should be mounted. The Code attempts to draw the line between legitimate defence tactics adopted for the benefit of all shareholders and steps which could frustrate an offer altogether and prevent shareholders even considering it. Actions by the offeree which are prohibited include the issue of new shares, options, warrants or convertibles, the sale or purchase of material assets, entering into significant contracts or agreements, particularly service contracts with the existing board, or purchasing or redeeming its own shares. To prevent the business of the offeree grinding to a halt during this period, there is provision that commitments outstanding before the offer is announced may be honoured and that any such steps may be taken if sanctioned by shareholders in general meeting.

In order to make sure there is every opportunity to open up the bidding, information supplied to one offeror by the offeree must be supplied to all other bona fide offerors if they ask for it specifically (they cannot simply ask in general terms for everything supplied to anyone else). This can raise particular problems where a competing offer is made after an MBO has been announced, where one offeror (management) has a vast amount of information on the company. The information to be provided to a rival suitor may be limited to say the information the MBO team have provided to their own financiers.

(iii) Timetable and procedural aspects

Other rules govern timetable and procedure or are essentially reactive, brought in to counter specific moves which have been seen as oppressive or unfair.

For a code to command general support in the market, a clear timetable is important. The offeror must have sufficient time to put his case and canvass acceptances and the offeree to reply fully without being exposed to a protracted siege. The main deadlines and typical periods allowed are: posting the offer document after the announcement of a bid (3 weeks), response by offeree company (2 weeks after posting), minimum period for offer to be open (3 weeks), minimum period for offer to be open after conditions are fulfilled (2 weeks), final date for closing (60 days after posting) and final date for revision (2 weeks before the 60 days' limit). However, if a competing offer is subsequently announced, these deadlines are relaxed so as to maintain an even timetable between the rival offers. If an offer is finally defeated or withdrawn, a fresh offer may not be made by the same offeror for a given period (say 12 months).

The Code is primarily written from the point of view of an offeror whose objective is to acquire 100% of the target company. However, provision is also made for partial offers and, in the UK, there is also a code governing substantial acquisitions of shares (SARs), introduced to tackle the sudden emergence of 'dawn raids' (see Section III (i) below). They regulate a grey area where a strategic stake may be accumulated without the trigger point being reached. The effect is to slow down the speed with which such stakes can be assembled and to require public announcements, which by alerting the market tend to increase the share price of the target company and make holders less inclined to sell.

II   TECHNIQUES – PRIVATE COMPANIES

There is in normal circumstances no alternative to carrying out the acquisition of a private company by negotiation with the directors or major shareholders, who are often the same people. Where the purchase is for less than the whole of the share capital, problems can arise with pre-emption rights. In order that the circumstances of the sale may be properly documented, the lawyers for the buyer and seller will prepare a comprehensive sale and purchase agreement. If a business has suffered serious financial problems, the seller may be a receiver or liquidator instead of the shareholders and directors. Additional steps will probably have to be taken to deliver the business or assets in a form acceptable to the purchasers.

(i) Pre-emption rights and restrictions on share transfer

(a) Pre-emption clause and fair value

The articles of association for a private company may well contain a pre-emption clause laying down procedures which a shareholder wishing to sell shares must follow. For example, a typical clause might provide that a vendor of shares must notify the directors of his intention and his opinion of a 'fair value' for the shares and appoint them as his agents for the sale. The directors may accept the opinion of value or request independent professionals such as the auditors of the company or a merchant bank to establish a fair price. This exercise will be done on a willing buyer, willing seller basis, taking into account the limited marketability of the shares in a private company. The result could be a lower figure for fair value than a shareholder expects.

(b) Inherent delays

Once a fair price has been established, notice is given to all other shareholders in the company of the number of shares to be sold and the price asked. Each has the opportunity within a certain period to state what maximum number of shares he wishes to purchase. The directors will then allocate the shares available on a pro rata basis, allocating any surplus shares to shareholders who have indicated they wish to purchase more than their pro rata entitlement. If all the available shares are not sold in this manner, the directors may well have a right to sell to a third party within some specified period, say 1 month. Only after these procedures have been exhausted is the vendor free to sell the shares to a third party of his own choice.

(c) Registration

Whether or not there is a pre-emption clause and whether or not the pre-emption procedure has been followed, the directors may still have the right to refuse to register the transfer of shares without giving any reason for their action. Without the purchaser being able to have his holding registered, it will be impossible to complete the transaction. Consequently the full co-operation of the board of directors of the company is in practice needed.

(d) Lack of marketability

It will readily be seen that these provisions can create major problems for a seller or purchaser of less than 100% of a private company. He can only carry the transaction forward to a certain stage and then has to await the pleasure of the existing shareholders. A purchaser may feel that if the shares are worth buying they are almost certain to be bought by one of the parties who has the right of first refusal. The vendor too is at a severe disadvantage. Once he has indicated he wishes to sell he is at the mercy of an expert whose view he cannot challenge setting a price for the shares which he believes is too low. In addition, he is forced to impose on the purchaser a significant delay while the pre-emption procedures are exhausted. For these reasons, a minority holding in a private company may be virtually unmarketable even if the underlying assets of the company are attractive. It is little wonder that minority shareholders of private companies press for the company to go public whenever possible so that such restrictions are lifted.

(ii) Sale and purchase agreement

The transaction negotiated between the principals is embodied in a sale and purchase agreement set out in the form of a legally binding contract between buyer and seller. Both sides will be advised as regards the terms of the contract by their own lawyers who will be responsible for the drafting and frequently take a leading role in the negotiations. A typical sale and purchase agreement will include the following main sections.

(a) Preamble

The date, identities of the parties to the contract, recitals giving a brief background to the transactions to be dealt with and definitions to assist in the reading of the contract.

(b) Details of the assets and price

The details of what is being purchased, the price to be paid and how it is to be satisfied will have been the subject of intensive negotiations between the principals probably long before the involvement of lawyers. For this reason, these sections of the contract should not cause difficulty at this stage. If they do, it is a sign that the negotiations have not really been concluded.

(c) Conditions

The conditions to which the transaction is subject will usually have been discussed, though they may not have been expressed in precise detail. Putting them down on paper may have the effect of making one or other of the parties believe that negotiations are being reopened. Making the deal conditional on a 'due diligence' exercise is conventional and, in many cases, essential, but can make the vendor feel it is baring its soul without even knowing the deal will go through. Some agreements have so many conditions that it is questionable whether it is worthwhile to proceed with a formal agreement at that stage. It may be better to try to satisfy the major conditions in advance, to establish that the transaction is a realistic one. The tests for satisfaction of conditions should be objective ones, not dependent on the subjective judgment of one of the parties to the contract.

(d) Warranties

The area which causes the most difficulty is the question of warranties to be given by the vendor. It may not be relevant for the purchaser to give significant warranties, particularly if the purchase is for cash. Assurances may be obtained that the purchase has been properly authorised according to the purchaser's internal rules and any external regulations, if applicable.

The vendor is likely to be asked to warrant the condition of the business being sold in considerable detail. Warranties will include the following aspects:

Financial position: that the balance sheets and other financial information provided about the company and its subsidiaries are correct and complete, that there have been no material adverse changes since the date on which the information has been provided and that the business will continue to be run in the ordinary course until completion.

Commitments and contingencies: that there are no material capital commitments, unusual contracts, guarantees or any other contingent liabilities outstanding, including current or threatened litigation, other than as disclosed.

Records and returns: that the books and records of the company are correct and have been kept up-to-date and that all tax returns and other statutory returns have been made when due.

Title and insurance: the group has good and marketable title to all its assets and that they are fully insured.

Agreements: that the group has complied with all leases, licence and franchise agreements, loan covenants and other agreements.

Dilution: that no shares of the company are under option and that there are no outstanding rights to subscribe for shares or securities convertible into shares.

A vendor will wish to limit the warranties as far as possible by stipulating minimum and maximum claims. The minimum level is to prevent time-consuming minor claims and the 'cap' protects the vendor from the possibility, for example, of a warranty claim greater than the payment the vendor has received. It is also useful to put a time limit (say 1 or 2 years) for any claims to be lodged. The vendor may seek to protect himself by a detailed letter of disclosure of items about which the purchaser is formally put on notice and which are then excluded from the warranties. Liberal use of such terms as 'material' may be sought to describe potential breaches of warranties. There should also be a trade-off between due diligence and warranties. If the purchaser has been allowed to complete extensive due diligence, he should be able to satisfy himself on many matters.

The purchaser will wish to make the warranties as broad and open-ended as he can. At its broadest, a purchaser may ask for a warranty that all information relevant to a purchaser for value has been fully disclosed to it and that the vendor acknowledges that the purchaser is making the acquisition in reliance upon such information. Care must be taken over what entity gives or guarantees the warranties – extensive warranties are no use if given by an insubstantial company. The purchaser may also seek structural safeguards, such as retaining part of the purchase money to offset against possible claims under the warranties.

(e) 'Boilerplate'

This is a term used to describe portions of the contract which may seem cumbersome and complex but which in time-honoured fashion rarely change, except to get longer. The procedures for handing over control at completion, for example, are not usually controversial. Clauses dealing with such matters as governing law, notices, confidentiality of information, costs and announcements are standard and normally grouped at the end of the contract.

(iii) Sales by a receiver or liquidator

(a) Need for speed

If a business encounters financial difficulties, it may come under the control of a receiver or liquidator whose main responsibility is to realise funds for lenders and other creditors within a reasonably short period. This may present an opportunity for an acquisition at an attractive price. The receiver may take the view that the value of the business will rapidly diminish unless a speedy sale can be concluded.

(b) 'Going concern' basis

The sale of a business as a going concern is likely to generate more cash than selling assets piecemeal. It is also a more convenient and usually a quicker process. However, a purchaser may be reluctant to buy a business with its associated liabilities and commitments, some of which may be difficult to quantify.

(c) 'Hiving down'

To facilitate a sale, a new subsidiary of the failed group may be set up by the receiver and the relevant assets 'hived down' to the new company. The new company will have a low share capital and the consideration for the assets hived down will be left outstanding and perhaps undetermined for the time being. If a purchaser agrees to buy the business he will purchase the share capital of the new company for a nominal amount and provide funds to it to satisfy the debt to its former parent. The debt will at this stage be crystallised at the amount that the purchaser has agreed to pay for the business.

Through the hiving down procedure, the purchaser can buy a business which starts with a clean sheet and the liabilities and commitments of which can be precisely assessed. This method is perhaps most appropriate for manufacturing concerns where stocks form a considerable proportion of total assets. If operations cease, much raw material and practically all work-in-progress may be valueless. Customers may no longer be willing to take finished goods unless they are contractually bound to do so in case after-sales service and support are lacking. In these circumstances, the receiver may well take a view of value which leaves some margin for a company engaged in a similar line of business to make an advantageous purchase.

(d) Lack of warranties

It is desirable that the purchaser should be able to assess the risks for himself. It is unlikely that the receiver or liquidator will be willing to give any warranties and to obtain a warranty from the vendor, the failed group, serves little purpose. In addition, it is unusual for a receiver or liquidator to accept any other terms of payment than cash.

III TECHNIQUES – PUBLIC COMPANIES

In the case of a public company, a wider range of procedures is open to the would-be acquiror. It may be feasible to acquire a significant stake in the target company, either as a preliminary to a full bid or with the intention of achieving control without making a full offer. Where a full bid is made, there may be a choice between a public offer based on market practices for share purchases or a legal procedure called a scheme of arrangement. An important consideration will be how to deal with shareholders who do not accept the proposals.

Whatever procedure is chosen, shareholders have to be informed of the details of the offer and the up-to-date position of the target company. The contents of documents published in connection with proposals made to shareholders of a public company are subject to review and control by various bodies.

(i) Acquisitions of less than 100%

(a) Dawn raids and SARs

The technique of buying a significant stake in the market rapidly and from as few shareholders as possible is called a 'dawn raid'. Stockbrokers with major institutional connections will be key members of the war-party, identifying significant holders who could be sellers and approaching them simultaneously with a firm bid.

In the UK, rules have been introduced as a supplement to the Code which govern substantial acquisitions of shares (SARs). The main rule prohibits the acquisition, in any period of 7 days, of 10% or more of the voting capital of a company if, by doing so, the acquiror would come to hold over 15% of the votes. The SARs do not apply to acquisitions below 15% or above the trigger point, since in that case the full Code applies. Once the holding exceeds 15%, the acquiror must announce this holding and each whole percentage point increase in the holding. The SARs do not require disposals to be announced or disclosed.

The effect of disclosures and enforced delays in the pace at which a significant stake can be built up have to some extent limited the effectiveness of the dawn raid as a tactic in the UK. However, elsewhere it can be decisive and, despite changes in regulations, the acquisition of strategic holdings (even if below 15%) can be a major blow to the target company's morale and a major boost to the offeror.

A dawn raid can have some drawbacks for the offeror. As set out in Section I above, depending on the percentage acquired, a raider may not be permitted to make a full bid without providing a cash alternative equivalent to the highest price paid for the shares during say the previous 6 months. If the trigger point is reached, the purchaser is required to extend an offer to all other shareholders, in cash or with a cash alternative at the highest price paid.

(b) Partial offers

With the consent of the Executive, a partial offer may be made for any nominated percentage of a company's share capital. Consent is usually a formality if the bid is for less than the trigger point, as the Code does not seek to regulate such holdings, although the SARs may still be relevant. Consent may not be given for a partial offer which is for over the trigger point percentage but less than 50%, as this would circumvent the normal condition that offers must be subject to a minimum of 50% acceptances, unless holders of more than 50% vote in favour of the proposal. Consent may not be granted at all if significant purchases have been made from the market in advance of the offer.

Market enthusiasm for partial offers varies widely. In the US, they are frequent. In the UK, and other countries which have adopted broadly the same system in the securities markets, the practice is to date relatively rare.

A partial offer is normally conducted on a tender basis. The offeror either fixes the number of shares he wishes to buy or he may indicate a range, with a maximum and minimum. He will also stipulate the price he is prepared to pay. Shareholders can tender any or all of their shares to the offeror.

If the offeror receives less than the stated minimum number of shares, the tender will lapse. If he receives a greater number, acceptances will be scaled down proportionately so that the offeror only purchases the number of shares he desires. A shareholder tendering all his shares may succeed in selling a larger percentage than the percentage for which the offer is made if other shareholders do not tender all their shares.

From the offeror's point of view, the procedure reduces the amount of funding required as compared to a full offer. As a minimum percentage of the shares will remain in public hands, the tender offer method ensures that the shares of the target company will continue to have a degree of marketability.

(ii) Choice of procedure for a full bid: offer or scheme

A full bid is an easier process for shareholders to understand than a partial offer and still leaves them with the option of assenting only a proportion of their holdings. The price of giving shareholders this choice may be uncertainty for the offeror about the final level of shareholding he will achieve. This uncertainty can be removed in some jurisdictions by the use of a legal procedure called a scheme of arrangement. The main areas of difference between a scheme and an offer are as follows:

(a) Need for co-operation of target's board

A scheme of arrangement is entered into between the company and its shareholders. The 'offeror' may have little or no involvement beyond providing the cash or other consideration called for under the scheme. Because of this, it is very difficult to employ a scheme of arrangement without the active co-operation of the board of directors of the target company. It may perhaps be argued that directors ought in any case to put advantageous proposals to shareholders for their decision. As a practical matter, it can be assumed that the option of using a scheme of arrangement is only available if it is supported by the target company's board.

(b) Expenses reduced

A scheme may be significantly cheaper to implement where transfer duties represent a substantial part of the expenses. Under the terms of a scheme of arrangement, existing shares of the target company are cancelled and new shares issued to the acquiring company. A cancellation and reissue of shares is not technically speaking the same as a transfer of existing shares. No payment of transfer duty therefore arises under a scheme, which can provide significant cost saving. No capital duty is incurred when the new shares are issued under the terms of the scheme, so there is no offsetting cost in this regard.

As a scheme is a fairly complex legal procedure which includes court hearings, legal costs are higher than for a straightforward offer. These additional expenses, however, should be outweighed by the saving in transfer duty. A scheme is particularly useful where a new top holding company is being created to merge two existing groups beneath it. If the groups involved are sizeable, the savings in transfer duty may be very substantial. However, capital duty will be payable on the entire share capital of the new holding company, which may turn out to be equivalent to the transfer duty. This is an argument for establishing the new holding company in a low-tax jurisdiction such as Bermuda or the Cayman Islands.

(c) Acceptance level required

There are important differences in the level of acceptances required. An offer is usually conditional on at least 50% of the total shares in issue being controlled by the offeror and must reach the high level of 90% acceptance (of the shares for which it is made) before the remaining shares which have not been assented to the offer can be acquired compulsorily. A scheme, on the other hand, has an apparently higher initial percentage level of support required. Normally, a scheme must be approved by a majority in number of shareholders present in person or by proxy at the shareholders' meeting convened to consider the scheme representing 75% in value of the shares represented at the meeting. It is important to note that the percentages relate to those present or represented at the meeting to consider the scheme, who may be quite a small number, and not to the total shareholding body. Consequently, it is possible for a scheme to be approved with total votes which would have resulted in an offer failing to become unconditional.

On the other hand, it is also possible for a 25% minority to block a scheme completely. A minority of this size could not be confident of preventing a public offer succeeding at least to the level where voting and management control of the company passed to the offeror.

(d) Time needed to obtain control

A public offer will be open initially for a minimum period of, say, 3 weeks, and may be closed on two weeks' notice after becoming unconditional. Voting control of the company can be immediately exercised if sufficient acceptances have been received. It takes approximately one month longer under a scheme to reach the stage where the shares of the target company are owned by the offeror. The scheme proposals must be approved by meetings of shareholders, the notice period for which is approximately the same as the minimum period a public offer must remain open for acceptance. However, the need to comply with court requirements imposes delays both before and after the posting of the documents to shareholders. Consequently, if taking voting and management control as quickly as possible is the main objective, a scheme will not be appropriate. Such instances are most likely to be unrecommended offers where, owing to the need for co-operation from the target company's board, a scheme is not a practical alternative in the first place.

If it is critical not simply to obtain majority control of the target but to acquire the entire issued share capital, a scheme is the quicker reliable route. Under the terms of a scheme, it takes no longer to acquire 100% control than it does to obtain the required approvals for the scheme itself, which is an 'all or nothing' procedure. If a public offer is made, it is extremely unlikely that all shareholders will accept it in the first instance and there is no immediate way to compel them to do so. The procedures for acquiring an outstanding minority are summarised below and take up to 6 months from the posting of the offer. Consequently, a scheme is a faster method of taking 100% control by 2 to 3 months.

(e) Degree of certainty

Because of the legal nature of the scheme and its use in agreed situations, from the first public announcement of the proposals, they are assumed to be virtually certain of success. The announcement of an offer does not carry a similar degree of certainty.

If a scheme is used, the offeror knows from the outset that he will acquire 100% of the company or none at all. No possibility exists for the level of acceptances to settle in a 'no-man's land', over 50% but short of 90%. This no-man's land is the most difficult outcome for an acquiror to finance. The amount to be paid out is considerably greater than the minimum required to obtain control, yet as minorities are still outstanding, no direct access to that company's assets is possible. This may not be a comfortable situation for the acquiror or his bankers.

(f) Privatisation

Because of the higher degree of certainty and the greater ease of 'mopping up' minorities who may be difficult to contact, a scheme is often used where a majority shareholder wishes to buy-out the rest of the shareholders and so privatise the company. In this instance, the co-operation of the board as a whole is likely since it will be controlled by the majority shareholder, who may however put forward terms which are not particularly generous. The interests of the minority shareholders will be protected to a degree by the establishment of a committee of independent directors (if any) to consider the terms of the scheme and the appointment of independent financial advisers. However, minority shareholders may face the choice of accepting unsatisfactory terms or rejecting them and risk jeopardising the prospects for their investment under a disaffected management. To discourage proposals which are arguably too low, the establishment of some guidelines on terms and procedures may be desirable, for example that the proposals should represent no more than a certain discount (say 10%) to net assets.

(iii) Dealing with small minorities who do not accept

Special procedures exist for acquiring small minorities who may not accept the offer. It is unlikely that all shareholders will accept even an attractive and recommended offer as a percentage will be uncontactable or unable to give good title, for example, where probate has not yet been granted.

If a sufficient level of acceptances of a public offer is received (typically 90% of the shares for which the offer is made) the offeror may, in due course, acquire the balance of the shares compulsorily through legal procedures. However, this is a lengthy process which takes up to 6 months to complete from the date the offer was originally made. It is open to shareholders who wish to do so to raise objections before the court. During this period, there will be minority shareholders outstanding in the offeree company, some of whom may be actively opposed to full absorption of their company in the new group. Revisions of the group structure and redeployment of group assets may not be possible until the minorities have been acquired.

As mentioned above, under a scheme, control of 100% of the shares of a company is obtained at completion of the required procedures. No question of outstanding minorities can arise and the outcome will be achieved some 2 to 3 months before compulsory acquisition of outstanding minorities would be completed if a public offer had been employed.

(iv) Contents of takeover documents

Whether a partial offer, a full offer or a scheme of arrangement is employed, a document will be required to be circulated to shareholders on behalf of the acquiror. In most jurisdictions the person sending out such a document is required to be licensed as a dealer or securities adviser in order to protect investors and assist the authorities in controlling the contents of the offer documentation. The contents of such a document are determined by law, stock exchange rules and other regulations including those contained in the Code. The main components of this type of document are as follows:

(a) Chairman's letter

This letter sets out the broad principles and terms of the acquisition and explains why it is being put forward and what benefits are expected from it. The tone of the letter will vary greatly depending on whether the proposals are agreed or not, or whether it is hoped that they will be agreed in due course. It is likely, at a minimum, to point out the (presumably superior) performance of the offeror and its management.

If the offer is agreed from the outset, the letter is more effective coming from the chairman of the target company. His views about the attractions of the offer may be felt by the shareholders of that company to be more relevant than those of the party making the offer.

(b) Offer letter

The offer letter will be written by the acquiror's financial advisers who make the offer on behalf of the acquiror. The letter will state the terms of the offer and describe the different elements in it. It will include the terms and conditions attached to the offer and explain the timing for acceptances and the level of acceptances required. The financial effects of acceptance will be spelt out with examples of the effect on capital value, income and possibly attributable net assets and earnings. More technical matters relating to the validity of acceptances, how to tender share certificates and when the consideration will be received will also be explained.

(c) Financial information

Financial information about the offeree company will be set out. The information given will normally be a summary of the past 5 years' results together with the latest audited balance sheets. If a forecast of results is being made, details of the basis and main assumptions will be supplied. Any material changes since the date of the audited figures will also be given, particularly an up-dated statement of the indebtedness and commitments of the group.

If the offer is in cash, a confirmation will be given by a financial institution that the maximum amount of cash required under the terms of the offer will in fact be available to the offeror. In the UK, the Code requires a description of how the offer is financed and the source of the finance.

Where the acquiring company offers its own shares or other securities in exchange for those of the target company, the offer document also serves as a prospectus. Financial information about the offeror similar to that required for a listing must be given, including a working capital statement and if possible a profit and dividend forecast for the current financial year.

Where a profit forecast is made by either the offeror or offeree it must be verified and reported on by the auditors and the financial advisers of the company making the forecast.

(d) Legal requirements

Differing levels of disclosures are required by the stock exchange and other official bodies in various markets. The disclosures emphasise dealings in shares, areas relating to any conflicts of interest which might arise and significant contractual arrangements which have been entered into.

(e) Notice of meetings

A scheme requires at least two meetings of shareholders. Other offer arrangements may require meetings to approve certain steps being taken, for example to issue substantial numbers of new shares or dispose of major assets. The notices convening the meetings will be attached to the offer document. The information included in the offer document forms the basis for shareholders' decisions on how to vote at the meetings.

The procedures for completing acquisitions are specialised and in their detailed application may depend on quite obscure tax or other legislation in particular countries. However, the principles underlying the techniques change much less than the techniques themselves. Negotiations for control of a private company may prove frustrating because it is only possible to follow a limited number of paths. The greater range of routes available in a public company acquisition and the provisions of the Code make the procedures more complex and at the same time provide scope for a greater range of tactics to be employed. A number of difficult choices face the acquiror. His task is to match the methods selected with his objectives and complete the transaction with a minimum of disruption, delay and expense.

CHAPTER 21

Roles of professional advisers

Mergers and acquisitions require a range of expertise to bring about a successful conclusion. Individuals who generate ideas are not always the most successful negotiators. Negotiating and dealing with people in turn demand different skills from the specialist task of devising the most efficient method of implementation from a tax, accounting or legal standpoint.

Merchant banks are often the prime movers in an acquisition. They put up ideas, offer advice and provide support with financing. Accountants will be involved from the evaluation stage and particularly in assessing such aspects as the impact on published results. Lawyers play a central role in the documentation and completion phases of the acquisition. Tax advice is often critical. It may be provided by accountants or lawyers working on the acquisition or by tax specialists. If the companies are listed, the help of a firm of stockbrokers will be highly desirable. Other professionals may be consulted depending on the specific type of acquisition under consideration.

(i) Role of merchant banks

Merchant banks have made a speciality of merger and acquisition work although it has little connection with classical banking business. In some cases, there is no significant outside funding required and the company's lawyers or accountants may have a closer relationship with the principals. However, it is the investment and merchant banks who have taken the lead in building large departments of full-time professionals and such departments now dominate the field. They are closely involved in all facets of merger and acquisition work from the initial identification of targets to the monitoring of completion procedures.

(a) Preliminary stages

Merchant banks actively go out seeking mandates to act for a buyer or a seller of a company. A mandate for a committed seller is preferred. All managements worth their salt wish to hear about opportunities. Few will say they are not interested in acquisitions. This is a far cry from actually concluding the deal.

It is a simpler matter to determine whether a potential seller is serious about a sale. There is a brand of seller who much prefers courtship to consummation. Usually, however, it will be possible to identify a convincing reason for a sale – retirement, diversification or financial pressures, for example. Once the parameters (price, terms, timing) have been established, one side of the transaction is firm. It should then not be too difficult a task to identify a buyer in the market-place.

Acting for a seller also has advantages when it comes to fees. A firm mandate to act exclusively can be obtained from a seller whereas few buyers will wish to commit themselves in this way. In addition, a seller who has received a satisfactory price is normally quite willing to pay a reasonable fee out of the proceeds. A buyer who is already facing large payments for the acquisition may be unwilling to shoulder heavy professional fees as well.

Merchant banks will try to keep lists of current buyers and sellers in their files. However, the chances of arranging a transaction 'off the shelf' in this manner are remote. Good deals tend to be done quickly. Deals which have been in the market for some time go stale. It is likely that a specific search will be needed to identify a target which is not being actively offered for sale. In a large market such as the US, an initial screening may be made by computer to identify a range of suitable propositions.

Merchant banks will assist, if desired, in assessing the price which may have to be offered to bring an acquisition to a successful conclusion. A merchant bank's approach will tend to be market-orientated, concentrating on the price needed for success which is not necessarily the same as a valuation.

The merchant bank will often be involved in the negotiating process. Questions of price and negotiations tend to merge. If a buyer is willing to pay a high price, the negotiator need not be very skilful. A merchant bank will seek some room for manoeuvre in negotiations to improve the chances of bringing the discussions to a successful conclusion. As merchant banks are often paid in this context on a 'no foal, no fee' basis, or with a modest retainer and a substantial 'success' fee, they have a strong interest in getting the deal done. This is not to say that they will not fight hard for their corner but they may also be inclined to feel that it is in their client's interest to show some flexibility.

(b) Advice on the Takeover Code

As set out in the previous chapter, takeover codes operate in the UK and a number of markets where practice is traditionally based on the UK system. The merchant bankers advising the offeror and offeree companies act as 'point men' in communications with the Executive administering the Code and are responsible for advising their clients on the terms of the Code. Documents have to be posted within 2 or 3 week deadlines which may involve an intensive period of negotiation with the Executive just before printing. In the period when acceptances are being sought, tactics regarding press announcements and advertisements, press conferences, public statements, market purchases and financing arrangements are discussed with the Executive on a daily basis.

While lawyers often assist in communication with the Executive, there is a non-legal culture about the process which discourages a legalistic approach. This reflects the 'voluntary vs legal' debate discussed at the beginning of the section on the Takeover Code in the previous chapter.

(c) Co-ordination

When negotiations have been concluded, the merchant bank will usually take the lead in co-ordinating documentation. Offer documents for public companies contain much legal and accounting information which the merchant bank will not have prepared. The merchant bank's role is to draw the various parts together into a consistent whole. This document will then be submitted to various regulatory authorities for their comments.

Once the document has been put together and cleared by the relevant regulatory agencies, the merchant bank will oversee the process of distributing it to shareholders. The merchant bank will also monitor response, often drafting in numbers of people to assist in contacting shareholders or soliciting proxies.

If a company meeting is involved and difficult questions are anticipated, a rehearsal may be held to prepare the executives involved for what may be ahead. A list of expected questions and model answers will be drawn up.

Throughout this period, in a public company takeover, the merchant bank will be monitoring the reaction in the market and watching for an opportunity to pick up shares in the target company at advantageous prices.

(d) Financing

When necessary, the merchant bank may arrange finance for acquisitions. Although merchant banks rarely do much straightforward lending, they may be involved in forming a syndicate of lenders and negotiating terms with them. If the takeover is being financed by the issue of securities, the merchant bank, in conjunction with the company's stockbrokers, may assemble a group of institutions to buy or underwrite the securities being issued.

(ii) Role of accountants

(a) Accountant's report

It is prudent for a purchaser to seek a full accountant's report on the business he is buying. Some sellers oppose an accountant's investigation, at least until a preliminary agreement has been signed. Others recognise it as a significant hurdle and prefer to get it out of the way at an early stage. Not only does the report represent a further substantial barrier at which the deal may fall, it can involve disruption to day-to-day business. The morale of existing staff must also be taken into consideration.

The basic methodology of the accountant's report is to take each significant item in the financial statements and examine it to ensure that any unusual or doubtful aspects are brought to the attention of those deciding the offer price. Any items of potential under- or over-valuation will be highlighted, together with items which may not be directly reflected in the balance sheet but could have an impact on value such as guarantees, litigation and lease obligations. Comments may be made on the adequacy of systems and the general competency of management.

The quality of earnings and the accounting policies adopted will be scrutinised by the accountants. It is normally possible for a company to produce better than average results for one year by including items which may previously have been held in reserve. Particularly in a private company there is no incentive for the owners to increase their tax bill by showing a high level of profitability.

Companies may follow different policies in accounting for profits. Certain sales of assets may be included in profits before taxation by some companies and treated as extraordinary items by others. Interest may be capitalised in some circumstances and not in others. In general terms, it is only to be expected that the sellers will groom their company for sale and present the figures in the best possible light.

The buyer should regard the accountant's report as a thorough check but not a substitute for thought and analysis of their own. In the final reckoning, the acquirors must form their own view of value.

(b) Impact on acquiror's accounts

An acquisition can have a significant impact on the balance sheet, profit and loss account and dividend paying ability of the acquiror. The acquiror's accountants are in the best position to assess this impact. The factors they will consider will include the following:

Cost of acquisition. The cost of acquisition is based on the consideration provided by the acquiror. In the case of cash or loan stock, it is the amount paid or the nominal amount issued. In the case of shares, it is the market value of the shares issued, unless some unusual factor makes the market price misleading, in which case some other measure such as net asset backing could be substituted. The expenses of the acquisition may also be added. If shares are issued at a premium over par, the expenses of acquisition may be deducted from the share premium created.

Goodwill. The cost of acquisition is compared with the 'fair value' (based on open market value) of the assets acquired.

There has been considerable debate about the correct method of accounting for takeovers, particularly where it may be argued that a merger has occurred. It is difficult to define a merger precisely but it would seem that to qualify the two companies of approximately equal size must come together in such a way that one does not dominate the other and that both sets of shareholders continue to have substantial equity interests in the new group. In such circumstances a 'pooling of interests' method may be used to account for the new group. The individual financial statements are aggregated with only the minimum adjustments. No goodwill arises.

The 'purchase' method of accounting for acquisitions is more frequently applied. Any excess of the cost of acquisition over the fair value of the net assets acquired will appear in the consolidated balance sheet of the acquiror as goodwill.

If goodwill is assumed to represent a payment made in anticipation of future income, it is appropriate to treat it as an asset to be written off against the income generated on a systematic basis over its useful life. The useful life will vary depending on the type of industry, the competitive environment and other factors affecting the particular company purchased. Periods of up to 40 years are used.

More extreme views of goodwill are possible. One view is that any goodwill should be written off as soon as an acquisition is made. Goodwill may be too nebulous a concept to account for on a long-term systematic basis. Perhaps a virtue should be made of the 'new broom' and all goodwill written off at the outset.

Others would argue that goodwill is not an asset which necessarily depreciates at all. As long as the company acquired thrives, and profits are maintained or increased, no write-offs are appropriate. For example, a company holding a licence to operate in a growth industry is likely to become more valuable rather than less, although presumably this should be reflected in the price paid.

The directors of predatory companies dislike goodwill appearing in their balance sheet. Banks and other analysts tend to regard it as an intangible asset to be deducted from the capital base of the group, increasing the gearing ratios. If the auditors insist on regular amortisation, the contribution the acquisition makes to the profits of the combined group can be severely reduced. This makes it all the more important to establish at the outset the auditor's view of the effect of the acquisition on reported earnings of the group.

(c) Pre-acquisition profits

When a company is acquired, the retained earnings of that company are designated as 'pre-acquisition'. They cannot be treated by the acquiror as distributable to its own shareholders. However, the new management may wish to write-down the value of the assets of the company acquired which can be done against pre-acquisition profits. The bulk of the profits in the year of acquisition may in this way be judged to have occurred post-acquisition and so can be distributed. 'Clearing the decks' allows the acquiror to report better profits from the acquisition in justification of its decision.

Where a new company is formed to control a group, the problem of pre-acquisition reserves is particularly acute, since the new company will initially have no distributable reserves.

If this structure is put into place by a scheme of arrangement, the opportunity can be taken as part of the scheme to reduce the capital and reserves of the new holding company from the aggregate cost of acquisition to the level of the share capital and share premium accounts of the subsidiaries. By this means, distributable reserves are created in the new holding company equal to the combined distributable reserves of the subsidiaries.

(iii) Role of lawyers

In an acquisition of any complexity, legal advice will be required at an early stage. Specific legal problems may arise as regards the powers of a target company's directors, actions which can be taken by its shareholders and the rights of holders of, for example, preference shares or loan stock. The procedure for the conduct of a meeting or arrangements for voting may be of great tactical significance in an attempt to take control of a company. Many lawyers are skilled negotiators and act as spokesmen rather than simply behind the scenes advisers. Their formal role will include:

(a) Heads of agreement

As the framework of an agreement emerges, lawyers may be involved in drawing up a preliminary summary of the transaction called a 'heads of agreement'. Opinions vary as to whether it is helpful to reduce the main terms of an agreement in principle to a written form, which is signed or initialled even though it is not legally binding. A heads of agreement can serve to clarify and record the intentions of the parties and to bring into focus any major areas of dispute. Some vendors regard a heads of agreement as a necessary stage before they are prepared to release sensitive information about their business.

Another view is that to sign an agreement that it not legally binding is to interpose an unnecessary step in the negotiations. Because the parties know the agreement is not binding, there may be a tendency to fudge difficult issues so that the meeting of minds is more apparent than real. The parties may feel that there is a substantial measure of understanding between them when in fact there is not. Frustration may set in later because negotiations appear to be going backwards. The transition from a heads of agreement to a legally binding contract can be as difficult as arriving at the heads of agreement in the first place.

(b) Formal sales and purchase agreement

If the principals intend to sign a formal sale and purchase agreement, the lawyers for both sides will play a prominent part in drawing it up. Successive drafts of the agreement may be used as a vehicle for advancing the negotiations so the role of draughtsman and negotiator become mingled. At this stage, the person drafting can insert ideas of his own as well as reflecting the results of discussions which can give rise to antagonism and accusations of bad faith unless fully disclosed and carefully explained. A lawyer may gain the trust of his opposite number as well as his own clients if he can fairly reflect in the documentation what has been agreed between the two principals. This approach is often ultimately more effective than a more adversarial style.

(c) Public offer

The lawyer's role in the formal stages of a public offer is pervasive. He will be closely involved in reviewing all aspects of the documentation with particular attention to the matters required to be disclosed by law and other regulations. The detailed terms of the consideration under the offer, its conditions and the rights of the securities which form part of it will be carefully examined and precisely worded. If the takeover is by way of a scheme of arrangement, the legal procedures will set the framework and timetable for the entire transaction.

(d) Tactics

A number of tactics, particularly in defence, are the province of the lawyer. Various provisions may be built into the company's articles of association, designed to repel an unwelcome bidder or make his bid prohibitively expensive. To be effective, such measures need to be introduced and worded with extreme care. The company's lawyer will be called upon to shepherd the directors through each step. Other defensive manoeuvres may include appeals to anti-monopoly legislation and contact with the bodies which administer it. The company will look to its lawyers to take the lead in organising the necessary presentations and meetings.

(e) Approvals

Offers and defences require a plethora of approvals by boards and individual directors. In a situation where their handling of affairs may come under close scrutiny, directors will seek such comfort as they can obtain that all the documents are accurate and complete. The lawyers will be responsible for organising the necessary verification procedures and documentation. They will also prepare detailed board minutes for use as an agenda for directors' meetings to ensure that all necessary areas have been covered. After documents have been approved, the lawyers will check that they have been cleared or filed with all the relevant authorities.

(iv) Tax aspects

Advice on tax may be provided either by accountants or lawyers involved in the transaction or by specialist tax advisers.

The taxation aspects of an acquisition are often the most technically complex part of it, particularly in countries such as the US and the UK. General guidelines can be misleading in particular circumstances but the following points are often relevant:

(a) Transfer duty

When shares are bought and sold, a duty is normally payable on the registration of the transfer. In a stock market transaction, the practice is for buyer and seller to pay their own duty. This practice may be followed in the acquisition of a private company. In the case of a public company, the terms of the offer may include a provision for the buyer to pay both buyer's and seller's transfer duty. In a cash offer, it is relatively simple to deduct the seller's portion of the transfer duty from the consideration and make a net payment. In the case of an all-paper offer where the selling shareholder receives no cash, it is rarely possible to recover a payment from an accepting shareholder of a public offer.

Various methods are available to eliminate or reduce the transfer duty payable. A scheme of arrangement, which works by cancellation and reissue of shares, does not technically involve a transfer and therefore no duty is payable. If a scheme of arrangement cannot be used, it is sometimes possible to reduce the value of the shares being transferred for example by the issue of new shares. Existing shares are converted to deferred shares carrying inferior rights and therefore having a low value. Transfer duty, which is charged by reference to value, is reduced.

(b) Capital duty

Where shares are issued as part of the consideration, it is likely that capital duty will be payable unless the acquiring company is domiciled in a country where such taxes do not apply. The duty is based on the value at which the shares are considered to have been issued. Loan capital does not normally attract such duty.

(c) Tax on income stream

When calculating the return from an acquisition, it is important for a purchaser to determine what return he requires in cash and where it is to be received. In the case of acquisitions outside the acquiror's own tax domicile, the dividends, interest, management fees and the other components of the return may be subject to withholding and other taxes. The appropriate domicile of the ultimate holding company will be influenced by political stability, ease of communications and access, taxes on capital and income and other expenses of operation.

In countries which permit grouping for tax purposes, it is likely to be advantageous if the immediate holding company for the investment is domiciled in the same jurisdiction as the investment. This may permit interest payable on loans used to finance the investment to be offset against the taxable profits of the acquisition. It is unlikely that the investment holding company will make profits on an unconsolidated basis if there is even a moderate amount of gearing in its capital strucure.

Countries which levy a withholding tax on dividends normally tax payments which may be made in place of dividends, such as interest on shareholders' loans, management fees and royalties.

(d) On sale of investment

The individual tax position of shareholders who receive an offer, particularly in cash, will be relevant. Shareholders may be subject to tax on a disposal which will reduce the apparent attractiveness. A share-for-share exchange on the other hand is not normally treated as a disposal until the shares received in exchange are themselves disposed of.

The tax implications of a disposal by a company require prior planning to enable the most suitable holding structure to be established. Where an investment is likely to be sold again, it may be useful to place it in an intermediate holding company. It may well be advantageous to sell an offshore company holding or controlling an investment rather than to sell the investment itself.

(e) Tax liabilities of company being acquired

In countries where the depreciation bases for tax purposes and for accounting purposes vary, it will be necessary to ensure that any discrepancy between the tax written down value and book cost of assets has been taken into account.

On occasions, a major item of value, or even the prime purpose of an acquisition, is a tax loss available to offset future profits earned by the company being acquired. There may be limitations on whether such tax losses can be fully utilised after a change of control of the business which require careful examination. If the nature of the business also changes, the continued availability of the tax losses will be further jeopardised.

In the case of private companies, tax liabilities may arise through the tax position of their previous controlling shareholders. An indemnity from the vendor in the sale and purchase agreement is usually considered sufficient to cover this point.

(v) Role of other professionals

Depending on the nature of the transaction various other professionals may be involved in one or more stages.

(a) Stockbrokers

In a public company takeover, firms of stockbrokers will have a particularly key role. They will normally handle the necessary liaison with the stock exchange authorities as regards public announcements, trading arrangements and clearance of the offer documents.

The stockbroker is in a position to offer informed advice on what price may be acceptable to major stockholders and will liaise with stockholders who are their customers to obtain their views on the situation. Research departments may be asked to put out brokers' circulars on the participants. Both the offeror and offeree companies may encourage market operations to provide support for their respective share prices and sometimes to destabilise their opponent's. There will however be strict limits as to how such operations may be carried out and what disclosure is required by law and/or the Takeover Code. This cut-and-thrust role in the market is very much the province of the stockbroker.

If the offer requires financial support through underwriting, the stockbroker will play a leading role in lining up a syndicate of underwriting institutions.

If a substantial volume of commissions is generated through dealings in the market, the stockbroker may be prepared to handle other functions for a fairly low fee. On other occasions where a stockbroker has provided a corporate finance advisory service without handling a large volume of market transactons, a higher level of fee will be charged.

(b) Valuers

If the companies concerned in a takeover have a substantial amount of fixed assets it may be desirable (or required) to commission a revaluation. The valuer chosen should be independent of the board and of sufficient reputation that his opinion will stand up under any cross-fire which may arise. He should be alert to the possibility of different valuations for different uses of the asset and should present a 'best alternative use' value so that this can be considered in negotiations and communications with shareholders.

(c) Public relations consultants

The appointment of public relations consultants to co-ordinate press and publicity activities has become standard in public company takeovers, particularly contested situations. In this capacity, they will assist in the preparation of press announcements and the parts of the offer documents which present the arguments for or against acceptance. They will also maintain contact with journalists to ensure that their client's side of the argument is getting its fair share of air-time. Many shareholders will find it more convenient to form their view of an offer's merits from press coverage rather than the documents sent to them. In bids where there may be a public interest aspect, such as broadcasting or banking, or where there are significant employment or anti-monopoly considerations, the role of the public relations adviser as lobbyist may be critical to the outcome.

(d) Others

In the closing stages of an offer, the registrars or receiving bankers may be heavily involved in counting acceptances. There have been occasions where two parties have claimed to have received over 50% acceptances.

A measure of double-counting and other mistakes are likely to occur under pressure. Last minute circulars and other documents may be required so that the less glamorous functions of proofing, printing and getting documents despatched can become highly critical.

Merger and acquisition work requires a decisive principal. Behind the high profile announcements and decisions, a great deal of teamwork and specialist support is required. Constant co-ordination is essential to ensure that the various professionals involved are not either treading on each other's toes or missing an important area on the assumption that someone else must be covering it.

CHAPTER 22

Disposals

It would seem logical for a management to spend as much energy and enterprise on identifying and preparing for disposals as it does on acquisitions. This rarely proves to be the case. Attitudes to disposals tend to be ambivalent at best, if not downright negative. Factors relevant to taking the decision to make a disposal are discussed in 'I Deciding to make a disposal' below. If it is decided that a business should be considered for sale, it should be groomed in advance to look its best on the day. 'II Preparing for and promoting a sale' below covers how to prepare a business for sale and other practical steps which may be taken to achieve a successful outcome. 'III Disposals made in special circumstances' below deals with such matters as defence against an unwanted takeover bid or a sale in connection with a flotation.

I DECIDING TO MAKE A DISPOSAL

The first element in taking the decision to make a disposal is subjective, an attitude of mind. The second is analytical, what specific criteria should be used to decide that an asset or business should be sold.

(i) Attitude

(a) Psychology of disposals

Acquisitions are associated with growth and achievement. Disposals tend to carry a connotation of decline and failure. The initial reaction to even an over-priced acquisition may be more positive than to a well-judged and lucrative disposal. At the opposite extreme is the equivalent of zero budgets, that everything is potentially for sale and that it is retention which must be justified.

It is important for senior executives to encourage the attitude that considera-tion of a business or an asset for disposal need not be any reflection on the executives responsible for it. The best use of an asset may change for reasons entirely unconnected with the performance of the business in which that asset is employed. For example, a plantation which gradually becomes part of the suburbs of an expanding city will inevitably be more valuable if redeveloped for residential purposes. It may be impossible for an industry whose profits are largely determined by world commodity prices to earn a return equal to that from redevelopment.

Apprehension about disposals among staff is partly rooted in a very practical concern about remaining employed. Particularly in the case of horizontal mergers, there is likely to be some duplication of functions, resulting in loss of jobs as the corporate structure is rationalised after the acquisition. This is likely to take a higher toll of the staff of the target than of the acquiror.

It is unrealistic to expect that executives employed in a company targeted for disposal will show any real enthusiasm in this respect. Potential damage to morale may make it difficult to involve such executives as fully in the planning and execution of a disposal as is desirable. A reputation for protecting the rights of employees in negotiations and attempting to offer displaced staff some alternative or out-placement help in finding a job in another organisation will assist in these circumstances.

(b) Management buy-outs

This negative approach will not exist where it is a group of executives themselves who are proposing the disposal through a management buy-out (MBO). However, there may be rivalry and personal conflict between the MBO group and other executives in the firm excluded from it, or between the MBO group and head office staff. MBOs and leveraged buy-outs in general are discussed in ch 19.

Many MBOs are proposed in the first instance by the vendor group. For a vendor, an MBO has the advantage of dealing with a buyer which is a known quantity and avoids the need to disclose possibly sensitive information to 'outsiders'. This also keeps the disposal more confidential until a deal is done. Other factors which may influence a vendor are the need for expertise, close local connections, difficulties in agreeing terms with a third party or lack of an external buyer.

(c) Planning for disposals

At the corporate level, planners and analysts should be encouraged to consider identifying group companies for disposal to be as much part of their job as sifting through acquisition candidates. Regular reporting requirements from group companies should be partly drawn up with an eye to keeping the necessary information readily available. This will enable an internal review of the company's businesses to be carried out on a regular basis. The objective will be to identify under-performing or superfluous assets.

A middle-level unit may be the most successful in identifying such assets. They do not have the emotional commitment of higher management to businesses they may have developed or acquired nor are their career prospects linked in to a particular area.

(ii) Measures of performance

In order to compile a reasonable basis for assessing a disposal, accurate measurement of the company's performance over time is required. If a business is to be retained, it ought to meet, or be capable of meeting, similar financial and other objectives which would be expected when an acquisition is made.

Most control systems are based on setting budgets and monitoring performance against them. Budgets tend largely to be expressed in numerical terms and,
on the financial side, some of the most important numbers will relate to capital
employed and profits. The way these figures are calculated and presented
becomes very important.

(a) Capital employed

Capital employed in a business must be properly assessed. Book values may not
properly reflect the worth of the assets being employed. Property may have
increased in value due to inflation or may have a higher value to an alternative
user. The best alternative use value should be adopted as the basis for analysis,
taking into account costs which would have to be incurred to realise this value.
Plant and equipment may have been written-off over a period of time but should
not for this reason be ignored. A company may appear to be making a
reasonable return but may, in fact, be running down by not earning sufficient
for reinvestment in up-to-date equipment. Working capital requirements and
whether they are managed tightly are also relevant. If cash can be released by
improved control of current assets, this benefit can be obtained without a sale.

(b) Profitability

The method of computing profits must also be monitored to see that the
information it produces is a fair basis for measuring performance. In a group of
companies, the allocation of overheads, for example, may be done in a rather
arbitrary way. Transfer prices between one related company and another may
not reflect the reality of the market in which case profits will be distorted.
Standard costs may be used which are out of line with actual costs. Tax
planning and other strategic corporate considerations may also affect the
results.

Apparently inferior performance can be caused by accounting policies. The
weak points occur in the same areas where a purchaser needs to be wary in
assessing the quality of an acquisition's earnings. Capitalisation or writing-off
of research and development and some types of interest expenses can make a
significant difference to the costs charged against earnings. The treatment of
disposals of assets can greatly affect the level of reported profits. Lower reported
earnings may also paradoxically reflect a period of growth for the company,
especially if costs are being incurred which are not capitalised but which may
contribute to performance over a prolonged period. For example, an increased
marketing effort may not bear fruit immediately. A management which feels it is
under the gun to produce good results may be tempted to sacrifice projects
which they realise are to the long-term advantage of the business but which will
penalise profits in the short term.

(c) Incremental costs/benefits

In monitoring a business for disposal, the analysis should reflect accurately
what the incremental costs and benefits of selling the business are. If a business
is sold, what income would actually be lost? It may be possible for other parts of

the group to assume some of the business of the unit which is being sold. Equally important, would all the costs being charged against the business be saved on a disposal? Would head office costs allocated to it actually be reduced? Would material sold to it or services provided by related companies generate income in its absence? Have the full costs of disposal such as those associated with any redundancies been fully taken into account? Could stocks be realised at book value if production ceases?

(d) Strategic considerations

It is important that decisions on disposals are not taken on a purely short-term view. If financial criteria are applied too rigidly, it may appear that a particular line of business can no longer be carried on profitably. This indeed may be the case, but the poor results may also be attributable to a low point in a normal business cycle. A loss-making business should not immediately be put up for sale. Its future potential should be assessed as would be done in the case of an acquisition. Indeed, on the theory of 'better the devil you know', it may be reasonable to set somewhat lower financial targets for a business familiar to management. The risk of a business of which management has significant experience can be more fully evaluated than for a new acquisition, so that a lower level of return may be acceptable.

The apparent attractions of alternative investments may also be illusory. During a property boom, it may appear profitable to close a factory and redevelop the site. However, conditions may change during the course of the redevelopment to make the expected earnings unrealisable. There is a risk of having the worst of both worlds, no longer having the cash flow from operations but being unable to carry through the alternative project.

Management has to consider the strategic implications of ceasing to carry out a certain type of activity. It may have a broad impact on the morale of employees and the reputation of the group in general. Such a decision should not be taken 'by default' by allowing return on investment criteria to dictate policy.

II PREPARING FOR AND PROMOTING A SALE

Once the monitoring system has alerted management that a business should be considered for sale, it is beneficial to spend some time preparing the ground so that the business can appear in as favourable a light as possible. This will assist in the task of attracting potential buyers. Buyers may need a certain amount of persuasion or assistance from the vendor to reach the stage where a formal offer is made.

(i) Preparations

It is a useful exercise for the seller to try to put himself in the buyer's shoes. What strong and weak points would he be looking for particularly? The seller can then examine these points to see if any improvements to the existing position can be made. The points to be considered might include the following:

(a) Profitability

If the business is likely to be valued on an earnings basis and there are certain loss-making activities, it is preferable to close down or transfer them to another group company before the business is offered for sale. The presentation of financial information should be adjusted to exclude the results of the business which is to be discontinued or transferred. If there are unfavourable internal pricing policies or particularly conservative accounting treatments consideration should be given to making appropriate changes. If the business has been financed largely by debt, it may be advantageous to recapitalise and value the business on earnings before interest and taxes.

It may also be advisable to curtail major items of capital expenditure. Increased depreciation charges will reduce the earnings of the company in the period before the benefits of the project come through. In any case, a potential purchaser is unlikely to have precisely the same technical requirements or assessment of the market needs.

(b) Balance sheet

The main items on the balance sheet should be examined to see if there is anything which might deter a potential purchaser. It is inevitable that the purchaser will scrutinise major balance sheet items in great detail so it is worthwhile anticipating any criticisms he might make. Independent valuations of the larger assets serve to defuse arguments.

(c) Commercial

If a lease on key premises is due to expire soon a renewal may be negotiated in advance. It may be easier for someone familiar with the landlord to obtain fair terms than for a newcomer. There is always a tendency for an outside party to allow some discount for real or imagined difficulties in this regard.

If there are valuable agreements or licences which a change of control could jeopardise it may be advisable for the seller to sound out the relevant parties in advance so that he can provide reassurance to the purchaser on these points at the outset.

(d) Inter-company accounts

If there are any inter-company dealings preparations should be made to put them on an arm's length basis. Any accounts outstanding should be settled. If the funding of the business has been on non-commercial terms negotiations should be commenced with outside banking sources to replace the internal facilities. Temporary agreements may be required to cover transitional arrangements on such matters as provision of technical assistance or computer services.

(ii) Timing

(a) Cycles – picking the right phase

Successful sales of businesses depend critically on timing. Most markets are subject to cyclical forces. Towards the end of the upward phase of the market, the profits generated by a business should be near their peak allowing an attractive price to be set. At the same time, a purchaser can still look forward to some further improvement in performance. The confidence of potential purchasers will be high, a very important factor in a bridging the gap between simply talking about a transaction and making a final commitment.

(b) Financing

It is at this point of the cycle that finance for acquisitions is also likely to be most readily available. The availability of finance can significantly influence a purchaser's judgment. Apart from making a purchase possible at all, the backing of a banker may provide some comfort to a purchaser that the transaction is financially sound. While no bank loses money on purpose, the record of banks in evaluating their customers' decisions near market peaks is not without blemishes.

(c) Indecision by seller

A major obstacle is often indecision by the seller who is loathe to part with a company that is apparently doing well. There is a tendency to assume good times will last forever. Some of the most successful managers of major groups of companies are people whose strengths include the ability, without emotion and at the correct time, to dispose of businesses they have built up. If a vendor delays until the business turns down, the attitude of potential purchasers will be substantially different.

(iii) Supplying information

(a) Preparing and controlling information flow

The initiative at the opening of negotiations lies with the offeror. However, the seller need not simply be a passive recipient of proposals from the buyer. He may have prepared a presentation on the company and have his own ideas about the structure of the deal.

The supply of information should be tightly controlled, perhaps by one individual, so that only properly vetted material is supplied. It is important to keep track of precisely what information has been supplied as the purchaser is in due course likely to ask for a warranty that all such information is correct.

(b) Reluctance

It will be of advantage to appear the 'reluctant' bride no matter how desirable a sale may be in actuality. This will mean not showing too much eagerness in negotiations. Supplying information will appear like drawing teeth. Many regrets will be expressed at the impending sale.

(c) When to withhold information

The provision of information can backfire. In acquisition negotiations, it is almost impossible to provide all the data a purchaser could want. At some stage, it may be counter-productive to provide further details. The receipt of such information spawns delays, pending its analysis by the purchaser. The moment of decision is postponed while the purchaser begins to flounder under mountains of paper. In these circumstances, he may become incapable of making up his mind. Moreover, it is likely that the analysis will itself suggest additional questions which may never have arisen at all unless prompted by the further information disclosed. While it can be thought unhelpful to refuse to provide all the information requested, it may prove that retaining some of the mystery is a better strategy than removing all the 'seven veils'.

(iv) 'Sotheby's' atmosphere

(a) Benefits for price

In obtaining a good price for a business, it is helpful to generate an aura of excitement as sometimes happens in an auction room. A spirit of rivalry, often involving companies well-known to each other, fosters an atmosphere where a higher price may be paid than can be justified objectively. Deadlines may be imposed which are not strictly required, but are designed to force a purchaser to overcome final doubts and create suspense, as when bidding reaches a climax before the hammer falls.

(b) Bringing a buyer to a decision

Buyers like to believe they are not the only party interested or they begin to wonder why. A little competition can do wonders for the enthusiasm of a purchaser. A seller may try to create the sense of a competing offer in the wings, although to quote rival terms if none exist is not legitimate. Skilful sellers have resorted to mysterious meetings and sudden business trips, accompanied by profuse apologies. If the seller can succeed in building up this kind of atmosphere, the chances of the deal being concluded will be substantially improved. A sense of occasion is created where the buyer must say yes or no.

(v) Use of intermediaries

(a) General role

In negotiating with potential purchasers, it is often advantageous to use a third party such as a merger broker or investment banker. This allows even a keen seller to avoid seeming too eager to sell and a buyer too committed to a purchase. It also may provide a purchaser with confidence if an investment banker has prepared a presentation on the company and reviewed the financial information provided.

A seller has probably more to gain than the purchaser from the use of an intermediary. While few people mind being known in the market as a buyer, for a seller to indicate a willingness to deal is often thought to display weakness. If the approach is made through an intermediary, the seller can always claim if the news leaks out that he was misinterpreted and that the intermediary was exceeding his instructions.

(b) Narrowing the gap

A third party using 'shuttle diplomacy' between principals has more chance of narrowing the gap between two sets of proposals. At times, he can be more shameless in insisting on price as the major factor than a seller, who will tend to emphasise other factors, even if price is the main thing.

A skilful intermediary will seek to make both parties feel he is on their side. As someone who is committed to neither and paid only if a deal is consummated, his interest lies in seeking ways to reconcile the objectives of buyer and seller.

(c) Acting as a buffer

If emotions run high, a direct meeting between the seller and the acquiror may be bad tempered. A clash of personalities can hinder the conclusion of a proposal which might otherwise have a good chance of success. An experienced intermediary can see the warning signs and intervene to avoid unnecessary antagonism.

(vi) Vendor finance

A seller may have to consider assistance to a purchaser in financing an acquisition. Insistence that the purchaser arranges funding for the entire purchase at arm's length may make the transaction impracticable, especially if the business being purchased makes poor collateral for bank borrowing.

(a) Taking paper

A willingness to take some shares in the purchasing company not only helps in raising the total amount required, but may promote a feeling of partnership. By accepting paper, the seller is expressing a degree of confidence in the management and business of the purchaser. Alternatively, a seller may agree to become a shareholder in a new vehicle formed to acquire a business or assets from himself. In this way, he retains an interest and avoids being thought anxious to sell out entirely.

(b) Deferred consideration

A vendor may agree that a portion of the consideration should be paid on a deferred basis. This is equivalent to the vendor being paid out in part from the cash flow of the business being sold, which some vendors find objectionable. The purchaser would, however, still have the obligation to pay if the cash flow falls short of expectations.

(c) Purchase note

A loan may be made to the purchaser by the vendor, secured on the business or assets purchased. This may be done so that an acquiror can complete a transaction for which sufficient third party financing is unavailable or as part of a package which the seller provides to attract a buyer, even though he could raise finance independently. In such circumstances, the seller cannot really regard the sale as being completed until the money is fully repaid. It may happen that the seller needs to continue with some management role in the business or even take it back if the purchaser fails to meet his commitments. For this reason, this structure is most suitable for a relatively simple asset such as an investment property or a hotel.

III   DISPOSALS MADE IN SPECIAL CIRCUMSTANCES

Occasions arise where a disposal is made not primarily because performance is below standard but for other tactical reasons. Some examples are given below.

(i) To raise money

(a) 'Selling the family silver'

A group may be forced by financial pressures to make a disposal in order to raise money. In this situation the normal logic is reversed. Instead of singling out a business with a disappointing return, one of the more promising assets of the group may have to be selected to ensure that the sum required is realised within a reasonable time.

(b) Taking the initiative

The bargaining position of the vendor will be weakened if he waits until the market is aware of his financial difficulties. A skilful operator has sometimes managed to take the initiative by proposing to merge with or even buy a rival company thus succeeding in setting in motion a process which eventually leads to an offer for his own company. This type of manoeuvre takes time and planning as well as skill to accomplish.

(c) Constraints on action

A group which has encountered financial difficulties often finds itself under a number of constraints. A sale of an asset which is heavily borrowed against may reduce gearing significantly but will not generate the free cash (after loan repayments) which may be necessary for survival. A disposal at a book loss may be sensible commercially but may draw the market's attention to problems. The accounting effects of a disposal may be critical if the company has little leeway on borrowing restrictions and other covenants contained in loan stock or bank loan agreements.

(ii) Defence against an unwanted takeover

A takeover may be launched principally because of a particular business or asset a group controls (sometimes referred to as a 'crown jewel'). In normal circumstances, this would probably be the last item the directors would consider selling. However, to deter a raider, approaches may be made to potential purchasers in order to put the prize beyond the raider's reach. Sometimes this may be done in such a way that existing shareholders of the group retain an interest in the asset for example by spinning it off into a separate company or by putting it in a partnership in which shareholders participate. This tactic has the merit of protecting the position of existing shareholders whereas to sell the asset outright simply to prevent a takeover seems in some sense self-defeating.

If the whole group is threatened with takeover, the directors may seek a defensive merger to make the enlarged group too big for a predator to swallow. Alternatively they may seek a more acceptable suitor called a 'white knight'.

(iii) Management buy-out

As discussed in Ch 19, in a diversified group, certain businesses may become neglected because of operating problems or a strategic decision to emphasise development in other areas. Administrative controls may deprive management of the flexibility to make key decisions and funds for expansion may be difficult to obtain. This may lead to a demoralisation of management and a decline in performance. It may even endanger the survival of the business if allowed to continue indefinitely.

It may therefore suit both the parent company and the management in question to arrange for a disposal of the business to the management. As MBO techniques and financing have become well established, it is always worthwhile for a vendor at least to put an MBO on the list of alternatives to be considered. Finance for the purchase may be provided partly by the vendor, by offering deferred terms or vendor finance, partly by management from their own resources and partly by outside investors.

(iv) Flotations

(a) Loss-making subsidiaries

When a group is being groomed for flotation, it may be preferable to sell or even give away a loss-making subsidiary. If the price of the flotation is being set by reference to a multiple of earnings, a loss incurred by one member of the group will reduce the overall valuation by a factor equal to the multiple being applied. On occasions a company has been disposed of to a private associate of the group going public, with an option to reacquire the business subsequently once the flotation is complete or the company restored to financial health.

(b) Value of listing

A listed company may be sold primarily for the sake of its listing. This is discussed in detail in ch 9. A purchaser wishing to obtain a listing for some of his interests may buy control of a listed company and inject assets into it either for cash or new shares. The listing which is being sold may be considered to have a value independently of the other assets of the company. This value will correspond roughly to the costs involved in going public via the full flotation process plus an intangible element for the added certainty and control which the shell route offers. The premium which the shell can command will also depend on the attitude of the stock exchange and other regulatory authorities towards obtaining listings via this route.

CONCLUSION

Disposals ought logically to occupy as much of management's time and attention as acquisitions do but this is rarely the case. Whereas acquisitions are associated with progress and growth, disposals carry a negative connotation. Nevertheless, a well-judged disposal can be critical in the development of a group. The technique of making a successful disposal is a subtle one. The type of personality which makes an executive an effective acquiror of companies will not necessarily mean he is a good salesman.

Sometimes a disposal is forced on a group by financial circumstances and there are other particular circumstances which may dictate policy in this regard. While the philosophy that everything for sale is anathema to many coporations it seems that greater attention to the merits of an organised disposal programme and policy could pay great dividends.

Index